A GUIDE TO CHILDREN'S REFERENCE BOOKS AND MULTIMEDIA MATERIAL

This book is dedicated to my husband Peter without whose unfailing kindness, support and patience it could never have been completed.

A Guide to Children's Reference Books and Multimedia Material

edited by

Susan Hancock

Routledge
Taylor & Francis Group

LONDON AND NEW YORK

First published 1998 by Ashgate Publishing

Reissued 2018 by Routledge
2 Park Square, Milton Park, Abingdon, Oxon, OX14 4RN
711 Third Avenue, New York, NY 10017, USA

Routledge is an imprint of the Taylor & Francis Group, an informa business

Copyright © Susan Hancock, 1998

The contributors have asserted their moral rights

All rights reserved. No part of this book may be reprinted or reproduced or utilised in any form or by any electronic, mechanical, or other means, now known or hereafter invented, including photocopying and recording, or in any information storage or retrieval system, without permission in writing from the publishers.

Notice:
Product or corporate names may be trademarks or registered trademarks, and are used only for identification and explanation without intent to infringe.

Publisher's Note
The publisher has gone to great lengths to ensure the quality of this reprint but points out that some imperfections in the original copies may be apparent.

Disclaimer
The publisher has made every effort to trace copyright holders and welcomes correspondence from those they have been unable to contact.

A Library of Congress record exists under LC control number: 97077938

Typeset in Sabon by Intype London Ltd

ISBN 13: 978-1-138-60998-3 (hbk)
ISBN 13: 978-1-138-61000-2 (pbk)
ISBN 13: 978-0-429-46029-6 (ebk)

Contents

List of contributors	vii
Preface and acknowledgements *Susan Hancock*	ix
Introduction:	xi
What is a reference book? *Susan Hancock*	xi
A brief historical survey *Pat Pinsent*	xi
1 About the Guide:	1
A guide to the reviews	1
Matching children and texts	3
National Curriculum tests *Susan Hancock*	5
2 Publications for pre-school children *Susan Hancock* with *Fiona Collins*	8
3 Publications for Key Stage 1 *Susan Hancock* with *Fiona Collins* and *George Raper*	16
4 Publications for Key Stage 2 *Susan Hancock* with *Fiona Collins* and *George Raper*	45
5 Publications for Key Stage 3 *Susan Hancock* with *Fiona Collins* and *George Raper*	101
6 Information playgrounds *Lisa Sainsbury*	145
Bibliography	188

Author Index	191
Index of Reviewed Titles	193
Subject Index	199
Index of Illustrators	202

Contributors

Fiona Collins MA is Senior Lecturer in Primary Education, language and literacy at the Roehampton Institute. Her particular interest is children's literature and she teaches this in both the Education and English faculties.

Susan Hancock MA is Project Manager for the National Centre for Research in Children's Literature at the Roehampton Institute.

Pat Pinsent MA BSc is Principal Lecturer in English at the Roehampton Institute. She is joint convener of the MA in Children's Literature. Her particular research interest is in equality issues in children's literature.

George Raper PhD is Lecturer in Science Education at the University of Warwick. He is Director of the PGCE course and co-ordinator of all Science courses, primary and secondary, for Initial Teacher Education.

Lisa Sainsbury MA lectures in English Literature at the Roehampton Institute, specialising in children's literature; she currently teaches on the MA in Children's Literature. She is presently involved in doctoral research on the subject of postmodernism in contemporary children's literature.

Milverton Primary School
Headteacher: Roger Smith
Project co-ordinator for the guide: Maureen Thurlow

Woodloes Junior School
Headteacher: Geoff Claridge
Project co-ordinator for the guide: Lyn Bentley

Aylesford School
Headteacher: Lesley King
Project co-ordinator for the guide: Graham Tyrer, Head of English and Curriculum Co-ordinator for Communications

Additional research by Peter Hancock, Resource Base Co-ordinator for Round Oak School and Service

Preface and acknowledgements

Educational issues have been pushed into prominence in recent years, with high profile press coverage of the introduction of the National Curriculum and the publication of 'league tables', giving performance data on a school-by-school basis. Many parents and carers are becoming increasingly aware of these issues and the surrounding debates, and rightly see themselves as being closely involved in the process of ensuring that their children derive maximum benefit from their years at school.

One of the ways in which parents and carers feel able to participate in their children's education is in the acquisition of information and reference books for the home. Publishers in the field, acutely aware of these developments, have responded by producing ever-increasing numbers of such books, many of which signal their relevance in the educational world by the use of 'insider' terms (such as 'National Curriculum Key Stages') that have become familiar to parents and carers over recent years.

At the same time, cuts in education budgets have put pressure on the availability of books within schools and have increased the need for these to be supplemented by judicious purchases for the home. There is a heightened awareness of the need to obtain value for money, and those responsible for buying books are under growing pressure to ensure that they make the right purchases. Mistakes are expensive; but few purchasers have the time or resources available to allow them to carry out the research necessary to ensure that the book they acquire is the best value (in both educational and monetary terms) for the children for whom it is intended. This is particularly true for reference works, such as encyclopedias, where the outlay can be a significant sum. For those homes with the necessary computer hardware, purchasing decisions are further complicated by the volume of reference material targeted at children which is now available in multimedia format.

For these reasons I have put together a team of specialists to review a variety of the reference books and multimedia reference material available at the present time and to comment on the issues involved in the purchase of such volumes. Never forgetting that the ultimate readers of these texts are the children themselves, further 'in-school' review panels have also had their 'say'. A series of reviews by pupils in Key Stages 1, 2 and 3 (with additional observations made by the teachers who introduced them to the books and watched the child/text interaction over a number of weeks) are included in Chapters 3, 4 and 5.

Overall I hope that this book will help reference work purchasers to make the most appropriate and informed choices from the many titles that are available to them.

Susan Hancock

Acknowledgements

Many thanks are due to friends and colleagues at the Roehampton Institute for their help and support during the writing of this guide. Particular thanks are due to Fiona Collins, Pat Pinsent and Lisa Sainsbury for their invaluable contributions and to Dr Kimberley Reynolds, Director of the National Centre for Research in Children's Literature, for her patient interest and thoughtful comments.

Warm thanks are also due to the participating schools: to the children for their enthusiastic cooperation; to the headteachers who allowed their pupils to review the books; and, particularly, to the school project co-ordinators, who gave both time and expertise, making it possible for the children to have a voice in the guide.

Introduction

What is a reference book?

With such a wide and varied range of non-fiction currently on the market for children, it is not always easy to decide which of these might qualify as reference works and which might be better classified as general information books. For the purposes of this guide my working definition of reference books has been those texts designed for 'dip in' reference rather than as a 'cover to cover' read. These have tended to fall into the following general categories: atlases; abc books, 'first words' books and dictionaries; encyclopedias. However, I have also included some books which, although they might individually be regarded as information books, belong to a coherent series capable of being built up into a 'mini-library' for reference purposes. Mini-libraries are useful in bridging the gap between information books and full reference works. They can offer younger children smaller, 'friendlier' volumes, collectable over a period of time, yet still teach retrieval skills, ranging from early awareness of subject matter (which book in the series to take from the shelf) to use of an index to find specific topic coverage within the selected book. Many have appealing subject matter which can encourage children to pick them up and use them; no mean feat considering the antipathy felt by many children toward conventional reference encyclopedias.

A brief historical survey

The history of books published for children epitomizes in itself the history of childhood and of attitudes to children throughout the ages. As Gillian Avery (1989) remarks, 'Children's books have always been particularly vulnerable to the ideologies of the age'. (p.95) The function of reference books means that their didacticism does not need to be concealed even to the imperfect extent that obtains in most children's fiction, since they are explicitly intended for the child to use as part of learning. They are subject not only to contemporary views about childhood, but also to current perspectives concerning 'knowledge' and how it should be imparted, and, in particular, the nature and purpose of reading.

Ultimately they reflect more directly than most texts what the arbiters of the period considered to be the purpose of human life.

Alphabet books

Within the genre of reference books, the texts designed to facilitate children's acquisition of reading are perhaps those with the longest recorded history. The notion that most people could not read until a fairly recent period, which was cited variously as somewhere between the early eighteenth century and the Elementary Education Act of 1870, has been challenged by a number of writers, such as Coleman (1981), who reveals a fairly high degree of literacy in medieval England. Clanchy (in ed. Brooks, R.G. & Pugh, A.K., 1984) quotes a statement by Sir Thomas More (1477-1535) which implies that as many as 60 per cent of the early Tudor population were able to read, though we must be careful not to assume that this ability was at a level we would find acceptable today. It does however imply that such readers had been taught the alphabet [as children]. Even before books were printed in England, this teaching process was carried out by means of the letters being set out at the beginning of a prayer book, a 'primer', the word deriving from the 'Hours' (which include 'Prime'), in both Latin and English. A significant number of primers, whose chief function was to serve private devotion, survive from the Middle Ages; and by no means all of these are associated with the wealthy (cf. Duffy, 1992, pp.209-98). Before the age of printing, books would have been scarce and expensive, so that to expose them to the grubby fingerprints of a child learning to read was scarcely desirable. Therefore, as an alternative to providing the alphabet within the book, it was often set out separately and mounted on a board covered with translucent horn. This 'Horn Book' generally also included some basic prayers. As printed books gradually became cheaper the function of teaching the alphabet was often transferred to them, though horn books also remained popular. A number of primers devoted to the alphabet are still extant from the sixteenth century onward. One of the most enlightened of the early manuals is John Hart's *A Methode, or Comfortable Beginnings for all Unlearned* (1570) which contains the first known picture alphabet and recommends a phonic method for teaching reading (cf. Avery, 1995, p.4).

With the Reformation, it became even more imperative to teach reading, so that children could become personally acquainted with the scriptures in English. This probably accounts for a growth during the seventeenth century of alphabet books directed towards children, who in many instances would be learning at their mother's knee and applying themselves to slowly decoding the catechism, the prayers and metrical psalms, and appropriate passages of the Bible. Among English alphabet books, probably the best known, though far from being the earliest to survive in a number of copies, is the one which starts 'A was an Archer' (c.1705). It was reprinted, both by itself and as part of other publications, for over 150 years, by which time it had been joined by a considerable range of other texts. Over the years, archers may have become less familiar to the infant commencing reading, and many alternatives were printed. Some attractive examples from various periods include *ABC: the Broadsheet King*, which begins 'A was an Acorn that grew on the Oak', the *Fairytale Alphabet*, the *Farmyard Alphabet*, *The Scripture Panoramic Alphabet* and the alliterative 'Arthur and Albert eating Apples'.[1] *The Alphabet of Peace*, published in 1856 to celebrate the end of the Crimean War, includes the couplet:

> N is Miss Nightingale, with her fair band
> Who solaced our sick in a far distant land.
> (Carpenter & Prichard, 1984, p.2)

Among other late nineteenth-century examples is the *ABC in 4 line verses*; the superscription on a copy of this reveals it to have been given for Christmas in 1888, hopefully to the joy of the recipient. Another is *The London Alphabet*, which includes:

> O for Omnibus
> U for Underground Railway
> Q for Queen Victoria now sits on the Throne[1]

Many early picture book alphabet books have been reproduced in facsimile in more recent years, and there seems no evidence of the trend to produce new ones having diminished.

Dictionaries

The place of the massive work of Dr Johnson (1755) in the history of adult dictionaries of English is well known, though he was by no means the first to attempt to supply this need; Cockeram's *English Dictionarie: or an Interpreter of Hard English Words* appeared in 1623. There seems however to have been little recognition of the desirability of children having an *English* dictionary more appropriate to their limited needs, though schoolboys' Latin requirements were not forgotten; *An Abridgement of Ainsworth's Dictionary of the Latin Tongue* (1758) omits 'several items less important to youth'. It would be interesting to know whether these items were omitted because of difficulty or possibly salacious content! A French text described as an educational dictionary of ancient and modern history appeared in 1837, but it seems to have been nearer what we would describe as an encyclopedia.[1]

Meanwhile a number of English dictionaries continued to appear, and though some of these, like Daniel Fenning's *New and Complete Spelling Dictionary* (c.1770), may well have been intended for younger readers as well as for adults, children were more usually supplied with spelling books as such, like *The Illustrated Webster Spelling Book*, adapted from vocabulary in the Webster dictionaries, and the many Mavor's *Spelling Books* which appeared throughout the nineteenth century, and whose twentieth-century counterparts are little books such as those by the prolific C.J. Ridout in the 1950s, *The Spell-well Word Books*. The prevalence of word and spelling books rather than dictionaries as such is probably related to the pedagogic stance of compilers and publishers. Children need *these* words, rather than the 'free-range' supplied by a dictionary. *Words I like to Read and Write* (1956) reveals its association with a well-known reading scheme by the sentences 'Janet and John ran home. Puppy ran *after* them'; the title pre-empts any alternative choices by the children.

Dictionaries the content of which clearly presupposes young readers, like the *Collins Etymological and Reference Dictionary* (many editions before 1948), occur in the first half of the twentieth century, but they are much more frequent from 1950 onwards. They can be roughly divided into two main categories: those which use sentences to *illustrate* (rather than define) the meaning of the words, quite often adding some pictures, and those which rely only on the pictures. The Preface of *Cassell's Picture Dictionary* (1952) makes clear its credentials to an adult audience; it is compiled by Mary Waddington, a Lecturer in Child Development at the University of London, and the vocabulary has been checked by thorough research. The words are all contextualized, and the chosen sentences reveal the author's intention to teach more than mere words; for the word 'afternoon' we have: 'After school dinner we say, "Good Afternoon". After tea we say, "Good Evening".'

The Introduction, again addressed to adults, of Collins' *The Children's Picture Dictionary* (1951) states its aim 'to amuse while it instructs' by including story and nursery rhyme characters, though the drama associated with the word 'cry' seems to reveal certain gender-based assumptions: 'Jack gave a cry when he fell off his bicycle. He gave a shout. Jill began to cry. Tears fell from her eyes. She was crying. She cried.'

By contrast with these explicitly didactic works, Publicity Products' *My Picture Dictionary: A Picture with Every Word*, has no preface, but it is possible to detect its American origin (Maxton Publishers, New York) from pictures such as the large showy vehicle which supports the line: 'I like riding in our *automobile*', a word which does not occur in the other works named above. More recently, Chambers' *Young Set Dictionaries* (1971/2) show the development from large pictures and a text mostly confined to nouns in *One*, through an increase in complexity of words, with the inclusion of some adjectives, in *Two*, to a wider range of words, supplied with definitions rather than illustrations, in *Three*. The third volume also has a Preface about how to use the dictionary; it differs from the 1950s examples by being addressed to the child reader.

Atlases

Globes seem to have come into use in the 1550s, but at that stage there would have been no attempt to distinguish between the child and the adult user. Instruction of the young seems however to be at the forefront of *A New and Easy Guide to the Use of the Globes and the Rudiments of Geography wherein the*

Knowledge of the Heavens and Earth is made easy to the meanest Capacity (4th edition 1779). Although a child reader is not explicit in the title, its author, Daniel Fenning, was also responsible for books for 'British Youth' on Arithmetic and Mensuration. This text, which uses the familiar question and answer technique ('Tyro' [learner] and 'Philo' [lover of the subject]); carries a number of maps, including one of what we should now term 'The British Isles' revealingly entitled 'The British Empire'. A picture of globes is accompanied by a quotation from Milton, 'E'er half the school authors be read, it will be seasonable for YOUTH to learn the use of the globes'. Works like Fenning's may be seen as precursors of the *Walker's Universal Atlas for the Use of Schools* (1811, 1828). These small books have no editorial matter and make no concessions to their young readers, being no more than a compilation of twenty or more maps.

The continued use of unannotated atlases like these may be presumed to lie behind the production of *Philips' Elementary Atlas of Comparative Geography.* Its date may be deduced as being before the First World War or the Russian Revolution, because of the map of the German Empire and the naming of 'St. Petersburg', respectively. G. Philip Junr, the compiler, clearly rejects the system of the Walker's atlases which gave no more attention to Great Britain than to the rest of the world. He claims that:

> in the present book – for the first time in an English Elementary Atlas – each map takes its place as an essential part of a *general scheme*, so ordered, that, while all the regions of the world are adequately treated, special prominence is given to the British Empire, and those countries which are of particular interest to British Scholars.

Thus, since this is the 'London' edition, it starts with lessons in map-reading based on Westminster Abbey, before maps of the Thames Basin and the County of London.

It is difficult in many atlases from the first half of the twentieth century to distinguish between, on the one hand the sensible pedagogical method of starting with what is familiar to the children, and on the other the natural desire to display the importance of the world role of Great Britain. Many of the children's atlases place the British Isles first before contextualizing them in Europe and the world, and they also tend to give many more pages of maps of England [sic] and its regions than of other parts of the world. Awareness of the ideological opportunities which atlases afford seems to have motivated the production of such books as *The Pupil's Empire Atlas* (1925, associated with the Empire Exhibition at Wembley in 1924) and the *Royal Primrose Atlas of the British Empire*,[1] by John Knight, issued for the Jubilee year of 1936 and carrying an advertisement for Knight's Castile toilet soap.

Probably because of the need to follow the campaigns, atlases seem to have been produced during the Second World War to a greater extent than many other texts for children, which were often simply reissued in their pre-war form. The *Collins Clear School Atlas* (c.1942) reveals its date by the shading of countries then under German occupation, but the *Modern School Atlas* (1943) (ed. Kermack) rather delightfully turns from theatres of war to locate, among its maps of products, Herring, Haddock and Plaice in the North Sea and Skate, Ray and Hake to the west of these islands. The precision might not be adequate to direct the fishing boats, however!

The imperialistic note is not surprisingly also to be found in other atlases shortly after the Second World War but before the total dissolution of empire. *My First Atlas* (1952) (for a younger reader than those described above) unites a child-centred pedagogic approach with an Anglocentrism fairly characteristic of the period. Sam and Susan, protagonists created in order to make it reader-friendly, appear on the front cover and the final page, but generally the reader is addressed directly. Orientation is achieved at the beginning: 'If you look at the sun at midday you are facing south' (presumably no sale in the Antipodes was envisaged!); and children are led through plans of classroom, house, street and town towards five big maps of the British Isles and a little one of Europe. The maps are surrounded with coloured pictures appropriate to national products; that for 'Wheat Growing' depicts two horses drawing a reaping machine. The result is an alluring combination of entertainment and propaganda.

Encyclopedias

One of the earliest books for children, the *Orbis sensualium pictus* by the Moravian Jan Comenius, could well be termed the first Children's Encyclopedia in miniature. Described as 'A World of Things Obvious to the Senses drawn in Pictures', with text in both Latin and the vernacular, it was published in Germany in 1658 and translated into English the following year. Beginning with the kind of catechism characteristic of many early books of instruction, which tells us so much about early teaching methods, it goes on to provide illustrated sections on subjects like God, The World, Fire, Clouds, Metals, Insects, Moral Philosophy, Astronomy and The Tormenting of Malefactors, finishing with The Last Judgement. Representative pages from the section on Man (36–44) indicate Comenius' approach. A numbered picture illustrates 14 different 'Deformed and Monstrous People', such as 'The Huge Gyant', 'One with two bodies', 'One with two heads', 'the great nosed' and 'the blubber lipped'. The final addition of 'the Bald pated' surely suggests that not everything should be read solemnly.

The development of the encyclopedia for children seems to have gone in parallel with that for adults. Classical writers who could be seen as contributing to the origin of this genre include Aristotle and Pliny, who would no doubt have expected the young to be among their readers. Probably the best-known early modern example of the genre is provided by the 28 volumes of the French *Encyclopédie* edited by Diderot and others (1751–72), even though it was antedated by a two-volume English work by Ephraim Chambers (1728); both of these were directed at adults. The children's publisher John Newbery, however, makes clear his pretensions to producing an encyclopedia for young people by the title *The Circle of the Sciences* (from 1745 onwards), since the word 'encyclopedia' derives from the Greek which means, 'Education within the

Circle'. These little books, generally again in a question and answer format, cover grammar, arithmetic, rhetoric, poetry, logic, geography and chronology. Other early precursors of children's encyclopedias seem to have been less ambitious in their titles. For instance, a schoolmistress, Richmal Mangnall, published *Historical and Miscellaneous Questions for the Use of Young People* (1800), which includes historical, biographical and later astronomical information. A schoolmaster, William Pinnock, published a series of *Catechisms* on subjects such as geography, mineralogy and music, beginning in 1817. These works seem to have inspired 'A Lady', Fanny Umphelby, to produce *The Child's Guide to Knowledge* (1825), which also uses a question and answer technique and carries an index. This came out in a number of editions, some with additional material. Its arrangement is at times curious, and the provenance of information, which generally lies with the answerer, sometimes changes to the questioner. It starts with common products such as flour and rice ('the principal food of the lower class of people in Asia') and arrives at tea and sugar:

> Q How were the SUGAR plantations formerly cultivated?
> A By negro slaves who were brought into the colonies from the coast of Africa.

Having established that the evil of slavery has been abolished through the efforts of British people, without further ado the text immediately goes on to: 'Q What sort of a plant is the SUGAR-CANE?'

The Religious Tract Society was prominent throughout the nineteenth century in its attempts to instruct and thereby to improve the morals of children, and while many of its publications are primarily devoted to fiction, periodicals such as *The Child's Companion*, *The Boys' Own Paper* and *The Girls' Own Paper* are full of informative material, though the organisation would make it difficult to use these regularly on a reference basis. While the structure of these publications is clearly not yet that of the encyclopedia proper, they are undoubtedly to be seen in the background of the *Children's Encyclopedia*, which was initially published in 50 fortnightly parts from 1908 onwards.[2] This evolved into the ten-volume work (1925) which has become the main progenitor of the multitude of later encyclopedias for children and thus deserves a good deal of attention in its own right. Arthur Mee, its editor, was prolific in his production of both magazines and books for children, such as *The Children's Newspaper* (1919–1965) and *The Children's Treasure House*, which was published as a companion to the Encyclopedia. Unlike most comparable works for adults and a good many later examples for children, his main opus eschews the alphabetic principle in the attempt to make the material interesting, though it could of course be argued that as a result of his organization, children needed to acquire a good range of skills in using contents and indexes.

The modern reader is immediately struck by the first two colour plates. The frontispiece is a picture of woman with her elbow on the window-sill looking soulfully out into the eyes of Shakespeare, balding but still young, standing in the garden and reading from a sheaf of papers. The picture is headed 'Shakespeare fancies a new rhyme', and beneath it are the words:

> In his cottage days at Stratford, we may be sure that Shakespeare fancying some new rhyme, would call Anne Hathaway to listen as he proudly read it over.

Fortunately the accuracy of the items in the remainder of the encyclopedia seems a little less suspect! The second picture is perhaps even more striking. Covered by a transparent page identifying the nationalities, it is a coloured rendering of the children of the world, the presumed readers, we suppose, of what follows: 'Brothers and Sisters are we all'. More than half the page is devoted to children of white European stock, surmounted by a row consisting of such 'suspect' peoples as Turks and Egyptians. Crammed into a tiny space in the far corner are a Pigmy and a Negro, next to Hottentots, Apache and Dakota Indians, a Mexican and a South Sea Islander. Though the editor's dedication is to 'Boys and Girls Everywhere', he clearly has no inkling that a high proportion of the population of the world could feel marginalized. This unashamed Eurocentric bias is inevitably reflected in the articles; the section on Literature starts with another picture of Shakespeare, devotes itself largely to English literature, and is described as 'Imperishable thoughts of men [sic] enshrined in the books of the world'.

The encyclopedia is divided into 19 groups of subjects, but these are split up between the ten volumes in the effort to provide an interesting reading experience for the child rather than to supply an exhaustive treatment of a single subject. Groups consist of areas such as Animal Life, History, Familiar Things, Wonder, Countries, the Bible and Power. There is an Atlas section, a considerable number of stories, poems and nursery rhymes, some suggestions as to things to make and to do, and a collection of 'School Lessons' in Reading (using the alphabet and sight-word methods), Writing, Arithmetic, Music, Drawing and French. The mixture of ambition and idealism of the undertaking is clear from Mee's Preface. He disavows any intention to cram the child's head with facts, but instead offers his work as a 'gift to the nation, a thing of measureless value to parents and teachers'. Finally he speaks for the provider of all the good things to be found within the Universe:

> I, Nature, give to you, to be yours for ever and ever, the right to the free enjoyment of this world. I give to you the years that are before you and the world that is about you.

His letter to the children concludes:

> It is a Big Book for Little People and it has come into the world to make your life happy and wise and good. That is what we are meant to be. That is what we will help each other to be. Your affectionate Friend, Arthur Mee.

The unconcealed pride in achievement is almost attractively naive, but some of the sentiments sound a little hollow from a production many of whose editions were produced between the wars in the period of economic depression and growing militarism. It was also a period when many publishers realised both the need for and the commercial attraction of producing encyclopedias of this kind for children. In 1933, Odhams Press, not to be outdone by the Educational Book Company, published *The Wonderland of Knowledge*, edited by Ernest Ogan, in

Introduction xix

12 volumes. This also adheres to the 'serendipity' plan of Mee, consisting of a similar set of sections, such as 'The Story of the Nations', 'Great Names in English Literature', and, not forgetting the desirability of keeping the reader active, 'Things to make and to do', which includes puzzles, tricks and magic. Central to these and other contemporary works is the greater technical facility in printing pictures, especially colour plates, so that they can be made attractive to children without undue expense. Like subsequent encyclopedias, the cost of such volumes could be spread, and the involvement by newspaper companies suggests the undertaking was profitable. Odhams, publishers of a number of periodicals, were joined by Associated Newspapers under Lord Northcliffe, who produced *The Treasury of Knowledge: General Knowledge Illustrated*. Although this is not specific to young people, its educational aim is emphasized by the tone of the Introduction from an eminent headmaster, J.F. Roxburgh, from Stowe.

It is easy today to detect the imperialistic bias in these productions and to ridicule their mixture of idealism and self-interest, but there is no doubt that they provided inspiration towards education for a large number of people in the inter-war years, and far from all of these were children. After the break in publication caused by the Second World War, there is a trend towards smaller works. *The New Encyclopedia for the younger generation* (1958) is a single volume translated from the French Larousse children's encyclopedia and divided into sections on 'The World in which we live', 'Our History through the ages', 'Living Beings', 'Machines in the service of man', and 'How do we live?'. The omissions, such as Art and Literature (Shakespeare gets one line), are as telling as the inclusions; the Eurocentric bias is still apparent, but perhaps as a result of the French origin, and probably also because of political changes, the British Empire does not feature in the same way as in the earlier works. The treatment of Africa, however, shows little advance on *The Wonderland of Knowledge* (1933); the proportion of space given is almost identical, and both seem to consider that any history of Africa prior to the advent of the white man is of minimal interest. 'The ancient city of Zimbabwe' does receive a mention in the later work, but it is implied that although the origin is not known it was certainly beyond the ability of native Africans to build it. Nor does the treatment of the topic of Slavery see much advance; the main reference is an item in the 'Machines' section, where The Slave is positioned between The Wheel and The Windlass. This encyclopedia is illustrated on every page, mostly with specially commissioned drawings and paintings. Like Mee, these editors have no mean opinion of their achievement:

> Few books have been as skilfully designed as this one; few books have provided as much pleasure or been referred to as often as this one will be.

An even slimmer volume (128 pages) is the 1970 *Encyclopedia for Boys and Girls*, which unlike those previously mentioned is organized alphabetically but has no contents page. The material on Africa, for example, is proportionately much greater and appears to be less distorted than that of its predecessors. All the illustrations are coloured and there is no foreword lauding the achievement of its editors.

Another trend of the post-war years is for volumes on single subjects, like the *Bible Encyclopedia for Children* (1964), whose items are arranged in alphabetical order, and the *Wide World Encyclopedias* (1969) with separate volumes on *Nature, History, Wildlife* and *Our World*. Similar to sections of encyclopedias are also the items in the very wide-ranging collections of books on single subjects, appearing from the 1930s onwards, with a break for the war. Dent (*The Story Book of Coal* (1936) and *The Story Book of Clothes* (1937)) and Penguin (*Our Cattle* (1948) and *Airliners* (1949)) have interesting examples in this genre, but probably the best known are the *Ladybird* series. Each of these small-format, 52 page books, reminiscent of the collections of articles in the larger-scale encyclopedias, is generally colourfully and accurately illustrated. There are several different sub-series, and the hundreds of titles include *British Wild Flowers* (1957), *British Railway Locomotives* (1958), *Stone Age Man in Britain* (1961) and *Your Body* (1967). The fact that three of the titles quoted here relate to Britain, while it is not entirely representative of the numerical proportions of the books overall, does nevertheless do justice to the national feeling displayed. For instance, of the 23 titles listed for the 'Adventures from History' series, which generally describe the lives of individuals, only Christopher Columbus, Marco Polo, Alexander the Great and Cleopatra are without direct connection to these islands.

In conclusion

The history of reference books published in Britain can be seen to reveal a good deal about the attitudes, both to children and to knowledge itself, which prevailed at the time of their publication. It also displays the inevitable limitations of the world-view of the adults who produced this material for children. Such limitations are easy to detect in material of past periods but no doubt equally present, though far less conspicuous to today's readers, in comparable reference books produced for children today.

Notes

1. Information concerning the titles of these books is derived from the Catalogue of the Renier collection at Bethnal Green Library of Childhood.
2. Information about the periodical publications for children is derived from Carpenter and Prichard (1984)

1 About the Guide

The Guide supplies information on over 250 recently published reference (book and multimedia) titles marketed for pre-school children and for pupils aged between 5 and 14 years (in Key Stages[1] 1, 2 and 3). Publications for Key Stage 4 pupils have not been included, although many of the texts reviewed as Key Stage 3 publications will still be of relevance to readers over 14 years of age. By Key Stage 4, the majority of young people are turning to texts marketed for adults and consequently have less need for age-specific reference books.

The texts have been reviewed by a specialist team consisting of the following members: Fiona Collins (Education Adviser), Susan Hancock (Humanities Adviser), George Raper (Science Adviser) and Lisa Sainsbury (Multimedia Adviser) (see the list of contributors for further information on team members). Three further review panels, each consisting of pupils from the following schools: Milverton Primary School (covering Key Stage 1 publications), Woodloes Junior School (covering Key Stage 2 publications) and Aylesford School (covering Key Stage 3 publications), have also looked at, and commented on, many of the reference books.

Multimedia productions are dealt with separately in what amounts to a complete guide within a guide. If you are looking solely for reference material in computerized form, this is reviewed in Chapter 6, where Lisa Sainsbury has set out her own introduction before going on to review a range of titles and offer helpful advice for would-be purchasers in this segment of the market. If you are interested in printed books, these are covered in Chapters 2 to 5.

A guide to the reviews

The specialist review team looked at the latest available editions of all of the books reviewed; however, with such a dynamic market, new titles and new editions are arriving on the scene almost daily, and it is always worthwhile checking with the relevant publishers' catalogues to see whether revised and updated versions are due for publication in the near future. This is particularly relevant with regard to atlases, where wars and the breakdown of larger states into smaller units necessitate rapid and frequent revisions of material.

Printed below is a sample of the format used for the majority of the book reviews:

[Publisher/Imprint where not included in book title] *Title*

Details relating to the publisher and date of publication are given, together with any relevant ancillary information.

ISBN

The International Standard Book Number, unique to each publication, is part of a world-wide identification system and can be useful when ordering books (the hardback and paperback numbers are both given where relevant).

Price

Cover or catalogue prices are given, where available, for guidance only. Purchasers should be aware that these frequently change and no guarantee of accuracy can be given.

Target age range

The education adviser here suggests the age range for which the text is suitable and notes whether this varies from the age range recommended on the cover of the book or in the relevant publisher's catalogue.

Coverage

Details of material covered by the book are given.

Language, layout and images

Here issues such as the accessibility of the language and attractiveness of the layout and images are discussed. Members of the team also look at whether the images contribute to the amount of information conveyed.

Retrieval devices

The inclusion of masses of information in a book is a waste of time if this is rendered inaccessible by poor retrieval devices. The team comment on successful and unsuccessful features here.

Children's assessments

Comments from pupils who reviewed the books are recorded in order to give a child's-eye view of the books examined. The children's own words and phrasing have been reproduced as written wherever possible; however, some minor amendments to spelling and grammar have been made where clarity of meaning might otherwise have been affected.

Other aspects

Other relevant items, if any, are commented on in this section, which often includes information on companion texts and awards achieved.

National Curriculum test results

Test scores relating to coverage of material from the National Curriculum are given here for many of the books reviewed in Chapters 4 and 5 (see the section on National Curriculum tests, pp 5–6, for details of these).

Minor changes to this format have been made for some texts. For example, dictionaries have a note of the number of headwords ('**Entries**'), instead of the section on '**Coverage**' and features such as '**Language**' may be given prominence as a separate section, instead of being considered together with layout and images.

Also included in each chapter is a section entitled 'Editor's personal selection'. This is a *personal* choice from those on offer, made after weighing up all aspects of the books examined, including cost, National Curriculum coverage, child-appeal and the opinions of all who reviewed them.

Matching children and texts

The range of non-fiction on offer today is much more exciting than it used to be; choosing reference books for children can be an enjoyable and rewarding experience. It is, however, easy for adult purchasers to be swayed by personal likes, dislikes and fond memories of childhood favourites when choosing books, forgetting that the needs and preferences of intended recipients are of paramount importance. If trying to raise an initial enthusiasm for reference books and to ensure that they are fully utilized, the child's individual capabilities and style and topic preferences should always be taken into account. It is pointless to buy a volume with masses of text if the intended recipient reads with difficulty and thrives on illustrations and diagrams (and vice versa). However, it is well worth encouraging children to try the new and unfamiliar; the library is a good first point of call for those wishing to test particular types of texts prior to purchase.

A recent survey of over 8000 children, sponsored by the British Library and carried out by the National Centre for Research in Children's Literature at the Roehampton Institute, London (this will be referred to as the 'Roehampton survey' in future chapters), asked a number of questions about the reading of non-fiction. Encouragingly, over three-quarters of the youngest children (aged between four and seven years) say that they read non-fiction; however, by the time they reach Key Stages 2 and 3, children are far less interested in this type of reading, as the table below (derived from the survey report: *Young People's Reading at the End of the Century*[2]) shows:

How often do you choose to read information books or other non-fiction?

% respondents who chose 'very often' or 'often'	GIRLS	BOYS
Key Stage 2: 7 yrs–11 yrs	25.5%	38.3%
Key Stage 3: 11 yrs–14 yrs	21.0%	35.7%

Children in these age-groups are even less responsive to the idea of using encyclopedias. Given a range of options, from activity books to CD-ROMs, children who took part in the survey were asked to identify the format in which they like to encounter their non-fiction reading.

When you are reading about these subjects [the children had previously been given a list of non-fiction topics] do you like:

Key Stage 2: respondents who chose 'YES'	GIRLS	BOYS
activity books	43.5%	41.4%
magazines	49.7%	39.7%
books with lots of pictures	34.3%	38.5%
books which give lists of facts and record-breakers	31.2%	43.6%
encyclopedias	19.8%	20.2%
CD-ROMs	28.7%	40.1%

Key Stage 3: % respondents who chose 'YES'	GIRLS	BOYS
activity books	20.2%	23.9%
magazines	63.6%	48.9%
books with lots of pictures	27.2%	34.3%
books which give lists of facts and record-breakers	24.8%	41.1%
encyclopedias	12.5%	16.7%
CD-ROMs	21.0%	42.8%

Clearly children are not attracted by the idea of using encyclopedias and need to be encouraged to discover just how interesting and useful they can be. Attractiveness and 'child-appeal' are not only cosmetic concerns, and the reviews which follow (in Chapters 2 to 5) will address these issues as well as examining the actual information which the books contain. To assist purchasers, individual chapters in the Guide contain further information, taken from the Roehampton survey, on factors relating to children's choice of books and subject areas which interest them. In addition, comments in Chapters 3–5, from pupils who carried out the assessment reviews, often suggest popular features to look out for and, conversely, reveal those aspects of reference publications that are poorly regarded by children in the target age range.

National Curriculum tests

Attention has been paid throughout the Guide to the requirements of the National Curriculum,[3] with information given on aspects to look out for in prospective purchases. Additionally, books aimed at pupils in Key Stages 2 and 3 were fully tested for coverage of material from the National Curriculum. These test scores are reported in the reviews for individual texts.

For dictionaries, technical vocabulary lists for a range of National Curriculum subject areas were constructed and checked in each book. Dictionaries were awarded one point for the inclusion of each *relevant* definition or half a point for the inclusion of a related word from which the meaning of the other might be deduced. Scores for individual subject areas were then added together to give an overall result which is reported as a percentage of the maximum possible score obtainable.

For other types of books, such as encyclopedias and mini-library sets, lists of topics were constructed for selected subject areas, in order to discover which of the books reviewed are likely to be most helpful for children researching school-based topics. Testers awarded one point for full coverage of each item on the list – only half a point if the coverage was judged to be particularly limited.

Many books, however, do not broach all aspects of any given subject area. For example, a Key Stage 2 reference book concerned with human biology would not be expected to cover science topics such as green plants as organisms, simple electrical circuits or the separation of mixtures of materials and so on. Results are therefore reported in two ways. The first mark reported for each text shows the score obtained as a percentage of the maximum possible score for the total subject area; although this presentation is biased against single topic books, it *is* relevant in that more individual texts will need to be purchased in order to cover all the aspects of that subject area which will eventually be studied by pupils. The second mark takes into account the stated portion of the subject area which the book claims to cover, giving the score achieved as a percentage of the maximum possible score for that portion only. For example, a Key Stage 3 reference book concerned with the twentieth-century world would be marked out of the total score obtainable in the test for coverage of that particular unit of the programme of study and not out of the total score for history coverage, since it would not be expected to include material from other, pre-twentieth-century, study units. Exceptionally, since the study of geography generally requires pupils to have access to an atlas as well as to a general reference encyclopedia (the latter covering themes as diverse as geomorphological processes and the causes and effects of population migrations), atlases were treated as a special case, and not marked as a percentage of total geography coverage.

The score achieved by an individual text should not be the only factor looked at in deciding on the suitability of any particular purchase. The depth and quality of analysis of topics, rather than simple coverage of relevant areas, is a significant factor and much more subjective to judge. However, the tests do at least give a guide to the amount of coverage of National Curriculum subject areas, and, as such, are of some use in assessing whether the volume to be purchased gives adequate assistance to pupils. It should, of course, be borne in mind that many of the books cover significant material which is *not* National Curriculum related, yet may well be both informative and interesting.

Notes

1. The Education Reform Act 1988 established four key stages to the National Curriculum (these are defined precisely in section 3(3–6) of the Act, as amended by the Education Act 1933). Key Stage 1 covers pupils aged between five and seven years, in year groups 1–2; Key Stage 2 covers pupils aged between 7 and 11 years, in year groups 3–6; Key Stage 3 covers pupils aged between 11 and 14 years, in year groups 7–9 and Key Stage 4 covers pupils aged between 14 and 16 years, in year groups 10–11.
2. Reynolds, Kimberley et al., *Young People's Reading at the End of the Century.* Survey report from the National Centre for Research in Children's Literature at the Roehampton Institute – awaiting publication. Further information from Dr Kimberley Reynolds, Director NCRCL, Roehampton Institute London, Downshire House, Roehampton Lane, London SW15 4HT.

3. Information relating to the National Curriculum contained in this Guide is drawn from the publication: *The National Curriculum England*, DFE Department for Education, published in London by HMSO in January 1995: ISBN 0 11 270894 3.

2 Publications for pre-school children (aged four years and under)

'abc' and first words books

The problem with choosing an 'abc' or first words book is the sheer volume of such publications that appear on the market on an almost daily basis. These range from sophisticated books, with artwork that clearly aims to tempt the adult purchaser rather than the child reader, to banal and unappealing concoctions, the latter churned out into what is presumably seen as a lucrative and easily filled market.

When selecting a suitable publication, practical concerns should of course be addressed. Has child-friendly lower case print been utilized? Is the book well constructed and of a manageable size for tiny hands? Do the pictures stand out clearly and distinctly from their background? Nor should the importance of beautiful and striking images be underestimated, even with the youngest of children; Margaret Meek emphasizes: 'The effect of illustrations on children's early understanding of stories [Meek here includes non-fiction] can be quite long-lasting, because striking pictures, those that remain in the memory, work, as ancient illustrators knew well, as icons'. (Meek, 1991, p.117).

Beyond these considerations, however, it is important to think carefully about the interests and age of the individual child for whom the book is intended. Learning should be a pleasurable experience. As children grow, their needs change; a simple 'abc' which appeals to a child at the age of two may well not attract the same child at age three or four. For younger children the naming of simple and familiar objects can be an enjoyable game. Older children have wider horizons and may appreciate seeing more varied characters, settings and objects (compare the illustrations offered in 'abc' and first word books with those which children enjoy in their favourite, fictional picture book reading; the pictures accompanying non-fiction need to be just as creatively constructed). Activities such as imaginative 'Can you find . . .?' games are useful ancillary features which help to make the learning process fun. Best of all is to have a range of books available; being prepared for children, even at this age, to have their own favourites, however illogical or idiosyncratic these may seem. As Elaine Moss reminds those of us who chose books for children: ' . . . a book by itself is nothing – a film shown in an empty cinema: one can only assess its value by the light it brings to a child's eye'. (Meek et al., 1977, p.142)

A selection to think about

[De Agostini] first word books: *I can say apple, I can say blanket, I can say boat* and *I can say teddy*, words selected by Ann Locke, illustrated by Louise Batchelor. De Agostini Editions Ltd: 1996

ISBN: 1 899883 17 7, 1 899883 19 3, 1 899883 18 5, 1 899883 16 9

Price: £1.99 each

Target age range: 18 months and upwards

Entries: Every book offers 12 words, one per page, each with an accompanying picture.

Language, layout and images
This little collection of first word books is ideal for parents and carers to share with toddlers who are just beginning to talk. The words used have been specially selected by a child speech therapist for children around this age and are printed in large child-friendly lower-case lettering. On each page, bright, clear watercolour pictures show happy, cartoon-style child characters playing with, or looking at, familiar named objects (such as 'doll', 'car', 'toes'), or carrying out named activities (such as 'kiss', 'blow').

Retrieval devices
The words are not in alphabetical order; there are no overt retrieval devices. However, for children of this age, picture retrieval is a useful early skill to acquire: 'Can you find the picture of . . .?'

Other aspects
These are wipe-clean board books; a sensible format for very young children.

a little Ladybird abc, illustrated by Elizabeth Tansley. Ladybird Books Ltd: 1988

ISBN: 0 7214 9582 6

Price: £1.50

Target age range: 18 months and upwards

Entries: 26 first words, one for each letter of the alphabet, are included in this tiny board book.

Language, layout and images
Every page has one or two separate letters, each accompanied by a relevant picture and word. These all relate well to young children, with cheerful, friendly animal characters (such as a cat, a duck, a mouse and an octopus) predominating. Lower-case, child-friendly print is used throughout.

The images are bright and clear, but putting two letters on one page (a & b, k & l, m & n, u & v share) is sometimes confusing. There is a good relationship between the words, letters and images, with pictures defining the words and linked to the relevant alphabet letter (for example the mouse's tail curves through the letter m and the octopus's tentacle through the o).

Retrieval devices
The book is arranged in alphabetical order.

Other aspects
This is again produced in a sensible, wipe-clean board format. Ladybird also publish *123*, *colours* and *opposites* in this series, plus an *abc learning frieze* for the child's bedroom. Although more imaginative ones are available, the learning frieze is well laid out, again with very clear bright images.

Collins First Word Book, by Evelyn Goldsmith, illustrated by Strawberrie Donnelly. HarperCollins Children's Books: 1995

ISBN: 0 00 197005 4 hardback

Price: £5.99

Target age range: Up to 5 yrs (although the range of words is fairly prosaic for more imaginative children at the upper end of the age bracket).

Entries: 300 first words

Language, layout and images
A collection of simple words is given, based around different themes and situations which are related to the experiences of children of pre-school age. A central picture gives the focus of the theme (such as 'On the farm', 'Spring cleaning' and so on) and relevant words are printed and illustrated along the edge of the page. These word definition strips are uncluttered and the everyday images are fairly simple but colourful. The images relate quite well to the words which are printed in child-friendly lower-case.

Retrieval devices
There is a table of contents giving titles and page references for the thematic vocabulary pages.

Other aspects
An introduction, aimed at parents, offers suggestions for further activities that might be undertaken with the book (such as 'look for the toddler's little teddy').

[Oxford] *My first alphabet book*, illustrated by Julie Park. Oxford University Press: 1995

ISBN: 0 19 910332 1 hardback, 0 19 910364 X paperback

Price: £4.99 hardback, £2.99 paperback

Target age range: 2 yrs and upwards

Entries: The number of first words is not specified; there are over 170, including the 'extras' listed at the back.

Language, layout and images
Relevant and interesting words, with a range of complexity, are given for each letter (for example the letter 'd' features 'dinosaur', 'dog', 'doll', 'donkey', 'door' and 'duck'). Each

letter is written in lower and upper case with images entwined to illustrate the words printed below. Both layout and images are lovely, encouraging children to look at and discuss the letters and words. At the end of the book a further list of words is given; children are challenged to go back to the letter pages and look for the depictions of these words, hidden amongst the defined images. There is an excellent relationship between the words and images.

Retrieval devices
The contents are organized in alphabetical order.

My Oxford Picture Word Book, illustrated by Val Biro, compiled by Sheila Pemberton. Oxford University Press: 1994

ISBN: 0 19 910332 1 hardback, 0 19 910346 1 paperback

Price: £7.99 hardback, £3.99 paperback

Target age range: 3 yrs and upwards

Entries: 500 first words

Language, layout and images
A good selection of first word entries are pictorially defined and set into an example phrase. The words relate well to the needs of this age-group, naming everyday objects and introducing less familiar words, such as those from fantasy and fairy tale settings. A useful list of commonly encountered words (such as 'end', 'very', 'under') is also included for children to refer to for help with spelling. There are also a number of illustrated vocabulary pages with various themes ranging from 'Numbers' and 'The calendar' to everyday scenes such as 'A picnic in the park' and fantasy scenes such as 'Once upon a time'. Overall, the text and images are uncluttered and well laid out, with a picture for every word. Lively images, with lots of animal characters, abound. The 500 headwords are printed in blue, so that they can be easily distinguished from the accompanying illustrative phrases. They are not, however, highlighted within the phrase (which would have been helpful for less fluent readers). The scenes at the back of the book are full of life and relate well to children in this age-group.

Retrieval devices
Words are arranged in alphabetical order and appropriately illustrated header letters are printed in upper and lower case at the start of each section. The letter for the page is further highlighted on an alphabet which is printed vertically on the side of each page. Some pages include more than one letter; where this occurs the highlighted letters on the alphabet at the side are colour-coded to match the appropriate header letter in the text. There is also an alphabetical index of words used at the back of the book and a table of contents at the front.

My Oxford ABC Picture Rhyme Book, with rhymes by Roger McGough, illustrated by Debi Gliori and compiled by Dee Reid. Oxford University Press: redesigned edition 1994, first published as *The Oxford ABC Picture Dictionary* in 1990.

ISBN: 0 19 910328 3 paperback

Price: £2.99 paperback

Target age range: 3 yrs and upwards

Entries: 200 first words

Language, layout and images
A selection of headwords, ranging from simple words (such as 'dog', 'doll', 'fox' and 'car') to more difficult ones (such as 'alligator', 'astronaut', 'hippopotamus' and 'skateboard'), are pictorially represented and set into an example phrase but not highlighted within it (see the review above). There is plenty of material, including games and activities, to 'stretch' imaginative four-, five- or even six-year-old children. The book is very well laid out, with a dictionary section and rhyme on the left hand page of each spread and activities and jokes on the right. Images of animal and human (both black and white, child and adult) characters are used throughout. Each double page has a picture crammed with items beginning with the letter of the alphabet featured on that page. The child reader is encouraged to identify these and check with the relevant list of words at the back of the book. The amusing rhymes, jokes and activities are a good way of making learning fun. There is an excellent relationship between the words and images.

Retrieval devices
Arranged in alphabetical order; the full alphabet is printed in lower case at the top of each left hand page and the letter for the page appears in bold black upper-and lower-case lettering on the right hand side.

[Oxford] *Fly with the Birds: an Oxford Word and Rhyme Book*, written by Richard Edwards, illustrated by Satoshi Kitamura. Oxford University Press: 1995

ISBN: 0 19 910319 4 hardback
(ISBN 0 19 910366 6 is noted on the back of the book as a paperback version; however, this was not available at time of writing, nor mentioned in any of the Oxford catalogues).

Price: £8.99 hardback

Entries: 100 first words

Target age range: 3 yrs and upwards

Language, layout and images
Written clearly with thematic poems and vocabulary pages, the book not only offers words relating to everyday objects (such as 'bed' and 'chair') but also moves into fantasy worlds with words such as 'unicorn' and 'dragon'. Movement from familiar scenes to fantasy settings is cleverly bridged by the poems. For example, a picture of a little girl playing in her bedroom and surrounded by a jumble of furniture is accompanied by the words: 'This is my castle with big thick walls,/And windows to spy from and dungeons and halls,/And stairs that wind up to a room where I hide . . .'. This is linked to another picture (hidden under a vocabulary flap) of the little girl in a castle, keeping an assortment of monsters at bay beyond a moat and raised drawbridge. The poem concludes: 'With monsters and goblins locked safely outside'.

  Wonderful images created by the award-winning artist Satoshi Kitamura illustrate and extend the meanings of the words and poems for the young reader. The layout is imaginative and made intriguing by the device of using the 'lift up' flaps to uncover the fantasy elements.

Retrieval devices
There is no contents page or other overt retrieval device, although the thematic pages may be said to move chronologically through the day, starting at the beginning of the book with waking up and dressing and ending with bath and bed.

Other aspects
Although marketed for children of three years and upwards, the book is particularly suited to five- or even six-year-old children. Potential purchasers should not be put off by seeing such an early start to the age range.

Other reference works for this age group

Pre-school children are not generally regarded as likely recipients for reference works, with the exception of the alphabet and first word books, dealt with above, that have long been associated with this age-group. Although this may be changing, as more parents become anxious to give their children a head start as they prepare for school, books published for pre-school children are still predominantly fiction and single-topic information books (in picture-book format). Designed to be read through, these are not particularly suitable for 'dip in' reference.

There is inevitably the odd borderline text which bridges the gap between early years reading and Key Stage 1 texts and these are worth looking out for. The atlas mentioned below is one of these; although not marketed for this age range, the simple format may well make it of interest to younger children.

The Oxford Infant Atlas, by Patrick Wiegand. Oxford University Press: 1992, reprinted with corrections 1994.

ISBN: 0 19 831687 9 paperback

Price: £2.80

Target age range: Although the atlas is marketed for children of five years and upwards, it is, as the title states, an 'infant' atlas, and best suited to children aged between four and five years. A full review of this book appears in Chapter 3, because of the age range recommended by the publisher.

More generally, the route into reference works may be being bridged by imaginative publishers using the mini-library approach (see Introduction). An example of this type of series is De Agostini's 'My First Weather Books' collection (reviewed below).

[De Agostini] 'My First Weather Books' collection: *Pete's Puddles, Suki's Sun Hat, Karl's Kite, Su's Snowgirl*, written by Hannah Roche and illustrated by Pierre Pratt. De Agostini Editions Ltd: 1996

ISBN: 1 899883 12 6, 1 899883 13 4, 1 899883 14 2, 1 899883 15 0

Price: £3.99 each

Target age range: 3 yrs and upwards

Language, layout and images
These are bright and colourful hardback books with appealing bold and simple illustrations.

Retrieval devices
Although there are no overt retrieval devices, with a series of this sort parents and carers can encourage children to look at familiar phenomena, such as the weather, and choose an appropriate book in the series to relate to their own experiences.

Other aspects
It is worth checking the De Agostini catalogue for new books aimed at pre-school children; they seem to have fresh and unusual ideas (no doubt, if these are successful, other publishers will follow suit) and will hopefully be adding other mini-library collections to those currently on offer.

Editor's personal selection

For this age-group, it is helpful to buy as many first word books as can be afforded, remembering that simple, clear, well-defined pictures in a durable format (such as the board book) are important for very small children. Be ready to buy new books as interests and abilities change, ultimately preparing older children in the age-group for the kind of texts they will encounter as they enter school.

The De Agostini first word books and *a little Ladybird abc* are good 'starter' texts for children of around 18 months and upwards; these can be followed by books such as *My first alphabet book* (Oxford) as children reach the age of about two. For three-year-old children, *My Oxford Picture Word Book* and De Agostini's 'My First Weather Books' are good buys. At the age of four, a child's library would be enhanced by inclusion of *My Oxford ABC Picture Rhyme Book*, together, perhaps, with *The Oxford Infant Atlas*. In addition, if funds allow, the [Oxford] *Fly with the Birds: an Oxford Word and Rhyme Book*, despite the price tag of £8.99, is a delightful and rewarding book to own. Purchasing all of these selections, over a three year period, would cost less than 50 pounds at today's prices.

		£
De Agostini first word books (board books)	4 @ £1.99	7.96
a little Ladybird abc (board book)		1.50
[Oxford] *My first alphabet book* (paperback)		2.99
My Oxford Picture Word Book (paperback)		3.99
My Oxford ABC Picture Rhyme Book (paperback)		2.99
Fly with the Birds: an Oxford Word and Rhyme Book, (hardback)		8.99
The Oxford Infant Atlas (paperback)		2.80
De Agostini's 'My First Weather Books' collection (hardback)	4 @ £3.99	15.96
TOTAL		47.18

3 Publications for Key Stage 1 (children aged between five and seven years, in year groups one and two)

Availability and suitability: the issues at Key Stage 1

A 'desire to know'

The programme of study laid down in the National Curriculum for children at Key Stage 1 makes it plain that children in this age-group should 'be encouraged to make use of a range of sources of information including dictionaries, IT-based reference materials, encyclopedias and information presented in a fictional form' (English, Key Stage 1, Reading). Pupils are also expected to 'use globes, maps and plans at a variety of scales' (Geography, Key Stage 1).

The acquisition of information retrieval skills is not, however, easy. Children must master alphabetical order and learn to use retrieval devices, such as an index and a contents list, to find relevant page references for the information they seek. In *Young People's Reading At the End of the Century*, the Roehampton reading survey mentioned earlier, even older children (Key Stage 2) reveal that they are more inclined to look through non-fiction information books and 'choose interesting bits' than they are to 'look at the index and contents list to choose what to read'. Yet Margaret Meek, writing in *On Being Literate*, suggests that: 'Although looking for information in books is a complicated business, young learners master it quickly if their interest is engaged and their desire to know makes them patient'. (Meek, 1991, p.176)

This engagement of interest and 'desire to know' would seem then to be crucial factors. If an attractive and appealing book contains information which children are keen to discover, there is at once a double incentive for pupils to master the techniques necessary to access the relevant material. Children are individuals, however; what appeals to one may not inspire another, so parents and carers need to be aware of what might spark such 'desire to know' in their charges.

Individual children themselves develop and change as they grow older. A reference book purchased for a five-year-old may well be outgrown within a year or so; there is just as much need to upgrade reference books as there is to upgrade the fiction read by children as they progress through Key Stage 1. Margaret Meek suggests that 'boring text books are usually either too difficult or too easy for the reader'. (Meek, 1991, p.172) Access to books which offer the right degree of challenge can be a significant factor in stimulating a love of non-fiction and the acquisition of those essential information retrieval skills that will stand children in such good stead in the years to come.

What might appeal to your child?

As part of the Roehampton survey, children in Key Stage 1 were asked about the non-fiction topics they enjoy. Results show that reading about 'animals and plants' is popular with both girls and boys. Girls also like reading about 'things to make' and 'other parts of the world', while boys prefer topics such as 'the stars and space' and 'sport'.

Children at this age are often keen to share their favourite reading with adults, and the children taking part in the survey were no exception. When asked if they would like to say what their favourite non-fiction books are, they supplied hundreds of names. Unfortunately many of the titles of non-fiction books are very similar, and it is not possible to identify beyond doubt the individual books referred to. However, an analysis of apparent subject matter, deduced from the names given, confirms the popularity of some of the topic preferences suggested above. Books related to natural history come out at the top of the list for girls (in second place for boys); with sport the most popular choice for boys (but not the girls – only one gave a sports title).

Pictures are also very important for children in this age-group. Over 60 per cent of the children questioned regularly choose books because they 'like the pictures inside'. Older children in Key Stage 1 often appreciate quite sophisticated artwork; 'naive' styles, which simulate the work of young children, are not generally popular. In *The Child and the Book: A Psychological and Literary Exploration*, Nicholas Tucker, drawing on research by Anthony Booth, reminds readers that: 'for children around the age of seven or so, there is usually a distinct preference for artistic styles that are developmentally superior to those which children themselves are adopting in their own drawings at the time'. (Tucker, 1990, p.27) Praise of 'real' pictures by pupils from Milverton Primary School (see below) seems to indicate that children in this age-group increasingly demand sophisticated photographic and computer images, as well as skilful illustrations, in their reference books.

Evidence from the children also suggests that clarity, both of pictures and text, good print size and well-spaced pages, appeal to the majority of the children, in all the categories of books. Such texts are approachable, and far less daunting to this age-group than the more cluttered approach of some books. Bearing out the findings of the Roehampton survey, pupils from Milverton Primary School greeted books featuring animals with pleasure whatever the type of text.

The 'Children's assessments' panel

The Key Stage 1 reference books were reviewed, under the guidance of their class teacher Maureen Thurlow, by a mixed ability group of Year Two children (aged between six and seven years) from Milverton Primary School, a large urban school situated close to the centre of Leamington Spa. Roger Smith, the Headteacher, writes:

> The children at the school come from a variety of social backgrounds and this is reflected in a very wide span of abilities. The school is fortunate to have a number of children whose parents speak other languages and is able to draw on this multicultural expertise. The school is also fortunate in integrating children with moderate learning difficulties into mainstream education.

He goes on to say:

> It is essential that children in Key Stage 1 have access to a variety of texts which include both fiction and non-fiction. As well as the basic skills necessary for learning to read, which can incorporate phonic, 'look and say' and mixed approaches, all children need to access information. To do this they have to have such higher order reading skills as how to use an index, a contents page . . . in other words, how to use reference books. These skills run parallel to other skills. It is no good waiting until children reach Key Stage 2. These reference materials need to be available in classrooms and accessible to children all the time.

Stressing the value of continuous access to texts, Roger Smith and his fellow teachers point out how this not only enables teachers and assistants to impart information-finding skills, but also encourages the children to work with and teach each other.

The market place

Most publishers of reference works for children seem to be aware of the need to supply dictionaries aimed at this age group, and there is quite a wide range of these for parents and carers to choose from. Other reference works are not so plentifully supplied, with a limited number of up-to-date atlases and encyclopedias on the market. More numerous are single-subject information books, some sets of which build up into mini-libraries (see Introduction) for children to own and use for reference as well as cover-to-cover reading material.

Evidence from the Roehampton survey shows that a potential market is there. Children questioned from this age-group are very responsive to non-fiction. Publishers, parents and carers need to get together to ensure that a plentiful supply of good non-fiction reaches and enriches the lives of eager young learners at the very start of their school career.

Atlases

National Curriculum requirements

The programme of study for Geography at Key Stage 1 requires that children learn how the localities they investigate can be represented on paper, using scaled reduction and pictures/symbols to record physical and human features. They must also be helped to acquire a sense of place, by locating areas they are studying in a broader geographical context: towns within regions; regions within countries; countries within continents. Maps and globes are important tools for children in the acquisition of such knowledge; atlases, which usually combine maps, representations of globes, and further required information about the interaction between human beings and their environment, are essential reference books for all children at this stage.

Notes on the children's assessments

Accessibility plays an important role in the success of any reference book. Children quickly become disillusioned if they cannot find the information they are looking for; conversely, the pleasure of succeeding in simple indexing tasks encourages further use of the text in question. Indexed atlases were well received by pupils from Milverton Primary School; looking for places seems to be a popular activity with many children at this age.

The children from Milverton looked at the atlases reviewed below, using them and discussing them with their teacher and with each other. They then used pre-printed worksheets to record their comments. The worksheets encouraged the children to think about different aspects of the atlases by asking the following questions:

- Does it have a contents page?
- Does it have an index?
- Is it easy to find places on the maps?
- Does it give you any information about countries?
- Does it have any pictures or photographs?
- What do you like about this atlas?
- What do you think could be better?

A selection of atlases

The Kingfisher First Picture Atlas, by Antony Mason, with maps by John Woodcock and Eugene Fleury. Kingfisher (an imprint of Larousse plc): 1994

ISBN: 1 85697 217 8 hardback

Price: £8.99

Target age range: 6–8 yrs

Coverage: In addition to its 40 pages, the atlas has a glossy, four-page-spread, foldout map of the British Isles. This features: main cities and towns; a question and answer box; a 'FACTS AND FIGURES' box; further iconic-style images, accompanied by snippets of interesting (though sometimes rather fanciful and stereotyped) information ranging from a paragraph about cricket, 'the national sport of England' to Celtic crosses, 'found throughout Ireland'. This could easily be detached from the book and used as a separate wall poster.

The atlas offers two maps (political and physical) of each of the seven continents (except Antarctica which has only one). An inset box on each political map locates the relevant continent on a small world map. Question boxes, which help to involve the reader and encourage the development of information retrieval skills, appear on each page, with answers located at the back of the book. The physical maps have small picture symbols including representations of the flora and fauna of an area (the inclusion of animals proved to be particularly popular with the children who reviewed the book). Additional features include a page of flags and the foldout map mentioned above. There is also information about the atlas and a helpful section about the making of maps, both global and local (the making of local maps and plans is a curriculum requirement).

Language, layout and images
The language is appropriate for readers in the recommended age-range. Images are thoughtfully laid out, with lots of interesting pictures and further information organized around the maps. The information is explained well, through a combination of text and image.

Retrieval devices
The simple letter/number grid system on each of the maps works well in conjunction with the index of place names at the back; however, only one page of some of the double-page spreads carries a number despite the fact that these 'missing' page numbers are referred to in the index. There is also a contents list at the front. Guidance on using the referencing system is given at the beginning of the book, together with other useful information about the atlas, including a list and explanation of the symbols used.

Children's assessments
The children, commenting favourably on the pleasing amount of information, say that the atlas is clear and easy to read. They suggest that 'real' pictures and a better contents page would, however, improve it. They particularly like the maps showing animals around the world. Of those reviewed, this is their second favourite atlas.

Ladybird Picture Atlas, illustrations by John Dillow, text by Anita Ganeri. Ladybird: 1994

ISBN: 0 7214 7560 4 paperback

Price: £3.99

Target age range: 6–8 yrs

Coverage: The atlas has maps of: The World (one political, one showing world environments); The British Isles; Northern Europe; Central Europe; Southern Europe; Eastern Europe and Northern Asia; Canada; USA; Caribbean and Latin America; Africa (unfortunately the capital city of Nigeria is still shown as Lagos and not Abuja); The Middle East; Southern Asia; South East Asia; China and Korea; Japan; New Zealand; Australia; The Poles. An inset box on each map locates the area in colour on a small world map. There are also 'FACT' boxes on each map, together with excellent supplementary pictures and information on topics ranging from music and dance to animals, sports and exceptional buildings, such as the Shwe Dagon Pagoda in Rangoon (these help to encourage children with a diverse range of interests to gain map reading skills by looking at topics which intrigue them and locating the activities, animals and places on accompanying maps). Small picture symbols are used throughout to depict farm animals, crops and industries and there are also pictures of some endangered species, encircled in red, for children to find as they look at the maps (again popular with the children who reviewed the atlas).

Additional features include a 'Continents and Oceans' frontispiece, showing the northern and southern hemispheres; two useful pages on how to use the atlas; and flags of the world. Unfortunately only one flag is shown for 'Czechoslovakia'; although elsewhere the separate states of the Czech Republic and Slovakia are acknowledged.

Language, layout and images
The language used is appropriate for young readers in the recommended age range and the layout of the book is uncluttered and effective. Contextualizing inset global maps use white and colour-coded areas to enhance clarity. Overall the atlas is colourful and appealing and the images and text work well together.

Retrieval devices
This atlas has no grid system but there are two indexes at the back giving page number references, one for place names and one for special features. There is also a contents list at the front. Guidance on using the atlas appears at the beginning of the book, together with other useful information, including a list and explanation of the symbols used.

Children's assessments
This is the children's favourite atlas; they like its accessibility and enjoy looking things up using the index. The animals (see above) are also popular.

The Oxford Infant Atlas, by Patrick Wiegand. Oxford University Press: 1992, reprinted with corrections 1994.

ISBN: 0 19 831687 9 paperback

Price: £2.80

Target age range: 4–5 yrs. Publisher's recommendation: 5 yrs and upwards.

Coverage: An opening picture of a space shuttle and an astronaut in space is followed by three images of the earth located in space, echoing the one on the cover. The last of these relates well to a globe depicting the same aspect of the earth on an adjacent page. Other pictures of the globe show it from four different aspects (bearing the caption 'Each side of the Earth looks different') and with children examining it from above and below to emphasize that it is spherical in shape.

There are four maps of the world showing: 'land' and 'sea'; 'big rivers', 'big mountains' and 'big deserts'; the seven continents; countries in colour (only seven named) and three 'big cities' (New York, Moscow and Tokyo). These are followed by two maps of Europe showing: 'big rivers' and 'mountains'; countries in colour (eight named) and four 'big cities' (Berlin, Paris, Rome and Madrid). Five maps of the British Isles begin with an impressive satellite image from space, followed by: 'Land and sea'; 'Rivers and mountains'; 'Countries' (including flags and symbols); 'Biggest towns' – showing 13 cities.

Language, layout and images
The language is extremely simple and straightforward, with little text on each page. The letters are in large, child-friendly lower case, giving the appearance of bold, neatly handwritten words. This might be regarded as a 'pre' first atlas taster and is much more of a 'read-through' picture book than a reference work.

Whilst the photographic images of space are 'high-tech' and very impressive, they are somewhat at variance with the almost child-like application of colour on the 'flat' maps which follow (see comments at the start of this chapter). Movement from the vastness of outer space through depictions of the world and Europe to the British Isles is a useful contextualizing device. This is backed up by a further image of the British Isles, viewed from space and showing the curvature of the earth, on the end sheet.

Retrieval devices

There are no retrieval devices: the book has no contents page and no index, and indeed the pages are not numbered.

Children's assessments
The satellite photograph of the earth from space and the colours and pictures are judged to be the atlas's best features; however, the children prefer to have an index and a contents page. This is the only one of the atlases reviewed here that does not have either of these features.

Other aspects
For classroom work, this is also available in a flopover version (£35.00); all the pages of the *Oxford Infant Atlas* are included, together with enlarged pictures for group work, plus wipeable acetate sheets for the teacher to add more information. There is also a workbook for use on its own or with the atlas (*The Oxford Infant Atlas Workbook*: ISBN 0 19 831782 4, paperback, 16 pages, £0.90).

Another atlas from Oxford University Press, *The Oxford Rainbow Atlas*, which may be suitable for this age group, is reviewed in Chapter 4 with the publications for Key Stage 2.

The pupils from Milverton also commented on some atlases from their classroom shelves: they like the pictures in *The Bartholomew Children's World Atlas*, which has a contents page but no index, while they prefer the big, clear writing in the *World Atlas*. They feel that the *Philips Junior Atlas* could be more colourful, although its depiction of mountains and lands is approved of. These three atlases are not as popular with the children as the *Ladybird Picture Atlas* and *The Kingfisher First Picture Atlas* reviewed at the start of this section.

Dictionaries

Most of the major publishers of dictionaries for children offer at least one book for this age range. They vary widely – from those which give simple pictorially defined lists of words to altogether more sophisticated dictionaries giving parts of speech, tense endings and so on. The appropriate choice depends very much on the age and ability of the individual children for whom the dictionary is intended. Reproduced below are definitions of a familiar word, 'television,' from each of the dictionaries reviewed, and also from the two encyclopedias dealt with later on; these help to convey the range of ability catered for.

The titles containing these sample definitions are listed alphabetically within publisher's recommended age range (where given). Those from encyclopedias are located at the end of the list.

Ladybird Picture Dictionary (no recommendation given by publisher, our education adviser suggests 4–6 yrs)
'a television set' [defined by a picture]

Chambers First Dictionary (publisher's recommended age range: 5–7 yrs)

> television
> A **television** is an instrument in the shape of a box with a glass screen. You use a **television** to watch programmes with pictures and sounds. The short word for **television** is **TV**. [no picture]

Collins First Dictionary (publisher's recommended age range: 5–7 yrs)

> television (televisions)
> A television is a machine that brings pictures and sound through the air by electricity. [no picture]

My First Oxford Dictionary (publisher's recommended age range: 5 yrs +)

> television (televisions)
> A television is a machine that receives sounds and pictures through the air. *We watched a tennis match on television yesterday.* [accompanied by a picture]

The Usborne First Dictionary (publisher's recommended age range: 5–8 yrs)

> television   televisions   A television is a machine that shows pictures and sends out sounds. Televisions receive signals through the air and turn them into pictures and sounds. [accompanied by picture]

Ladybird Dictionary with colour illustrations (publisher's recommended age range: 6 yrs+)

> **television** also **TV** *noun* **1** the sending and receiving of pictures and usually sound by means of

electrical waves; 2 TV set an apparatus in a box, for receiving these pictures and sound. [no picture]

The Oxford Illustrated Junior Dictionary (publisher's recommended age range: 6 yrs+)

television a machine that picks up programmes sent through the air and changes them into pictures and sound so that people can watch them. [no picture]

The Usborne Picture Dictionary (publisher's recommended age range: 7 yrs +)
'The children are watching television.' [defined by a picture]

Kingfisher Child's World Encyclopedia (publisher's recommended age range: 4–7 yrs)
Appearing under the section 'Everyday machines in the home' there is a picture of two children watching television, with the caption: 'Television is one of the commonest machines in a home. We spend hours using this machine!'

Televisions are also mentioned in connection with industry (as a Japanese export) and energy: 'When we watch the television, listen to the radio or feel a room warm up, energy is being used.'

Kingfisher First Encyclopedia (publisher's recommended age range: 5 yrs +)
Here televisions appear in the section on inventions: 'Television brings pictures and sounds from all over the world into our homes. We watch the TV to learn and to relax.' [accompanied by photograph of children watching a television] They are also mentioned under the heading 'drama': 'You can also watch drama on the television. . . .'

These variations show that publishers' views on the type and amount of information suitable for a particular age group are not necessarily consistent even within the same publishing house. Purchasers need to consider more than the age range suggested on the cover or in a catalogue when choosing a suitable text for an individual child or particular group of children.

National Curriculum requirements

It may be helpful to bear in mind that, amongst its numerous requirements, the National Curriculum states that children in this age-group should not only be taught to read and write the letters of the alphabet but also to focus on plurals, spelling patterns in verb endings, and the relationships between root words and derivatives in order to find out 'what can be learned about word meanings and parts of words from consistent letter patterns' (English, Key Stage 1, Reading). Also, in developing the vocabulary necessary to enjoy the literature they are required to read, children need to encounter not only words that are associated with the everyday world around them, but also the words needed to respond to books about imaginary or fantasy worlds and books that recount traditional folk and fairy tales. The recognition of alliteration, rhyme and sound patterning in poems and chants is yet another skill which needs to be acquired. In all these areas of the programme of study for English, the right first word books and dictionaries can be of immense help.

Notes on the children's assessments

The children from Milverton Primary School did not utilize formal worksheets when reviewing the dictionaries; however, the books were again used and discussed in the classroom. Some of the children then wrote short reviews.

Pictures and retrieval devices are important for the majority of the children who wrote reviews. The most popular dictionaries with the children are: *My First Oxford Dictionary*, *The Usborne Picture Dictionary* and *The Usborne First Dictionary*.

A selection of dictionaries

Chambers First Dictionary Chambers (an imprint of Larousse plc): 1995

ISBN: 0 550 10662 6 hardback

Price: £9.99

Target age range: 5–7 yrs

Entries: 1500 headwords

Language and coverage: A wide range of everyday headword entries with simple, to-the-point definitions are to be found in this dictionary for Key Stage 1 children. Irregular plurals, tense endings, comparative and superlative forms are included in brackets, following the headword, where appropriate. There are also spelling and pronunciation tips, coloured 'sound-alike' boxes (for example: 'Another word that sounds like **bare** is **bear.**') plus occasional word origin boxes for added interest.

Layout and images
The print is clear and well-defined and the layout well spaced. Headwords are clearly shown in bold print in the accompanying definitions and example sentences. Colourful and attractive drawings, including cartoon-style characters, and photographic images abound. There are lots of children in both photographic and cartoon versions, with ethnic minority groups well represented. Well-matched images extend the definitions offered to the child. For example, a child pictured taking slow and obviously reluctant steps is shown dragging a satchel (long handle fully extended) along the floor behind her. The definition reads 'If you **drag** something, you pull it along slowly. Katey is **dragging** her school bag along behind her.'

Retrieval devices
The entries are in alphabetical order, and an alphabet printed vertically on the side of each sheet highlights, in colour, the relevant letter for that page (only **x** and **y** share a

page). At the beginning there is a useful section on how to use the dictionary. A contents box also gives page numbers for the illustrated vocabulary sections.

Children's assessments
Rachel thinks that the dictionary has a nice cover and good pictures, but is 'a bit of a boring book'.

Other aspects
Additional features include: a spell checker for commonly used words; written lists of days, months, measurements and numbers; a series of analogue clocks showing the hour, half hours and quarter hours, with accompanying longhand captions. The word-play activities are likely to be popular with children and there are useful illustrated vocabulary pages covering topics such as 'Animals', 'Cars' and 'The human body'.

Collins First Dictionary, by Ginny Lapage. HarperCollins Publishers Ltd: 1995

ISBN: 0 00 197001 1 hardback
Price: £7.99
Target age range: 5–7 yrs
Entries: The cover states 1500 headwords; inside the book, in the note to parents and teachers, a figure of 2000 headwords is given. The cover figure is more accurate.

Language and coverage: Colour-coded headwords are explained in exact but simple language. Entries are extended by the inclusion of plurals for nouns, parts of verbs (third person singular present tense, present participle, past tense and past participle) and the comparative and superlative forms of adjectives. Extensions are bracketed for clarity. Numbered definitions are given for words with more than one meaning and headwords are numbered where they appear more than once; for example when both noun and verb functions are defined. Some entries include helpful example sentences, which appear in italics under the definition given.

Layout and images
The bright, attractive pages are well laid out and spaced, with lots of colourful cartoon-style pictures. The alphabet appears on each page in upper and lower case and the first and last word for each page is displayed at the top. Page numbering is at the edge of the sheet but, rather unusually, placed half-way up. In general the images relate well to the words; however, clarity is sometimes sacrificed in order to achieve comic effect.

Retrieval devices
The alphabet at the bottom of each page helps children to locate entries, as do the words at the top. The appropriate letter is highlighted on the alphabet at the bottom; however, a different colour is used from that in which the head letter for that section appears. Where more than one letter shares a page, the highlighted letters are in the same colour, perhaps a little confusing for younger readers. At the beginning of the dictionary a helpful page of instructions for parents and teachers is included.

Children's assessments
Zach is concerned that it is a 'babies' book and too silly for him, although other children commend it for the colour coding and the printing of headwords in blue.

Ladybird Dictionary with colour illustrations, illustrations by Mike Nicholls and Judith Wood of Hurlston Design. Ladybird Books Ltd: 1988

ISBN: 0 7214 1632 2 hardback

Price: £3.50

Target age range: 7–9 yrs. Publisher's recommendation: 6 yrs and upwards

Entries: 4000 headwords

Language and coverage: The definitions are quite exact and without the benefit of example sentences. Quantity of words rather than clarity of definition would seem to be the guiding principle. The relevant part of speech is given before each definition. A six-year-old would have to be quite a fluent reader and speller to use this dictionary; it is much more suitable for a bright seven-year-old or even children of eight years and upwards.

Layout and images
The layout is dense and compact (using a small typeface) and only occasionally relieved by illustrations or diagrams. The images, of which there are one or two per page, are simple coloured line-drawings, set in coloured boxes. A limited number of illustrations extend the definitions of a few of the words; however, many of the images are more for decoration or further interest, rather than for the purpose of explication (for example, a cowboy boot is depicted alongside the word 'boot' and a drawing of a carved wooden chair from Tutankhamen's tomb appears under the word 'wood').

Retrieval devices
Alphabetically organized; there are a few ideas on how to use the dictionary at the front. The relevant letter appears in a blue box on the side of each page.

Children's assessments
Francesca, Becky and Tom feel that the dictionary is 'boring', Tim complains that the writing is too small and there are not enough pictures.

Other aspects
Two pages at the end of the book give useful metric and imperial measurements and cardinal and ordinal numbers.

Ladybird Picture Dictionary, compiled by Geraldine Taylor, illustrated by Gaynor Berry. Ladybird Books Ltd: 1993

ISBN: 0 7214 7558 2 paperback

Price: £3.99

Target age range: 4–6 yrs

Entries: over 750 headwords

Language and coverage: Simple and explicit language is used, well suited to the needs of younger children. There is a half page of notes for parents and teachers, with some suggestions for activities.

Layout and images
The entries are arranged in alphabetical order. Each headword is printed in a box,

accompanied by a defining image and contextualized in a short phrase: for example, for 'planet' the phrase is 'the planet earth'. Unfortunately the relevant word is not highlighted in any way within the phrase, presenting difficulties for some struggling readers. Not all letters are allotted a separate page.

As with the language, all the drawings are both simple and explicit, relating well to the words. The characters, particularly the animals, are quite appealing; however, the cartoon-style images of human characters tend toward the stereotypical.

Retrieval devices
A clearer layout (there are three columns of words on each page) would have been preferable; it would also have been helpful to have had an alphabet on each page. There is however a useful index of words, with page numbers, at the back of the book, and a contents list at the front.

Children's assessments
This is more popular than the older *Ladybird Dictionary with colour illustrations*. Hannah thinks it is 'BRilliant [Hannah's capitals]', an interesting book using lots of colour and words that she can read.

Other aspects
At the back of the book are a number of well-presented and colourful illustrated vocabulary pages: 'My body'; 'Clothes'; 'Families'; 'Food'; and 'Shops'. There are also further lists of words, such as numbers (illustrated on an abacus), days, months, shapes and colours. Additional features include illustrated pages of 'Doing words' and 'Opposite words', plus a spelling list of 'Words we write a lot'.

My First Oxford Dictionary, compiled by Evelyn Goldsmith, illustrated by Julie Park. Oxford University Press: 1993

ISBN: 0 19 910236 8 hardback; 0 19 910275 9 paperback

Price: £7.99 hardback, £4.99 paperback

Target age range: 5-7 yrs

Entries: 1500 headwords

Language and coverage: There are clear and simple definitions, and many of the headwords are put into an italicized example sentence related to the child's understanding. Headword entries are also extended by the inclusion of plurals, tense endings, and comparative and superlative forms (bracketed for clarity), wherever these are appropriate.

Layout and images
Clearly laid out, with headword entries in coloured print and similarly coloured lines between entries, the dictionary looks appealing and fun. Many of the words are illustrated with bright and colourful pictures, including lively-looking children in good multicultural representations. The images extend the word definitions.

Retrieval devices
The entries are in alphabetical order, with each letter (other than x, y, z) starting on a new page. The head letter appears in upper and lower case and surrounded by a colourful picture. An alphabet, colour-coded to match the relevant header letter, is printed vertically on the side of each sheet with the letter for that page circled and printed in bold black.

The first and last word on each page are also shown at the top of each sheet in a similarly colour-coded box. Delightful characters with names beginning with the appropriate letter of the alphabet balance on the page numbers (for example, cats are depicted on pages 17 to 27 where the 'c' words are located). The illustrated vocabulary pages (see below) are cross-referenced from the alphabetical section. A detailed page of introduction for parents and teachers is included in the front.

Children's assessments
Sophie says that: 'the pictures are nice and the colours on the pictures are excellent.' She also feels that 'the writing is good', while Ethan and Talus find the book colourful and comment that it is easy to find things in. This is one of the Milverton children's three favourite dictionaries.

Other aspects
A special picture section shows illustrated vocabulary pages covering: 'Colours and Shapes'; 'Opposites'; 'Fruit'; 'Vegetables'; 'Flowers'; 'Trees'; 'Animals in the Wild'; 'Dinosaurs'; 'Farm Animals'; 'Pets'; 'Your Body'; 'Transport'; 'Time'; and 'Seasons'. There are also lists of days, months, numbers, commonly-used words and family words. The dictionary, which is a winner of the Duke of Edinburgh English Speaking Union Book Award, has a companion activity book with games, puzzles, activities and exercises. *My First Oxford Dictionary Activities* (30 pages, with line drawings, in paperback ISBN 0 19 910394 1: price £1.99) is now available to enhance and encourage use of the dictionary.

The Oxford Illustrated Junior Dictionary, compiled by Rosemary Sansome and Dee Reid, illustrated by Barry Rowe. Oxford University Press: 1994, first published 1989

ISBN: 0 19 910330 5 hardback, 0 19 910331 3 paperback

Price: £8.99 hardback, £5.99 paperback

Target age range: Although the Oxford University Press catalogue suggests that the dictionary is suitable for children aged six years and upwards, the cover indicates an age range of seven years and upwards. On the basis of the cover guideline, the book has been reviewed with the Key Stage 2 publications (see Chapter 4).

The Usborne Picture Dictionary, by Angela Wilkes, revised by Sarah Wedderburn and illustrated by Colin King. Usborne Publishing Ltd: 1991, based on a previous edition first published in 1984

ISBN: 0 7460 1797 9 paperback

Price: £6.99

Target age range: 6–8 yrs. Publisher's recommendation 7 yrs and upwards.

Entries: 1200 headwords

Language and coverage: Everyday words are pictorially defined and used in example sentences which are simple and to the point. There is a short 'How to use this book' section, ostensibly addressed to the child reader, but with parents and carers in mind.

Layout and images
The layout is well spaced, with words laid out in boxes, each containing a definition and a picture. Amusing cartoon characters are introduced by name at the front and used throughout; however, there are no multicultural images.

Retrieval devices
A clearer layout (there are three columns of words on each page) might have been preferable. Alphabetical order is used, but no full alphabet is given on individual pages (although one does appear in upper and lower case on the front cover). Letters in some instances share a page.

Children's assessments
The children are impressed with the colour coding and the colourful pictures in the dictionary and find it 'easy to read'. This is another of the children's three favourite dictionaries.

Other aspects
The dictionary has lists of 'Useful words': numbers, days, months, seasons and countries and continents. The lists of countries and continents are not very helpful; 31 countries (the Soviet Union is still listed among these) are featured and only five of the seven continents. Additional features include an extremely useful page detailing parts of speech; this has definitions, examples and illustrative sentences with the relevant part of speech underlined.

The Usborne First Dictionary, by Rachel Wardley and Jane Bingham, designed by Susie McCaffrey and Sue Grobecker, illustrated by Teri Gower and Stuart Trotter. Usborne Publishing Ltd: 1995

ISBN: 0 7460 2348 0 hardback, 0 7460 2347 2 paperback

Price: £12.99 hardback, £9.99 paperback

Entries: over 2500 headwords

Target age range: 7–8 yrs. Publisher's recommendation 5–8 yrs.

Language and coverage: Meanings are quite clearly defined and an italicized example sentence is given for many of the words (with the relevant word highlighted in bold print). Tense endings, plurals and comparative and superlative forms are given, where relevant, directly beneath the headword (these appear in the same black print as the word definitions and do not stand out from each other very well). Some of the headwords are followed by ideas for alternatives, included in colour-coded 'Some other words for' boxes (for example 'fast' is followed by a box which offers 'quick, swift, rapid and speedy'). Everyday opposites are also given for some entries and these are preceded by a distinguishing colour-coded symbol.

Layout and images
The layout is a little crowded with three columns per page. Picture illustrations and photographic images (including multicultural images) extend many of the definitions given. The images and text are tidily integrated and the images relate to and complement the example sentences.

Retrieval devices
There are introductory pages to advise on use of the dictionary. Added word games

encourage children to enjoy using the book. A full alphabet is included at the base of each page (lower case on one side of the spread, upper case on the other), with the relevant letter highlighted in the same colour as it appears at the start of each letter section. The coloured header letters are also printed in upper and lower case.

Children's assessments
Victoria and Lianne like the 'real' pictures and are particularly impressed by the 'real motorcycle'. They also comment favourably on the 'colours at the edge' and 'the abc at the bottom'. Laragh considers that this is 'a fun book because it has lots of pictures' and also 'a strong book very easy to understand'. Both Laragh and Douglas feel that it is 'exciting'. This is one of the children's three favourite dictionaries.

Some of the more advanced word books marketed for pre-school children can still be valuable resources for children in their early years at school. Good examples of these are the [Oxford] *Fly with the Birds: an Oxford Word and Rhyme Book* and *My Oxford ABC Picture Rhyme Book* (full reviews of these appear in Chapter 2). Children as old as six and seven years enjoy the jokes in the latter.

Encyclopedias

Very few full general encyclopedias are on offer for this age-group; the reason for this is perhaps suggested by certain of the criticisms levelled at the two reviewed below. In order to cover the quantity of material demanded by a multi-subject volume the publisher must choose, it seems, between one of two undesirable options. On the one hand, if the material is to be covered as deeply and comprehensively as it needs to be, the resultant book is likely to be too large to be handled comfortably by a small child, and to sell at a price that may be off-putting to a purchaser (who will be aware that its useful life must inevitably be shorter than that of an encyclopedia designed for older children). On the other hand, a smaller, cheaper book will tend towards being a rather superficial survey of the material which it offers; in other words a picture book guide to topics to be followed up elsewhere.

However, if purchasers are prepared to pay fairly large sums for encyclopedias for this age group, despite appreciating that they have a relatively short 'shelf-life', they can be a helpful introduction to the use of reference works. Certainly the children from Milverton Primary School *enjoyed* those they reviewed.

National Curriculum requirements

At Key Stage 1 the subjects included in the National Curriculum are: English, mathematics, science, technology (design and technology, and information technology), history, geography, art, music and physical education; so that any encyclopedia has a wide range of material to cover if it is to function as a useful general reference work for children at this stage. With so much to do, it is important that the texts have a clear idea of the needs of the age-group they aim to serve; not always the case with those reviewed, as comments from the specialist review panel will show (see individual book reviews).

Notes on the children's assessments

Six children were asked to write their own reviews of the two encyclopedias they examined. These are reproduced in the children's assessments sections below, with some spelling errors amended for clarity.

A selection of encyclopedias

Kingfisher Child's World Encyclopedia. Kingfisher (an imprint of Larousse plc): 1994
ISBN: 1 85697 256 9 hardback
Price: £25.00

Target age range: 6–8 yrs if read independently, or for younger children if mediated by an adult. Publisher's recommendation: 4–7 yrs. The book is very large and heavy for children in the early years of the recommended age range to handle.

Coverage: Material is arranged thematically under the following main headings: 'The Universe'; 'Our Planet Earth'; 'The Sea'; 'All Kinds of Animals'; 'Plants'; 'When Dinosaurs Lived'; 'My Body'; 'Machines'; 'Science'; 'People and Places'. A variety of topics are covered under each heading; for example, the section on plants has sub-headings for: 'Plants'; 'Living and Growing'; 'All Shapes and Sizes'; 'Food and Drink'; 'Decoration'; 'In danger'; 'Ideas'.

The book also offers a range of activities for children to do and has a helpful explanatory page showing the symbols used and detailing the functions of the directional arrows and the word boxes used. A nice touch is the inclusion of snippets from multicultural legends, myths, folk and fairy tales and well-known children's literature (including *Alice in Wonderland*, *Treasure Island* and *Chitty Chitty Bang Bang*).

Language, layout and images
The target audience is not always consistently addressed; at times fairly demanding words are used, yet at others very obvious questions are asked; for example, the question 'Can you find a steering wheel?' appears alongside a picture of a car with a steering wheel labelled.

There are some beautiful photographic images and friendly, funny cartoon characters; both styles are appreciated by children in this age range. The layout is well thought out and clarity is assisted by the judicious use of arrows and boxes.

Retrieval devices
A somewhat confused table of contents refers to the ten main sections. The contents lists associated with individual sections are much more helpful and straightforwardly laid out. There is also an index with page references at the end of the book.

Children's assessments

Child 1: 'It is easy to read. It tells you all about it and it is interesting because it tells you about animals and people and stuff. The writing is spaced out. I like the nests and eggs and the book is very good because it tells you about the earth and all things that you want to know.'

Child 2: 'I like the way they set it up. The contents are good. There are lots of things to look up. It is very good. There are lots of nice pictures. I like it a lot. It gives me lots of things to think about.'

Child 3: 'It is easy to read. It is spaced out. It is interesting it shows you everything. Many animals are good. I really like the animals.'

Other aspects

Whilst it is difficult to cover so many topics in any depth in one volume, the encyclopedia does at least offer a good introduction to many areas which are included in the Key Stage 1 programme of study for Science. There are pictures of flowering plants, including labelled diagrams showing roots, stem, leaf and flower. The making of materials such as glass is shown with the aid of diagrams and pictures. Activities such as the making of a simple circuit (with adult assistance) are suggested. Concepts such as transparency, translucence and opacity are demonstrated in helpful text/image combinations, as are those of light and dark (with activities suggested to enable children to investigate these for themselves). Life processes are explored with the aid of cross-sectional diagrams, including human growth, nutrition and reproduction.

Other subject areas in the National Curriculum are not allotted quite so much coverage. Traditions are touched upon (by continent, including religious and other festivals) but there are no pages on famous men and women. Although literature of the variety laid down in the programme of study for English is included, it is in tiny 'taster' paragraphs.

All in all the encyclopedia contains a considerable quantity of basic material for adults and the young children in their care to share and build upon, but the size (not child-friendly) and price (not adult-friendly) are both negative features.

Kingfisher First Encyclopedia. Kingfisher (an imprint of Larousse plc): 1996

ISBN: 0 7534 0054 5 hardback

Price: £12.99

Target age range: Although the book is marketed for children aged five years and upwards, parts of the text are perhaps better suited to older children in Key Stage 1 or even those at the beginning of Key Stage 2. However, the plentiful pictures may well appeal to younger children. Coverage is really rather mixed. For example the National Curriculum for Key Stage 1 expects children to learn to name the leaf, flower, stem and root of a flowering plant; in the encyclopedia under 'Flower' the parts labelled are the petal, stigma and stamen – prior knowledge of leaf, flower and stem is assumed, although a root is later labelled on the diagrammatic representation of a seed developing (shown under the heading 'Plant'). Conversely, the section labelled 'Inventions' shows pictures of items familiar to the majority of children, such as the telephone, refrigerator and television; these are accompanied only by a brief and very bland description of each (see the wording which is used to describe a television, reproduced at the start of the dictionary section).

Coverage: 90 topics are covered, ranging from single page coverage of areas such as 'Electricity' and 'Drama' to two double-page spreads for 'Animals' and for 'Weather'.

Language, layout and images

On the whole the language used is comparatively simple; however, a range of more complex or unusual words is introduced. The text is organized into small paragraphs, amplified by an accompanying image or images; a single-page glossary at the end of the book offers definitions for some of the more unfamiliar terms. For example 'submersible' is defined in the glossary as 'a small submarine used especially for underwater exploration'. Unfortunately, nothing on the 'how to use your book' page indicates that the glossary is there or how to use it, and when a defined word appears in the text there seems to be nothing to indicate that an explanation of the term will be given later.

Clear, fair-sized print is used throughout, with headings appearing slightly larger and emboldened. Sequential pictures are numbered for clarity, and arrows point to the appropriate image for the paragraph. There are small, coloured fact boxes and 'find out more' boxes which suggest related topics which may be of interest. These do not offer a comprehensive cross-referencing scheme; for example, the topic entitled 'Inventions' shows 'the wheel', but there is no cross-reference to the section on 'Machines', where diagrams explaining wheel and axle movement appear (the index does not pick this up either). There are well-produced and colourful photographs, maps, diagrams and illustrative pictures throughout, with plentiful multicultural images. The images assist in explaining and extending the text.

Retrieval devices

There is a 'how to use your book' page which covers aspects of the layout, including the use of sequentially-numbered diagrams, arrows and fact boxes and the use of child-friendly cartoon characters as symbols to indicate follow-on pages and 'find out more' boxes. No reference is made in this guide to use of the index or glossary which appear at the end of the book. There is a full contents list at the front, giving page numbers for the alphabetically organized topics. The index has a fairly comprehensive cross-referencing system.

Children's assessments

Child 1: 'I think this book is very good because it explains a lot and the writing is spaced out and it tells you how to use the book. The information is very useful. The pictures are good. The writing has an arrow pointing to the pictures. There are lots of pictures. It explains things very easily.'

Child 2: 'I think that it is very good because it has lots of pictures in it and it is very useful because it tells you about useful things. It is very interesting. It has useful information. It tells you about lots of different things. It is very easy to read because it has big writing.'

Child 3: 'I think they show you a lot about things and they explain very well. The pictures are very good. On page 21 there is a pretty fountain and there are animals that I've never seen before.'

Other aspects

This volume is not so large and heavy as the *Kingfisher Child's World Encyclopedia* and only half the price, but it is rather more superficial and far less helpful for Key Stage 1 children.

Mini-libraries

Mini-libraries, small collections of information books from a publisher's series, may be a partial answer to the problems encountered with the general encyclopedias reviewed above. These sets of books may be collected over a period of time, looked through as individual information books, and then retained on the shelves for later reference if a query on the topic they contain arises. The consistent format often used in a small series may then facilitate the use of these as multi-volume sets. A slight drawback to this approach is that whilst a contents list and index may be present in each book, there is unlikely to be an index system for the whole series.

Some of the material presented in such books may appear to be of little relevance to school work; however, a child learning how to look up facts related to a hobby or general interest is still acquiring information retrieval skills and may also be laying down an interest in non-fiction books that will encourage further use of these later on.

A selection of mini-libraries

Collins 'Little Gems'. HarperCollins Children's Books: 1996. A series of pocket-sized hardback books

ISBN: various (see individual titles)

Price: £2.99 each

Target age range: 5–7 yrs

Language, layout and images
Although the language used is quite accessible, the Key Stage 1 review panel reports that, if approached independently, the text is better suited to the more fluent readers in this age-group. However, our reviewers feel that less fluent readers can still glean much from the photographs, fact boxes and diagrams. The books are an ideal size for the age range suggested and pleasantly tactile, with a kind of padding inside the hardback cover.

Retrieval devices
All the books have a contents list and an index.

Children's assessments
The children on the Milverton Panel did not write individual reviews of the mini-library collections; however, their teachers' comments are recorded at the end of this section.

Other aspects
Designed for the leisure-time reading of enthusiastic 'hobbyists' and collectors of facts, these are probably of limited educational value in terms of the range of topics offered. They are however fun and child-friendly and can encourage the acquisition of information retrieval skills.

Individual volumes in this series are:

Cats, written by Sarah Allen, designed by Louise Morley

ISBN: 0 00 197912 4 hardback

Coverage: The book has lovely photographs and details of 25 different breeds of cat. Organized by type (long-haired, short-haired), rather than in alphabetical order, breeds covered range from the Abyssinian to the Turkish Van. Little 'cat facts' boxes accompany each cat, and the top rim of each page has a strip of amusing, tiny cartoon images of cats: playing with wool, chasing mice, and even knitting and playing with mice. There is a contents page at the front of the book and an index with page references at the end.

Dinosaurs, written by Dougal Dixon, illustrations by Peter David Scott
ISBN: 0 00 197910 8 hardback

Coverage: The contents of the book are organized by geological period: Triassic, Jurassic, Cretaceous. It begins with an introduction, details of fossil evidence and a general description of the different eating habits of the various types of dinosaurs: meat-eaters, swallowing plant-eaters, chewing plant-eaters. There are plenty of diagrams, including one of the geological time periods in which the dinosaurs lived. Drawings of different dinosaurs and their habitats are followed by pages of different species (36 in all), accompanied by 'dinofact' boxes and scale pictures showing the length and height of each creature. A section on families discusses ways in which different dinosaurs are thought to have cared for their young (recording any evidence uncovered in support of these theories); theories of why the dinosaurs might have become extinct are also discussed. The view that they may have evolved into birds: 'some scientists think that the similarities between birds and dinosaurs are so great that we should think of birds as dinosaurs' is aired. A contents list appears at the front, and at the back is an index with page references and a helpful pronunciation guide.

Dogs, written by Sandy Ransford, designed by Jacqueline Palmer and Simon Brewster

ISBN: 0 00 197911 6 hardback

Coverage: 42 dogs are depicted, each with photographs, text and a fact box. The book is organized by general type (hounds, terriers, working dogs, gun dogs, utility dogs, toy dogs) rather than in alphabetical order. The top rim of each page has a strip of amusing, tiny cartoon images of dogs: chasing, digging, sheep penning, fetching sticks, chasing cats and even pampered on cushions. There is a contents page at the beginning of the book. An index, with page references, at the end shares a spread with a height chart on which different breeds are compared.

Horses and Ponies, written by Sandy Ransford, designed by Charlie Webster

ISBN: 0 00 197913 2 hardback

Coverage: The book has lovely photographs. It records details of 33 different breeds of horses; these are again organized by type (heavy horses, middleweight horses, lightweight horses, and ponies) rather than in alphabetical order. As with the other books, information is disseminated by means of general text, fact boxes and the photographs of actual animals. There is a contents page at the beginning of the book. An index at the end, with page references, shares a spread with a height chart on which different breeds (shire horse, Welsh pony, Falabella) are compared with a child in terms of size.

Superbikes, written and designed by Charlie Webster and Mike Morris, consultant Michael Potter
ISBN: 0 00 197905 1 hardback

Coverage: The motorbikes are presented in alphabetical order. 26 are shown, ranging from the Aprilia RS250 to the Yamaha GTS1000. Each superbike occupies a double-page spread, with two or more photographs on each, together with text, a factfile box (detailing engine, performance, and power output) plus a picture of the flag for each country of origin. There is a contents page at the beginning and at the end an index, with page references, shares a spread with a labelled cross-section of a typical 'superbike'.

Supercars, designed by Louise Morley

ISBN: 0 00 197914 0 hardback

Coverage: 26 cars are included, in alphabetical order, ranging from the AC Cobra to the TVR Griffith 500. Each car occupies a double-page spread, with two or more photographs on each, together with text, a factfile box (detailing engine, performance, and power output) plus a picture of the flag for each country of origin. There is a contents page at the beginning of the book. At the end, as with the 'superbikes', there is an index with page references and a labelled cross-sectional diagram of a typical 'supercar'.

[Ladybird] 'Big . . .' series. Ladybird Books Ltd: 1995

ISBN: various (see individual titles)

Price: £2.99 each

Target age range: 4–6 yrs

Language, layout and images
There are good descriptions, in clear simple language, designed to help the young reader. More difficult words appear in bold and are explained in a glossary. The layout is lovely, with big, bold, colourful pictures; the text is well displayed on a coloured background. The images really support the text.

Retrieval devices
There is a clear table of contents and a well-spaced index. The headings are large and bold.

Children's assessments
The children on the Milverton Panel did not write individual reviews of the mini-library collections; however, their teachers' comments are recorded at the end of this section.

Other aspects
At the back of the book a large diagram, with key, shows the sizes of each of the creatures (or trucks) relative to each other. On the page on which the creature or truck appears,

an inset box shows a silhouette of it, alongside those of an adult and a child (in the *Big Bugs* book hands are shown). These are very helpful features for children learning about scale and relative size. A foldout frieze is also included in the books. This is an excellent series; the publishers have really thought about their young readers and the books are attractive and appealing.

Individual volumes in this series are:

Big Animals, written by Mary Gribbin and illustrated by Peter Bull

ISBN: 0 7214 9632 6 paperback

Coverage: Nine animals are featured, ranging from the elephant to the kangaroo.

Big Bugs, written by Mary Gribbin and illustrated by Andrew Tewson

ISBN: 0 7214 9634 2 paperback

Coverage: Some very strange creatures, ranging from the goliath beetle to the jumping spider, are introduced.

Big Ocean Creatures, written by Mary Gribbin and illustrated by Peter Bull

ISBN: 0 7214 9636 9 paperback

Coverage: Nine fascinating sea creatures are shown, ranging from the blue whale to the giant clam and the elephant seal.

Big Trucks, written by Mary Gribbin and illustrated by Julian Baker

ISBN: 0 7214 9633 4 paperback

Coverage: From a dumper truck to a combine harvester, nine trucks are shown in their work environment.

Additional titles, published in this series since the above were reviewed, are:

Big Buildings (ISBN: 0 7214 9658 X)
Big Farm Animals (ISBN: 0 7214 9660 1)
Big Machines (ISBN: 0 7214 9635 0)
Big Wonders of the World (ISBN: 0 7214 9659 8)

Usborne 'Starting Point Science' series. Usborne Publishing Ltd (various dates)
20 small books, each having 24 pages and covering single topics, form the core of the series.

ISBN: various (see individual titles)

Target age range: 6 yrs and upwards

Language, layout and images
Although the language used is generally relevant to this age-group, there is no glossary to explain the scientific words embedded in the text. The relationship between the words and the colourful, cartoon-style illustrations is very good, with the images supporting the text for less fluent readers. Good use is made of cross-sectional diagrams. However, the pages (on which the space allotted to words and to images is roughly equal) are rather 'busy'. The Key Stage 1 review panel found this rather off putting. These books may be better suited to children at the beginning of Key Stage 2, who tend to have more experience of complicated picture texts (such as those found in comics and magazines).

Retrieval devices
There is a contents list and index for each book; both work well.

Children's assessments
The children on the Milverton Panel did not write individual reviews of the mini-library collections; however, their teachers' comments are recorded at the end of this section.

Other aspects
Individually the books are a manageable size and quite reasonably priced (particularly the combined volumes discussed later). Additional features include some quizzes, suggested activities (for example, *Where does Rubbish Go?* has details of how to 'make your own paper') and fact boxes. The books are written in quite an informal, chatty style and very much addressed 'to' their young readers. For example, the excellent *Where do Babies Come From?* (consultants: Dr Kevan Thorley and Cynthia Beverton of Relate, Marriage Guidance Council) attempts to explain baby 'behaviour' to older siblings who may be experiencing jealousy ('Babies cannot wait for things. They have not learned to think about other people's feelings and if they do have to wait long, for something like food, they may even become unwell. . . . Brothers and sisters can sometimes feel left out.') and offsets explicitly labelled body diagrams with many more 'cuddly' pictures of loving family scenes.

Individual volumes are:

What Makes it Rain?, by Susan Mayes

ISBN: 0 7460 0274 2 paperback

Price: £2.99

What Makes a Flower Grow?, by Susan Mayes

ISBN: 0 7460 0275 0 paperback

Price: £2.50

What's Under the Ground?, by Susan Mayes

ISBN: 0 7460 0357 9 paperback

Price: £2.25

Where does Electricity Come From?, by Susan Mayes
ISBN: 0 7460 0358 9 paperback
Price: £2.99

The above four titles won the 1989 Science Book Prize (The Science Museum).

What's Out in Space?, by Susan Mayes
ISBN: 0 7460 0430 3 paperback
Price: £2.99

How Does a Bird Fly?, by Kate Woodward
ISBN: 0 7460 0694 2 paperback
Price: £2.25

How do Animals Talk?, by Susan Mayes
ISBN: 0 7460 0600 4 paperback
Price: £2.25

Why is Night Dark?, by Sophy Tahta
ISBN: 0 7460 0428 1 paperback
Price: £2.99

What's Inside You?, by Susan Meredith
ISBN: 0 7460 0602 0 paperback
Price: £2.50

Where does Rubbish Go?, by Sophy Tahta
ISBN: 0 7460 0627 6 paperback
Price: £2.50

Where do Babies Come From?, by Susan Meredith
ISBN: 0 7460 0690 X paperback, 0 7460 0691 8 hardback
Price: £2.99 paperback, £2.95 hardback

Where did Dinosaurs Go?, by Mike Unwin
ISBN: 0 7460 1016 8 paperback, 0 7460 1017 6 hardback
Price: £2.50 paperback, £3.50 hardback

Why do Tigers have Stripes?, by Mike Unwin
ISBN: 0 7460 1300 0 paperback, 0 7460 1301 9 hardback
Price: £2.25 paperback, £3.50 hardback

Why do People Eat?, by Kate Needham
ISBN: 0 7460 1302 7 paperback, 0 7460 1303 5 hardback
Price: £2.25 paperback, £3.50 hardback

Why are People Different?, by Susan Meredith
ISBN: 0 7460 1014 1 paperback, 0 7460 1015 X hardback
Price: £2.25 paperback, £3.50 hardback

What Makes you Ill?, by Mike Unwin and Kate Woodward
ISBN: 0 7460 0692 6 paperback, 0 7460 0693 4 hardback
Price: £2.25 paperback, £3.50 hardback

How do Bees Make Honey?, by A Claybourne
ISBN: 0 7460 1765 0 paperback, 0 7460 1766 9 hardback
Price: £2.99 paperback, £3.99 hardback

What's Under the Sea?, by Sophy Tahta
ISBN: 0 7460 0968 2 paperback, 0 7460 0969 0 hardback
Price: £2.25 paperback, £3.50 hardback

What's the Earth Made Of?, by Susan Mayes
ISBN: 0 7460 1709 X paperback, 0 7460 1710 3 hardback
Price: £2.99 paperback, £3.99 hardback

What Makes a Car Go?, by Sophy Tahta

ISBN: 0 7460 1650 6 paperback, 0 7460 1651 4 hardback

Price: £2.50 paperback, £3.50 hardback

Aware that individual titles might well be combined into a general encyclopedia or mini-library, Usborne have gone some of the way towards grouping these core texts into multi-volume sets. They have approached this in two ways.

The first method groups four unconnected topics into one volume: thus the first four titles published (one to four of the above list) appear as Volume 1, the next four as Volume 2 (five to eight inclusive), the next as Volume 3 (nine to 12 inclusive) and the following four as Volume 4 (13 to 16 inclusive). Under this scheme, titles 17 to 20 do not yet appear in a combined set. The combined volumes retain the individual contents lists at the front of each section (former book), but a combined index is given at the back of the volume. This makes for rather oddly assorted and confusing individual volumes; although once all four have been collected a fairly broad range of science subject matter is included in the set. Details of these volumes, which all represent considerable savings on the individual prices, are as follows:

Usborne Starting Point Science Volume 1, combining: *What Makes it Rain?*, *What Makes a Flower Grow?*, *What's Under the Ground?*, *Where does Electricity Come From?*

ISBN: 0 7460 1106 7 paperback, 0 7460 0481 8 hardback

Price: £4.95 paperback, £6.95 hardback

Usborne Starting Point Science Volume 2, combining: *What's Out in Space?*, *How Does a Bird Fly?*, *How do Animals Talk?*, *Why is Night Dark?*

ISBN: 0 7460 0655 1 hardback

Price: £6.95

Usborne Starting Point Science Volume 3, combining: *What's Inside You?*, *Where does Rubbish Go?*, *Where do Babies Come From?*, *Where did Dinosaurs Go?*

ISBN: 0 7460 1090 0 paperback, 0 7460 0970 4 hardback

Price: £4.95 paperback, £6.95 hardback

Usborne Starting Point Science Volume 4, combining: *Why do Tigers have Stripes?*, *Why do People Eat?*, *Why are People Different?*, *What Makes you Ill?*

ISBN: 0 7460 1306 X paperback, 0 7460 0481 8 hardback

Price: £4.99 paperback, £6.99 hardback

The second method combines topics thematically in three volumes; this is much more helpful. Again there are four missing titles, but not the last four this time. Details of the three themed books, which also offer considerable savings over the purchase of the sets as individual books, are as follows:

Usborne Starting Point Science: Earth and Space, combining: *What's the Earth Made Of?*, *What's Under the Ground?*, *What's Under the Sea?*, *What Makes it Rain?*, *Why is Night Dark?*, *What's Out in Space?*

ISBN: 0 7460 1970 X paperback, 0 7460 1971 8 hardback

Price: £5.99 paperback, £7.99 hardback

Usborne Starting Point Science: Life on Earth, combining: *Where did Dinosaurs Go?*, *How Does a Bird Fly?*, *How do Animals Talk?*, *Why do Tigers have Stripes?*, *What Makes a Flower Grow?*, *How do Bees Make Honey?*

ISBN: 0 7460 1972 6 paperback, 0 7460 1973 4 hardback

Price: £5.99 paperback, £7.99 hardback

Usborne Starting Point Science: You and Your Body, combining: *What's Inside You?*, *Why do People Eat?*, *What Makes you Ill?*, *Where do Babies Come From?*, *Why are People Different?*

ISBN: 0 7460 1857 6 paperback, 0 7460 1858 4 hardback

Price: £5.99 paperback, £7.99 hardback

Children's assessments

Roger Smith summarizes the general points raised by class teachers in respect of the mini-library sets:

> The children liked the Collins Little Gem books and the Ladybird First Discovery books. This was despite the fact that the Collins books were too difficult for them to read independently. They did however have excellent pictures and illustrations and the children used them to talk about with each other and with adults. The Usborne Science books appealed to only a few children who had very good reading skills. Many were put off by the amount of information on the page.

Editor's personal selection

The paperback version of *My First Oxford Dictionary*, together with its companion *My First Oxford Dictionary Activities*, is an excellent purchase for children between the ages of five and six. For children from about the age of six

The Ladybird Picture Atlas and also the Ladybird 'Big . . .' series (selecting, say, four titles on subjects that appeal to the intended recipient) are good buys. If any of the topics covered by the Collins 'Little Gems' series are of interest to intended recipients, these are popular and inexpensive books and it would be worth purchasing two or three relevant titles, as the start of a collection.

		£
My First Oxford Dictionary (paperback)		4.99
My First Oxford Dictionary Activities (paperback)		1.99
Ladybird Picture Atlas (paperback)		3.99
Ladybird 'Big . . .' series (paperback)	4 @ £2.99	11.96
Collins 'Little Gems' series (hardback)	3 @ £2.99	8.97
TOTAL		31.90

If feeling extravagant, add the *Kingfisher Child's World Encyclopedia* to the above selection (suitable for children from about the age of six); especially if there are younger brothers or sisters to pass it on to. This one may be worth trying in the library first, in order to judge whether children find the size and weight 'off-putting'.

When looking for books for children aged seven years, just before they move into Key Stage 2, the Usborne 'Starting Point Science' series, preferably in combined paperback volumes, such as the three: *Earth and Space, Life on Earth,* and *You and Your Body,* could be considered. These should not be purchased too early; recipients need to be fluent readers of both written and picture texts.

Additional purchases	£
Kingfisher Child's World Encyclopedia (hardback)	25.00
Usborne Starting Point Science: Earth and Space (paperback)	5.99
Usborne Starting Point Science: Life on Earth (paperback)	5.99
Usborne Starting Point Science: You and Your Body (paperback)	5.99
TOTAL	42.97

4 Publications for Key Stage 2 (children aged between seven and 11 years, in year groups three to six)

Availability and suitability: the issues at Key Stage 2

Choosing and interacting

Responses from Key Stage 2 children questioned in the Roehampton survey provide a snapshot of the way that children aged between seven and 11 years choose their books. The survey also reveals what interests these children in terms of non-fiction subject matter.

For those that choose books on the basis of the appearance of the cover, the pictures there are of prime significance; although a number of children also feel that it is important for their books to look 'up-to-date/modern'. Many of the girls questioned regularly opt for books from a series, whilst boys reveal that they often choose books that have featured in film or TV versions – this is supported by the boom in books about dinosaurs since the film *Jurassic Park* was released!

Active participation becomes important for children at this age, with books about 'things to make', sport (boys only) and hobbies topping the list of preferred non-fiction topics. An analysis of the children's favourite non-fiction titles reveals that books on natural history are still popular with most readers in this age range; books about history are also widely picked by both girls and boys. Predictably, however, boys list sports titles more often than any other category of non-fiction books.

Participation is also a keynote in the National Curriculum in all subject areas. For example, in Key Stage 2, pupils learn to plan and carry out experiments and to record the evidence they produce (science) and to observe, collect, record and analyse evidence about geographical features (geography). They are also encouraged to use a range of sources, including artefacts, pictures and photographs, to find out about aspects of the periods they are studying in history.

Reference books that include simple, well-thought-out experiments, interesting quizzes and achievable 'build it/ make it for yourself' activities can be helpful for young readers. Such additional features give children enjoyment and, at the same time, benefit them academically by encouraging the development of a delight in active enquiry into all fields of knowledge.

The 'Children's assessments' Panel

Children from Woodloes Junior School volunteered to use and review some of the publications marketed for Key Stage 2, with the kind permission of their headteacher Geoff Claridge. Under the guidance of their class teacher, Lyn Bentley, a class of Year Five pupils (aged between nine years and ten years) prepared the reviews reproduced in the 'Children's assessments' sections below – some spelling has been amended in the interests of clarity. Pupils were free to choose those they wished to write about; consequently not all of the texts have a written review.

The importance of presentation (easily-readable print size, well-presented photographic images of 'real' objects, uncluttered layout) is apparent throughout the children's reviews. It is clear that illustrations are thought of in two ways: amusing and imaginative cartoon characters and scenes are acceptable, as are professionally drawn diagrams; however, whenever material objects, living creatures and plants, or landscapes are portrayed, photographic and computer-generated images are greatly preferred to any other form of artistic impression.

The children are also quick to spot mistakes; they find omissions even more frustrating. Significantly, a number of texts were not even chosen for review by the children; if books do not appeal to young readers, they are in danger of being 'left on the shelf', however good their content may be. Overall, the children expect high quality, up-to-date texts, with a good range of easily accessible information.

National Curriculum testing

The publications in this chapter were tested for coverage of material from the National Curriculum, unless it was felt that they were oriented more towards hobbies and general interest rather than towards school work. See Chapter 1, pp.5–6, for details of how the tests were carried out and the way that results are presented.

The market place

The recent explosion in quantity of reference material is most noticeable in the provision for children in this age range. Numerous general dictionaries (observation of children on the review panel for this age-group shows that they still find dictionaries the most useful of their reference books) have appeared on the market; these are joined by a steady stream of single subject dictionaries and encyclopedias, mini-library collections and even general encyclopedias.

Visual appeal is the order of the day with traditional text-based volumes increasingly pushed to one side by attractive and eye-catching books. The latter often contain masses of high-tech images and/or imaginatively-drawn cartoon-style illustrations to tempt readers to pick them up.

The range of atlases aimed specifically at this age-group is the only disappointing category in terms of both quantity and quality of provision. Revised editions of these are often not as fully updated, in an ever-changing world, as they claim to be, and children are quick to spot errors and omissions. Relevant and interesting geographical material is, however, well supplied in encyclopedia format.

Atlases

National Curriculum requirements

At school, in Geography lessons, children in this Key Stage learn about the physical and human features that characterize localities. Three locations are studied: the pupils' own local area, a contrasting locality (of similar size) in the United Kingdom, and an area (also similar in size) situated in either Africa, Asia (excluding Japan), Central or South America. They also investigate the following geographical themes: rivers, weather, settlement and environmental change. Amongst other requirements, pupils are taught to interpret maps and plans and to make their own, utilizing different scales. They use co-ordinates and four-figure grid references; engage in measuring distance and direction; follow routes and find various locations utilizing the contents pages and index of an atlas. Atlases are essential to the majority of these tasks, as are encyclopedias which cover the geographical themes mentioned above. Access to these at home, preferably texts which encourage young readers to look for places or features and stimulate an interest in other lands, peoples and places, can be a useful first step in the acquiring of essential geographical skills and the fostering of an enthusiasm for the subject at school.

Notes on the children's assessments

The children who chose to review the atlases used them over a period of a week, recording their comments in a lesson at the end of that time. They did not utilize formal worksheets, but were encouraged to identify both positive and negative aspects, looking at ease of use, accuracy and any other features they felt to be relevant.

A selection of atlases

The Oxford Junior Atlas, editorial adviser Patrick Wiegand. Oxford University Press: 1993 (first published 1985).

ISBN: 0 19 831697 6 hardback, 0 19 831696 8 paperback

Price: £5.99 hardback, £4.40 paperback

Target age range: 8–11 yrs

Coverage: The user guide offers a clearly set out introduction to the use of symbol, colour-coded areas and scale. A cartoon crow character, and boxes showing a photograph of a particular feature accompanied by its symbol and name, are particularly helpful.

The atlas includes a political map of the world and lists countries and their capital cities by continent (the capital city of Nigeria is incorrectly shown as Lagos). Satellite pictures of the globe (from a satellite 35 900 kilometres away from the earth), followed by others homing in first on Italy and then on Naples and Mount Vesuvius (from a satellite 1450 kilometres away from the earth), add another dimension to understanding of the earth as a planet in space and of scale and distance.

There are 17 pages of maps of the British Isles, showing the largest built-up areas, transport routes, land height and other physical features, together with topic maps, including those featuring energy, historical sites, and countryside and wildlife. Continental maps and then world topic maps follow, showing wars, famines, food, raw materials and so on. A useful feature is the inclusion of a tiny (to scale) inset outline map of the British Isles alongside continental maps, bearing the legend: 'This is the size of the British Isles compared with . . .'.

Language, layout and images
Simple, child-friendly language is used throughout. The world maps and those of whole countries and continents are well laid out, with attractive inset photographic images and drawings. Satellite images are also incorporated to good effect. However, the regional maps of England, Wales, Scotland and Ireland are extremely dark in colour. This makes it difficult to pick out all the transport routes and the names of towns shown, and gives these maps a heavy, crowded appearance. The text explains features of the maps and other images succinctly.

Retrieval devices
In addition to the contents list, the contents page includes outline maps of the World and of the British Isles. These have ruled-off segments with the relevant page references printed inside. A gazetteer of the British Isles, at the back of the book, includes page references and simple grid references.

Children's assessments
'This atlas is easy to use, but it says Czechoslovakia instead of the Czech Republic and Slovakia [page 28]'

National Curriculum test result: 83%

The Oxford Rainbow Atlas, editorial adviser Patrick Wiegand. Oxford University Press: 1993 (first published 1987).

ISBN: 0 19 831695 X hardback, 0 19 831694 1 paperback

Price: £5.50 hardback, £4.40 paperback

Target age range: 6–8 yrs

Publications for Key Stage 2

Coverage: The use of symbols, colour-coded areas and scale is explained well, and distance is imaginatively contextualized: for example, the distance between John O'Groats and Land's End is given, together with a note that the journey would take thirty days on foot, two days by car and three hours by aeroplane.

The earth is shown as a planet, and there are maps of the British Isles showing countries, biggest towns, hills and rivers, and holidays. Interest is added by the inclusion of locations associated with traditional characters/stories (such as Robin Hood, Dick Turpin). Whole world maps show countries (Lagos is incorrectly shown as the capital of Nigeria), wonders, record-breakers (such as 'windiest ever', 'hottest ever', 'driest place'), hot and cold places, and animals.

Language, layout and images
Simple, clear and child-friendly language is employed throughout. Vivid photographic images and pictures enhance the layout.

Retrieval devices
The contents page includes outline maps with ruled-off segments enclosing the relevant page references printed inside. The contents list itself does not show these page numbers; confusing for children used to finding page references from this source. There is a map index with page references.

Children's assessments
Not chosen for review

Other aspects
This is a pleasant and undemanding starter atlas, with some imaginative features, but will soon be 'outgrown' by children in Key Stage 2.

National Curriculum test result: 50%

The Usborne Children's Atlas of the World, by Jenny Tyler and Lisa Watts, illustrated by Bob Hersey. Usborne Publishing Ltd: 1994 edition, first published in 1979

ISBN: 0 7460 1851 7 paperback

Price: £5.99

Target age range: 8–11 yrs

Coverage: Designed to aid awareness of the way in which places fit into a wider geographical context, an interesting comic-strip feature shows pictures moving from local to planetary scenes as an envelope in the corner of each acquires its address, line by line, picture by picture, ending up as: You, Your House, Your Town, Your Country, The Earth, The Solar System, The Milky Way, The Universe. Concepts such as latitude and longitude are explained with the aid of a cartoon pirate who has lost his buried treasure; other amusing activities include a jungle journey which teaches children about the use of scale.

Pictures and maps show physical and human features such as: earth's resources; land shaped by the sea; currents and tides; seasons; hot and cold areas; hot and wet areas and so on. Helpful information on understanding and using maps is also included.

Language, layout and images
A fairly simple chatty style of writing is used. The atlas does not have a modern 'feel' to it, although the information contained appears to be up to date. The images are not

particularly attractive, though the use of cartoon-style drawings may amuse some children. The comic-strip approach, with pictures and captions, is a useful aid to understanding some of the concepts explained.

Retrieval devices
There is a contents list, a map index (with some co-ordinates), and a general index.

Children's assessments
'Bad things about the atlas: I wanted a picture of the whole of Europe but it only had Eastern Europe and Western Europe. Also you can't see the borders of the countries.'

Other aspects
Although suitable for children who enjoy this style of presentation, the atlas is unlikely to have universal appeal.

National Curriculum test result: 83%

The Usborne Picture Atlas, (by Jenny Tyler and Lisa Watts, ISBN 0 7460 113 4 paperback, price £3.95) is referred to later under the entry for *[Usborne] The Children's Encyclopedia of Our World*

Atlases considered with publications for Key Stage 1 which would also be suitable for the early years of Key Stage 2 are:

The Kingfisher First Picture Atlas, by Antony Mason, with maps by John Woodcock and Eugene Fleury. Kingfisher (an imprint of Larousse plc): 1994.

ISBN: 1 85697 217 8 hardback

Price: £8.99

Target age range: 6–8 yrs
(See Chapter 3 for full review.)

Ladybird Picture Atlas, illustrations by John Dillow, text by Anita Ganeri. Ladybird: 1994

ISBN: 0 7214 7560 4 paperback

Price: £3.99

Target age range: 6–8 yrs
(See Chapter 3 for full review.)

One of the atlases considered with Key Stage 3 publications would also be suitable for the upper years of Key Stage 2:

[Kingfisher] Pocket Atlas, by Jill and David Wright. Kingfisher Books (then Grisewood & Dempsey Ltd): revised edition 1993, first published in paperback in 1987 and in hardback in 1983

ISBN: 0 86272 276 4 paperback

Price: £4.99

Target age range: Aimed at children aged between nine and 13 years, the *Pocket Atlas* is likely to appeal to Key Stage 3 pupils. However, the wealth of photographs and 'easy read' fact boxes make it accessible to younger children, and those in the upper years of Key Stage 2 might also enjoy it. (See Chapter 5 for full review.)

Dictionaries and related texts

Good dictionaries are a very important part of any child's reference library. It is an advantage for children to have access to these at all times, even to the extent, perhaps, of having a full-size dictionary at home and a smaller version (pocket-sized or sufficiently portable to be easily transported in a satchel or school bag) to carry around.

In order to see how the dictionaries marketed for this age group differ from those aimed at children in Key Stage 1 (reviewed in Chapter 3), sample definitions of the word 'television' have been taken for comparison and are listed below, in alphabetical order by title within publisher's recommended age range:

The Oxford Illustrated Junior Dictionary (Publisher's recommended age range: 6+ or 7+)

> television a machine that picks up programmes sent through the air and changes them into pictures and sound so that people can watch them [no picture]

Collins Primary Dictionary and ***Collins Pocket Primary Dictionary*** (Publisher's recommended age range: 7+)

> television A television is a piece of electrical equipment. With a television people can watch programmes of pictures and sounds that have come through the air. [tiny cartoon-style picture of child and dog watching television; the television is depicted complete with flex and plug in socket]

The Oxford Junior Dictionary (Publisher's recommended age range: 7+)

> television *noun* televisions
> a machine that picks up programmes sent through the air and changes them into pictures and sounds so that people can watch them. [no picture]

also

> telly *noun* tellies (*informal*) television

Collins Children's Dictionary and ***Collins Illustrated Children's Dictionary*** (Publisher's recommended age range: 8+)

52   A Guide to Children's Reference Books

television (televisions) *noun*
A television is a piece of electrical equipment. On a television, people can watch programmes of pictures and sounds that have come through the air. [no picture]

The Oxford Primary School Dictionary (Publisher's recommended age range: 8+)

television *noun* (televisions)
1 a system using radio waves to reproduce a picture on a screen. 2 a television set. 3 televised programmes.
television set, an apparatus for receiving pictures sent by television

also

telly *noun* (tellies) (*informal*) 1 television. 2 a television set.

Chambers Children's Illustrated Dictionary (Publisher's recommended age range: 9+)

television [omitting pronunciation guide] *n.* 1 the sending of pictures and sound in the form of radio waves to be reproduced on a screen in a person's home, etc. 2 (also **television set**) an apparatus with a screen and speakers which is able to receive radio waves and reproduce them in the form of pictures and sounds.

A further encyclopedic entry, accompanied by a simple diagrammatic representation of the process (not all of the labels shown in this diagram are explained, either here or elsewhere in the dictionary; for example 'Encoder', 'Decoder'), amplifies the definition as follows:

In television broadcasting, pictures are converted into electrical signals by cameras and sounds are converted into signals by microphones. The signals are sent to transmitting aerials. Receiving aerials pick up the signals and feed them to television sets which change the signals back into pictures and sound.

Collins Junior Dictionary (Publisher's recommended age range: 9+)

television televisions
1 (n) Television is the system which allows you to receive sounds and pictures sent over a long distance on a television set.
2 (n) A television is the piece of electrical equipment that receives pictures and sounds transmitted by the television system.
3 (n) Television is all the programmes you can watch on your television set. [no picture]

The Usborne Illustrated Dictionary (Publisher's recommended age range: 9+)

television
1 (*n*) a piece of equipment with a screen, that receives and shows moving pictures with sound. This simplified diagram [a cross-section of a cathode ray tube] shows how moving pictures are produced inside the cathode-ray tube of a television. Radio waves are converted into electrical signals which make beams of electrons sweep continuously across a fluorescent screen. As the

beams hit the screen's phosphor strips they create constantly changing dots of coloured light which the viewer sees as moving images.
2 (*n*) the sending of sounds and moving pictures along radio waves to be picked up by a television set.

The Usborne Pocket Dictionary (Publisher's recommended age range: 9+)

television 1 (*n*) a piece of equipment with a screen, that receives and broadcasts moving pictures and sound. 2 (*n*) the sending of sounds and moving pictures along radio waves to be picked up by a television set. [no picture]

National Curriculum requirements

In addition to learning to spell more complex, polysyllabic words, children at this stage should be further developing their vocabulary. This includes not only acquiring the vocabulary necessary to respond to a range of literature (such as: modern and 'classic' children's fiction; poetry; multi-cultural myths, legends and traditional stories) but also the acquisition of the technical vocabulary needed for a variety of National Curriculum subject areas. Each of the dictionaries reviewed in this chapter has been tested on coverage of this technical vocabulary (see Chapter 1, pp. 5–6 for details of the testing procedures).

Simple definitions are not enough for children in the upper years of Key Stage 2; they also need, for example, to be able to identify and use the standard written forms of nouns, verbs, adjectives and so on. Good dictionaries designed for children in years five and six (children from nine to 11 years of age) will include a wide range of relevant words and also identify parts of speech and spell out the derived forms of root words.

Notes on the children's assessments

Dictionaries were left on the children's desks for four weeks; comments were written at the end of this time. The dictionaries were analysed, by looking at prefaces and indexes, depth of definitions, ease of use and attractiveness. Missing test definitions were noted.

Class teacher Lyn Bentley writes:

> The main joy was having one dictionary between two pupils; having a dictionary on each table meant that they were used much more than usual. The 'Using the dictionary' books: *Using the Oxford Junior Dictionary*, *Using The Oxford Illustrated Junior Dictionary* and *Using the Oxford Primary School Dictionary* were extremely useful. The class completed lots of activities and dictionary competency really improved. The children each had different favourites; most popular were: *Chambers Children's Illustrated Dictionary*, *The Oxford Primary School Dictionary* and *The Usborne Pocket Dictionary*.

A selection of dictionaries

Chambers Children's Illustrated Dictionary, Editor-in-Chief John Grisewood. Chambers (an imprint of Larousse plc): 1994. The text for the dictionary entries is abridged and adapted from the New Edition of ***Chambers Pocket Dictionary*** published in 1992.

ISBN: 0 550 10651 0 hardback

Price: £19.99

Target age range: 9–12 yrs

Entries: not specified

Language and coverage: Quite sophisticated language is used, making it better suited to fluent readers. Each headword is accompanied by a pronunciation guide, its part of speech and definition (or definitions). An example sentence is often included. Irregular plurals of nouns are given; derived forms are supplied where the spelling of the main word changes.

Layout and images

The layout is fairly dense, but interspersed with numerous related images (including explanatory diagrams) and boxes with further information. The images are carefully drawn and extend the meanings of some of the more difficult words. Topic boxes giving additional encyclopedic information have well-integrated images and text; however, technical labels are not always defined elsewhere in the dictionary.

Retrieval devices

The dictionary is organized in alphabetical order, with the first and last word for each double-page spread given at the top. There is no contents list featuring the supplementary information pages which are located at the beginning and the end of the book. A useful section at the front offers guidance on use; this has clear, colour-coded boxes to explain the different types of information which follow the headwords.

Children's assessments

'Here are the things in my dictionary: headword entries, parts of speech, other forms of the headwords, definitions, numbers, example phrases, derived words. I didn't know all of them.'

Liked by most of the children, this shares the title 'most popular dictionary' with *The Oxford Primary School Dictionary* and *The Usborne Pocket Dictionary*.

Other aspects

There is a wide range of additional features. These include a brief history of the development of the English language and lists of: 'Countries of the World' (listing the adjectival form, capital city, currency and language); 'Counties of the United Kingdom and the Republic of Ireland' (including outline map); 'US States' (giving the abbreviation, capital city and symbolic bird and flower); 'Presidents of the United States'; 'Rulers of England, Scotland and Great Britain'; 'Prime Ministers (since 1900) of the United Kingdom, Canada, Australia, and New Zealand'.

Altogether this is an interesting volume, which is effectively an encyclopedia and dictionary combined; it is filled with wide-ranging facts and information and very good for browsing. The encyclopedic entries do have a slight transatlantic bias; for example, under 'Hughes' is an entry for the American poet *Langston Hughes*; *Ted Hughes*, the British poet laureate, is not mentioned. However, it is still pleasing to see a good range of writers (including contemporary figures such as Toni Morrison), musicians and artists mentioned.

National Curriculum test result: Overall score: 91% (joint second place)

Collins Children's Dictionary, written by Evelyn Goldsmith. HarperCollins Publishers Ltd: 1995, first published as *Collins Junior Dictionary* in 1992

ISBN: 0 00 196476 3 hardback

Price: £5.99

Entries: 5000 headwords

Target age range: 9–11 yrs. Publisher's recommendation 8 yrs and upwards.

Language and coverage: Passive formal language is used in the definitions. Parts of speech are given, as are derived words such as the plural form for nouns, tense endings for verbs, comparative and superlative forms for adjectives and so on. Some example sentences are included, where further clarification of a definition seems necessary.

Layout and images
There are no images to break up blocks of text; however, headwords appear in a brownish-red colour which helps them to stand out. There is little space left and the print is quite small. Overall it rather lacks 'child-appeal'

Retrieval devices
A short user guide appears at the front of the dictionary. The first and last words of a double-page spread are printed in a strip at the top of the page.

Children's assessments
'This dictionary has not got volleyball, has not got athletics. At the front is just a page on how to use the dictionary. We didn't understand it very well. There is nothing at the back. We don't like brown words. There are no pictures to help.'

National Curriculum test result: Overall score: 41% (eighth place)

Collins Illustrated Children's Dictionary, written by Evelyn Goldsmith, illustrated by Gary Rees. HarperCollins Publishers Ltd: 1995, first published in 1992 as *Collins Junior Dictionary*

ISBN: 0 00 197003 8 hardback

Price: £7.99

Target age range: 9–11 yrs. Publisher's recommendation: 8 yrs and upwards

Entries: 5000 headwords

Language: This is an illustrated version of the *Collins Children's Dictionary* discussed above. It is quite dense and best suited to fluent readers.

Layout and images
Although the layout is rather dense, the headword entries are in a bright blue colour which helps them to stand out. There are between one and three images on each page;

these include amusing though rather stereotypical characters. There is quite a good relationship between the pictures and the text, with almost a story in each picture to extend the definitions given.

Retrieval devices
These are discussed in the entry above.

Children's assessments
'The typing is the right size for me and I like the pictures, but it hasn't got the things in that I'm looking for.'

Other aspects
The illustrations help to make this version slightly more appealing than the plain *Collins Children's Dictionary* discussed above.

National Curriculum test result: See the entry above

Collins Junior Dictionary, compiled by Ginny Lapage. HarperCollins Publishers Ltd: 1995, first published in 1990 as *Collins First Reference Dictionary*, second edition published in 1992 as *Collins Illustrated Children's Dictionary*

ISBN: 0 00 196477 1 hardback

Price: £7.99

Target age range: 9–12 yrs

Entries: 10 000 headwords

Language and coverage: The language is quite sophisticated and the book is set out like an adult dictionary. Parts of speech are given in abbreviated form; plurals and derived words are also supplied. There are some example sentences, where these are needed to enhance clarity. A user guide gives relevant details about these features and gives a key to the abbreviations used.

Layout and images
The layout is uncluttered, with good clear images. The images relate well to the text, and assist in defining some of the headwords.

Retrieval devices
A bright red letter appears on the side of each page, an excellent aid to finding the relevant section of the alphabet quickly, and the first and last words of each double-page spread are written in large letters at the top. Symbols accompanied by page numbers are used to indicate helpful cross-references.

Children's assessments
'It tells you how to use the dictionary. It has very good diagrams, not overcrowded though. At the back are pictures of endangered species. At the front are spelling lists and useful words. Letters at the side of the page are useful for flicking through. Makes it quicker.'

Other aspects
Short appendices list days of the week, months of the year, numbers, question words, irregular verbs, and short forms (such as 'I'm'). There is also a colour section on endan-

gered species (with picture pages featuring the east coast, the highlands and open grasslands and heath) for added interest.

National Curriculum test result: Overall score: 74% (sixth place)

Collins Primary Dictionary, written by Evelyn Goldsmith, illustrated by Penny Dann, consultant editor Ginny Lapage. HarperCollins Publishers Ltd: 1995, first published in 1989 as *Collins First Dictionary*, second edition published in 1992 as *Collins Illustrated First Dictionary*

ISBN: 0 00 190055 2 hardback

Price: £7.99

Target age range: 7–9yrs

Entries: 3000 headwords

Language and coverage: The language is quite personal and child-friendly. Some words have a guide to pronunciation: such as 'lead... (as in feed)', 'lead... (as in fed)'. Parts of speech and derived words are not given. A short and basic user guide is included.

Layout and images
The layout is well spaced and illustrated with really imaginative and colourful cartoon-like drawings. The images really bring the text to life.

Retrieval devices
Headwords are printed in bold and the starting letters are colourful and striking. The first and last word appear at the top of each page.

Children's assessments
'At the beginning it doesn't tell you much about the dictionary. I have noticed some words that are not in my dictionary: athletics; volleyball; detailed; slap; thief; stutter; generation; solve; appendix.'

National Curriculum test result: Overall score: 24% (eleventh place)

Collins Pocket Primary Dictionary, written by Evelyn Goldsmith, illustrated by Penny Dann, consultant editor Ginny Lapage. HarperCollins Publishers Ltd: 1995, first published in 1989 as *Collins First Dictionary*

ISBN: 0 00 196475 5 hardback
Priced at £3.99, this is the pocket edition of the dictionary discussed above. The illustrations have suffered in size, clarity and number in order to make this truly a pocket volume.

Children's assessments
'I like the big writing and the detailed pictures. It has got a lot of variety of words, but it has not got some words in it. The dictionary is called a pocket dictionary but it doesn't fit in a pocket.'

The Oxford Children's Dictionary, compiled by John Weston and Alan Spooner, illustrated by Bill le Fever, Paul Thomas, Kathy Baxendale, and Celia Hart. Oxford University Press: 1994, first published in 1976

ISBN: 0 19 910321 6 hardback

Price: £7.99

Target age range: 8–11 yrs

Entries: 20 000 headwords

Language and coverage: The language used is appropriate for the targeted age group. In addition to the definitions and some example sentences, the dictionary includes the part of speech, plurals and derived forms of words.

Layout and images
Small coloured drawings help to break up the text and relate well to the words they illustrate. Blue-coloured headwords are used to enhance the clarity of the layout.

Retrieval devices
The full alphabet, with the relevant letter highlighted, appears at the bottom of each page. First and last words appear in a matching colour-coded block at the top. The colour-coding, although repeated, is quite useful, with enough colours to ensure that the correct letter is accessed. A very brief user introduction appears at the front of the book.

Children's assessments
'This book isn't that good because they only tell you about one thing, which is about the meanings. It does not tell you that it helps you spell words and that it's in alphabetical order. There wasn't much at the front of the book and nothing at the back. It didn't tell you how to use the dictionary. There are a few pictures but they are not very good.'

Lyn Bentley notes that the majority of the children are not impressed with this dictionary and adds: 'there is little information about using the book, it has very few small pictures and definitions tend to be much shorter than in other dictionaries.'

National Curriculum test result: Overall score: 85% (joint fourth place)

The Oxford Illustrated Junior Dictionary, compiled by Rosemary Sansome, Dee Reid, illustrated by Barry Rowe. Oxford University Press: 1994, first published 1989

ISBN: 0 19 910330 5 hardback, 0 19 910331 3 paperback

Price: £8.99 hardback, £5.99 paperback

Target age range: 7–10 yrs. The Oxford University Press catalogue lists this dictionary as being for children aged six years and upwards; however, on the cover of the book, the suggested age range is seven years and upwards.

Entries: 5500 headwords

Language and coverage: Definitions are clear and simple, with occasional example sentences. No parts of speech are given and, in general, no plurals or derived forms of words are supplied; however, some irregular plurals and derived words are used in the example sentences.

Layout and images
Numerous nicely-drawn colour illustrations enhance the layout. Headwords are printed in red, adding clarity. The images illustrate the words well.

Retrieval devices
An alphabet with the relevant letter highlighted in red appears at the top of each page. A contents list gives page references for the appendices.

Children's assessments
'At the back of the dictionary there are the days of the week, the planets, the months, the continents and places and people's names, colours and numbers and lots of diagrams and pictures. At the top of the page it has got all the alphabet and the letter is in a different colour so it's easy to find. The writing is not too big or too small so it's easy to read. The book hasn't got volleyball in, or athletics.'

Other aspects
Additional features include appendices with: places, peoples, continents, planets, days of the week, months of the year, colours, flat and solid shapes. There are also vocabulary pages; these cover a variety of diverse topics: scientific equipment, parts of a camera, musical instruments, playing-cards, dogs, fish, fruit, vegetables, parts of the body, ships and boats, parts of a bicycle, parts of a car. Some of the words defined pictorially here do not appear in the main body of the dictionary (for example 'tripod').

A companion paperback is also published: *Using The Oxford Illustrated Junior Dictionary* (Oxford University Press, ISBN 0 19 910362 3, priced at around £1.50). This has line drawings, games and activities and is very useful for teaching children to use the dictionary.

National Curriculum test result: Overall score: 40% (tenth place)

The Oxford Junior Dictionary, compiled by Rosemary Sansome, Dee Reid, Alan Spooner. Oxford University Press: 1995, first published in 1978

ISBN: 0 19 910304 6 hardback

Price: £5.50

Target age range: 7–10 yrs

Entries: 6500 headwords

Language and coverage: Straightforward, child-friendly language is used in the definitions. Parts of speech are given in full and all plurals, plus derived words, are supplied. Example sentences are included wherever they are needed to enhance clarity.

Layout and images
There are no illustrations, but the layout is well spaced and the headwords are printed in colour.

Retrieval devices
An alphabet printed at the top of each page has the relevant letter of the alphabet highlighted.

Children's assessments
'We like this dictionary because we understand it. These are the headings: headwords,

parts of speech, numbers, definitions, example phrases, derived words. It tells you about months, names, days, units of time, shapes and solid shapes. It said that a dictionary is a book where you can find out what a word means and how to spell things and the word dictionary is a noun.'

Lyn Bentley adds that children find the highlighting of the relevant letter of the alphabet a useful retrieval aid.

Other aspects
Additional features include appendices listing countries, continents, shapes, numbers, days of the week, times of day, and months of the year. A small paperback book of exercises and games has been published to accompany the dictionary: *Using the Oxford Junior Dictionary* (ISBN 0 19 910363 1, Oxford University Press: 1995, priced at around £2.00). Teachers of Key Stage 2 children report that this is very useful.

National Curriculum test result: Overall score: 47% (seventh place)

The Oxford Primary School Dictionary, compiled by A.J. Augarde, Colin Hope, John Butterworth, illustrations by Peter Bull. Oxford University Press: 1994, first published 1993

ISBN: 0 19 910335 6 hardback

Price: £5.99

Target age range: 8–11 yrs

Entries: 25 000 head words

Language and coverage: The language used is quite sophisticated, without forfeiting clarity. Parts of speech are given in full; plurals and derived word forms are all supplied. Some help with difficult pronunciations is also given.

Layout and images
The layout is clear and uncluttered; it is enhanced by the inclusion of a number of black-and-white illustrative drawings. The images are used to clarify the meaning of some of the words.

Retrieval devices
The first and last headwords for each spread are given at the top of the page. A user guide helps young readers to understand the format of the dictionary.

Children's assessments
'The definition was very good and explained everything clearly. At the beginning of the dictionary it tells you about it and also explains: vowels, consonants, syllables, simple words, compound words, adjectives. At the back of the book it tells you about weights, measures, lists of countries, punctuation, spelling, nouns, adverbs. Everything in this book is quite easy to understand. It needs more colour inside, but it's very clear. I like this dictionary because it's easy to understand by my age group.'

Much more popular than *The Oxford Children's Dictionary*, this is one of the children's three favourite dictionaries.

Other aspects
There are special notes which highlight common grammatical errors. Appendices give:

prefixes and suffixes, punctuation, spelling and grammar rules, countries, weights and measures. Some American equivalent words are supplied, for example 'checkers' for 'draughts'.

Also available is a companion paperback: *Using the Oxford Primary School Dictionary* (Oxford University Press: 1995, priced at around £3.00, ISBN 0 19 910307 0). This has exercises, games, quizzes and puzzles and is a very useful and 'fun' way to teach children to use their dictionaries.

National Curriculum test result: Overall score: 93% (first place)

The Usborne Illustrated Dictionary, editor Jane Bingham. Usborne Publishing Ltd: 1994

ISBN: 0 7460 1333 7 paperback, 0 7460 1334 5 hardback, 0 7460 2129 1 luxury edition (luxury edition has dust jacket, bookmark and gold blocking)

Price: £8.99 paperback, £10.99 hardback, £13.99 luxury edition

Target age range: 10–13 yrs. Publisher's recommendation: 9 yrs and upwards

Entries: over 10 000 headwords

Language and coverage: The language is quite sophisticated. Headwords are accompanied by an abbreviated word class (these are explained in the user's guide) and a definition. Where necessary, example sentences are given, as are pronunciation guides. Irregular plural forms are shown for nouns and derived word forms are also given. Usage guides indicate if a word is old-fashioned, poetic, informal or slang.

Layout and images
A few images (a mixture of photographic images, drawings and diagrams) appear on each page. Text is arranged in three columns, but does not have an overcrowded feel, despite the amount of information on each page. The text associated with diagrams or pictures appears in smaller type (labels) or in italics (longer explanations). Where there are images they extend the definitions well.

Retrieval devices
The dictionary has coloured strips for each letter of the alphabet along the side of each page. The colours are repeated, but sufficient different ones are used to ensure that these are not close enough together to cause confusion. The relevant letter appears on each page in the coloured area, and first and last words are repeated in a strip at the top of each page. At the front is a useful section entitled 'Your Dictionary: A User's Guide'. This contains guidance on using the dictionary; it also discusses parts of speech, giving definitions and example sentences (the relevant part of speech is underlined in colour in these). There is an index of picture labels at the back of the book.

Children's assessments
Not chosen for review, see review of abridged version below.

Other aspects
Additional features include: hints and guidelines on writing English (including punctuation); a short history of the English language and a section on English as it is spoken around the world today; lists of 'Countries and Nationalities', 'Days of the Week', 'Months of the Year', 'Measurements' and 'Numbers'.

The dictionary received a 'SUBSTANTIAL CONTRIBUTION TO CHILDREN'S LITERACY' award from the U.K. Reading Association in 1995.

National Curriculum test result: Overall score: 91% (joint second place)

The Usborne Pocket Dictionary, edited by Rachel Wardley. Usborne Publishing Ltd: 1995, an abridged version of the *Usborne Illustrated Dictionary* first published in 1994

ISBN: 0 7460 2349 9 paperback

Price: £4.99 paperback, £7.99 hardback

Target age range: 10–12 yrs. Publisher's recommendation: 9 yrs and upwards

Entries: over 8000 headwords

Language and coverage: This is an abridged version of the *Usborne Illustrated Dictionary* discussed above.

Children's assessments
'The dictionary tells me that you can find a word. If you can't find a word there is help. There were too many pictures in the book and loads of headings. At the back of the book there is an index saying what's in the book. I understood this dictionary because it was medium size writing and if you didn't understand the writing if you look at the picture you know what it is.'

The children appreciate the handy pocket/satchel size, voting it one of their three favourite dictionaries. Lyn Bentley comments that the children find the featuring of letters in the corner of each page a useful retrieval aid.

National Curriculum test result: Overall score: 85% (joint fourth place)
A selection of other aids to word usage, spelling and grammar is reviewed below:

The Oxford Children's Thesaurus, compiled by Alan Spooner. Oxford University Press: 1994, first published 1987

ISBN: 0 19 910323 2 hardback

Price: £7.99

Entries: 70 000 similar and related words

Target age range: 8–11 yrs

Language and coverage: Clear and effective language is used and some examples of usage are given. Words and phrases that should be used carefully are accompanied by bracketed warnings.

Layout and images
The layout is well spaced; there are no illustrations.

Retrieval devices
Entries are organized alphabetically, with headwords printed in green. The choice of colour for the headwords is not altogether successful (effectively a 'lowlight' rather than a highlight) and could be confusing for children.

Children's assessments
Not chosen for review

Other aspects
This is a companion volume to *The Oxford Children's Dictionary*.

[Oxford] *Spell it yourself.* Oxford University Press: 1995, first published in 1962

ISBN: 0 19 834138 5 hardback, 0 19 910342 9 paperback

Price: £5.50 hardback, £3.50 paperback

Entries: over 8000 root words

Target age range: 8–12 yrs

Language
Instructions for use are written in clear, child-friendly language and the book contains a good selection of root words with their derivative forms. No definitions are given as the book is purely an aid to spelling.

Layout
The layout is clear and uncluttered.

Retrieval devices
The alphabetical order is broken up into two-letter sections: for example, the first page has a section headed 'ab' (which runs from 'abandon' to 'abyss') followed by a section headed 'ac' (running from 'academy' to 'actual'. The two relevant letters also appear in larger print at the top of each column in which they appear. Root words appear in bold, with possible endings shown in lighter italic print. An index to these sections and to the additional feature pages appears at the end of the book. A two-page instruction section, at the front, explains how to use the book. There is also a contents list, which gives page references for the additional word lists (see below).

Children's assessments
Not chosen for review

Other aspects
The book also has lists of boys' names, girls' names, numbers, countries and peoples of the world, parts of speech, useful words to learn (very helpful), contractions, homophones, multiplication tables and a note for teachers and parents. It is an extremely useful book with a reasonably-priced paperback edition.

The Mini Oxford School Speller. Oxford University Press: 1995.

ISBN: 0 19 910357 7 vinyl.
This is a pocket-size version of the book discussed above. Priced at £2.99, it has a wipe-clean vinyl cover and is ideal for carrying about. The text is virtually that of the full-size book, omitting only some of the feature lists at the end. Lists included are: parts of speech, lists of useful words to learn and homophones. Despite the size, the layout remains clear and readable.

Children's assessments
Not chosen for review

Single-subject dictionaries and encyclopedias

A wealth of single-subject dictionaries and encyclopedias are now published for children in Key Stage 2, sparked in all probability by the introduction of the National Curriculum and attendant public interest. Science and geography receive the most coverage in reference works of this kind. The National Curriculum requirements with regard to geography have already been considered in the section on atlases (towards the beginning of this chapter); information relating to science is discussed below.

National Curriculum requirements

The Key Stage 2 programme of study for science aims to foster the development of an enquiring mind with regard to natural and everyday phenomena and to ensure the teaching of skills necessary to devise and carry out experiments and record the evidence from this research (see the beginning of this chapter). Three main subject areas: 'Life Processes and Living Things'; 'Materials and their Properties'; and 'Physical Processes' are covered. Not all of the subject dictionaries and encyclopedias concerned with science carry information about every one of these areas; quite a few concentrate on the first of these, covering animal, plant and/or human life processes, whilst others pick out topics of popular interest, such as the Earth in space (part of the study of physical processes).

Notes on the children's assessments

A classroom chart was kept, recording the number of times the children used the various reference books. By comparison with the dictionaries, which were in constant use, the children did not appear to find the encyclopedias very helpful. Lyn Bentley suggests that the information is often not detailed enough, while the vocabulary used tends to be too difficult.

The children who chose to review these books used them over a period of a week, recording their comments in a lesson at the end of that time. They were encouraged to identify both positive and negative features, looking at aspects such as the pictures, print size and clarity as well as at ease of use, accuracy and the relevance of the information supplied.

A selection of single subject dictionaries and encyclopedias

Kingfisher Visual Encyclopedia of Science, by Michael Allaby, Neil Curtis, Brian Williams and James Muirden. Kingfisher (an imprint of Larousse plc): 1995. The material in this book was first published in four individual volumes in 1993.

ISBN: 1 85697 385 9 hardback

Price: £17.99

Target age range: 10–13 yrs

Coverage: Selected topics from 'Planet Earth', 'The Living World', 'Stars and Planets', and 'Science and Technology' are covered. Each sub-topic is usually allocated two pages; enough text is included to help with project work and there are also good visual representations – photographs, drawings and sectional diagrams in full colour. Topics covered in the section on 'Planet Earth' range from examinations of land and water to a look at weather and climate. 'The Living World' includes a section on the human body as well as looking at the plant and animal kingdoms. 'Cosmic time', 'The Solar System' and 'Space exploration' are among the topics discussed in 'Stars and Planets'; whilst the section dealing with science and technology includes such topics as: matter and energy; force and motion; space and time; light and sound; and electricity. Overall the information is well packaged, using maps, illustrations, easy-to-read tables and charts and numerous fact boxes.

Language, layout and images

The text is very readable and child-friendly. The book has a thoughtful and spacious layout with excellent colour images (including some beautiful photographs of animals and landscapes) which are linked clearly to the text. Many of the diagrams are extremely informative, with good use made of a range of graphical techniques. Consequently, the reader will instantly get a good feel for such topics as the structure of the heart, diversity of colour in the bird population, or the architectural wonder of bridges, cathedrals and national monuments.

Retrieval devices

Topics are arranged thematically and accessed via an overall contents list; contents lists for each former volume; and a comprehensive index.

Children's assessments

'The things I like about it: I like the information about dogs, but there's not very much on rabbits or giraffes. The writing's very clear and it's got words in I can understand. It is good because I found out a lot of things I didn't know, like a giraffe is nearly six metres tall and a male king penguin of the Antarctica keeps its eggs warm beneath a flap of skin on its feet. The pictures are very colourful and clear and it's all the right colours.

The things I don't like about it: I don't like the hard words in it like sediment, continental and Marianas. The writing's too small so that I can hardly read it, but it's very, very clear and above all it is a really good book.'

Other aspects

Our science adviser considers that this is a much more useful reference book for science topics than the *Kingfisher Children's Encyclopedia* (see later in this chapter). An attractively-produced volume, it has a great deal of material of relevance to children in this age group.

National Curriculum test results
Science
Coverage of total subject area: 92%
Coverage of topics broached: 92%

The Oxford Children's A to Z of Geography, by Dick Bateman. Oxford University Press: 1996

ISBN: 0 19 910354 2 hardback, 0 19 910086 1 paperback

Price: £8.99 hardback, £4.99 paperback

Target age range: 7–9 yrs

Coverage: Definitions are given for around 400 geographical terms (such as 'erosion', 'reservoir', 'tributary' and the like).

Language, layout and images
The language is clear and defines terms quite well. An uncluttered layout is interspersed with numerous illustrations, diagrams and photographic images. Text definitions are amplified by the images, particularly the diagrams, which are well executed and very helpful.

Retrieval devices
The book is arranged in alphabetical order with headwords highlighted in blue. It has no contents page, index or user guide. Some related topics are cross-referenced within the text.

Children's assessments
The book was not chosen for review. Lyn Bentley notes that *The Oxford Children's A–Z of Geography* was little used by the children, other than for art landscapes. She adds: 'there are very few words under each letter and those that are there are mostly irrelevant to this age-group. There are some useful photographs, but mainly they are too small.'

Other aspects
This is useful for acquiring the technical vocabulary associated with the subject at this level; however, the alphabetical arrangement militates against any in-depth coverage of relevant topics. The paperback version is quite reasonably priced.

National Curriculum test results
This can really only be treated as a dictionary; coverage of the test words for the technical vocabulary associated with geography produced a score of 77%. By comparison, a number of the dictionaries, tested on the same words, scored rather better:
Chambers Children's Illustrated Dictionary: 100%
Collins Junior Dictionary: 85%
Collins Primary Dictionary: 81%
The Oxford Children's Dictionary: 81%
The Oxford Primary School Dictionary: 100%
The Usborne Illustrated Dictionary: 100%
The Usborne Pocket Dictionary: 100%

The Oxford Children's A to Z of the Human Body, by Bridget and Neil Ardley. Oxford University Press: 1996

ISBN: 0 19 910318 6 hardback, 0 19 910085 3 paperback.
See comments on *The Oxford Children's A to Z of Geography* reviewed above.

The Oxford Children's A to Z of Science, by Terry Jennings. Oxford University Press: 1996

ISBN: 0 19 910317 8 hardback, 0 19 910087 X paperback

Price: £8.99 hardback, £4.99 paperback
See comments on *The Oxford Children's A to Z of Geography* reviewed above.

Others in the series, are:

The Oxford Children's A to Z of Mathematics, by David Glover
ISBN: 0 19 910360 7 hardback, 0 19 910090 X paperback

The Oxford Children's A to Z of Music, by Humphrey Carpenter
ISBN: 0 19 910310 0 hardback, 0 19 910089 6 paperback

The Oxford Children's A to Z of Technology, by Robin Kerrod
ISBN: 0 19 910359 3 hardback, 0 19 910088 8 paperback

The Usborne Illustrated Encyclopedia: Science & Technology. Usborne Publishing Ltd: 1996

ISBN: 0 7460 1796 0 hardback, 0 7460 1795 2 paperback

Price: £12.99 hardback, £9.99 paperback

Target age range: 10–12 yrs. Publisher's recommendation: 9–12 yrs

Coverage: 48 topics, ranging from 'Atoms and Molecules' to 'Plastics and Natural Polymers', are covered. There are appendices giving key dates (for example: '1810 The first electric lamp was demonstrated in London, England.'), an A–Z of scientists and inventors (ranging from Ampère to the Wright Brothers) and scientific data such as equations, symbols and measurements.

Language, layout and images
Fairly formal language is used throughout, with a significant number of scientific and technical terms employed. Although there is a glossary, the presence of a word in it is not signalled from the text. The layout is quite dense; however, the text is neatly arranged under headings and sub-headings. Well-drawn diagrams and illustrations help to clarify the subject matter.

Retrieval devices
The encyclopedia is in thematic order with a detailed table of contents and a comprehensive index. Some user guidance is given in a small box at the beginning.

Children's assessments
'The things I like about it: the pictures are good (excellent) because they are clear and they explain things step by step and there isn't much writing.

The things I don't like about it: the print is quite good but very small. If someone picked up this book with something wrong with their eyes and didn't have glasses they couldn't read it.'

Other aspects
Although there is much useful information in the book, too much has been attempted in too small a space. This has led in some cases to oversimplified, single-paragraph explanations of advanced scientific theories.

National Curriculum test results
Science
Coverage of total subject area: 44%
Coverage of topics broached: 94%

The Usborne Illustrated Encyclopedia: The Natural World. Usborne Publishing Ltd: 1994

ISBN: 0 7460 1689 1 hardback, 0 7460 1688 3 paperback.

Price: £12.99 hardback, £9.99 paperback

Target age range: 9–12 yrs

Coverage: 54 topics are covered, ranging from 'How Plants Live' to 'Seas and Oceans'. There are additional sections on endangered species, evolution and classifying the natural world. A world map and 'See for yourself' activity boxes are other useful additions.

Language, layout and images
The language used is fairly straightforward (less formal and technical than that used in its companion volume: *The Usborne Illustrated Encyclopedia: Science & Technology*). Although there is a glossary, the presence of a word in it is not signalled from the text. Neatly arranged, though quite dense, the text is amply illustrated with numerous helpful and well-drawn diagrams and illustrations.

Retrieval devices
Material is thematically ordered (in what appears to be a somewhat jumbled fashion), with a detailed table of contents and a comprehensive index. Some user guidance is given in a small box at the beginning.

Children's assessments
'**The things I like about it:** I like the way they set out the pages and the writing because it's just how I have it. The pictures are very good and there are lots of them. You can find what you're looking for and there are not very hard words which is good. The price is good and its very useful.

The things I don't like about it: I don't like the front cover very much because it's crowded.'

  Lyn Bentley adds: 'The format of *The Usborne Illustrated Encyclopedia: The Natural World* is better suited to older children, although individual pages are popular (for example the page on turtles). However, it was not used very often as a reference book, as the vocabulary is too sophisticated and the print too small.'

Other aspects
Short, fairly basic explanations are given in this volume, making it useful as a first point of reference. Those requiring more detailed information may find that it covers a little too much in insufficient depth.

National Curriculum test results
Science
Coverage of total subject area: 19%
Coverage of topics broached: 70%

The Usborne Geography Encyclopedia, by Carol Varley and Lisa Miles. Usborne Publishing Ltd: 1992

ISBN: 0 7460 0954 2 hardback

Price: £9.95

Target age range: 7–11 yrs. Publisher's recommendation: 8–12 yrs

Coverage: There is a very good section on the making of maps, and small inset global maps contextualize the areas discussed. The account of physical geography includes information on: rocks; landscapes; how water shapes the earth; weather and climate. Coverage of human geography looks at peoples; settlements (including an interesting sub-section on town planning); transport and communication. Other features include maps of the world and reference sections on 'World Facts' and 'Nation Facts'.

Language, layout and images
The language is clear, quite simple and to the point. There is also a glossary, with words highlighted in bold, to help the young reader. Each double-page spread covers a different topic, the title of which appears in bold, highlighted on a coloured band at the top of the page. Clear images and the use of boxes to separate different subjects contribute to the well-spaced layout of the book. With images that amplify the text and clear arrows to point out particular aspects, there is a very good image/text relationship.

Retrieval devices
Topics are thematically arranged, with a clear table of contents and subject index. A good cross-referencing system of footnotes is signalled by asterisks in the text. There is also a map index; this utilizes a simple grid system and is very easy to work with.

Children's assessments
Not chosen for review

Other aspects
An up-to-date volume, with 'Did you know' questions and activities, this is a very good introduction to all aspects of geography and quite reasonably priced for a hardback volume of this size. It is also available as part of a combined volume: *The Usborne World of Knowledge Encyclopedia*. (see the section on general encyclopedias later in this chapter).

National Curriculum test results
Geography
Coverage of total subject area: 94%
Coverage of topics broached: 94%

The Usborne Living World Encyclopedia, by Leslie Colvin and Emma Speare. Usborne Publishing Ltd: 1992

ISBN: 0 7460 0344 7 hardback

Price: £8.95

Target age range: 7–11 yrs. Publisher's recommendation: 8–12 yrs

Coverage: 55 topics are covered (primarily habitat-related, such as 'Survival on the grasslands' and 'Winter in the northern forests') ranging from 'The story of the Earth' to 'People and parasites'. There are additional sections on endangered species and on the classifying of living organisms.

Language, layout and images
The language is clear, to the point and comparatively child-friendly. The inclusion of a glossary, which explains words highlighted in bold in the text, is very helpful for young readers. The layout is well spaced, with boxes used to separate different subjects. Images are plentiful and clear; they amplify the text well. Arrows are used to good effect to point out the relationship between the images and the words they support. This is another helpful feature for readers at the start of the recommended age range.

Retrieval devices
Topics are thematically arranged, with a clear table of contents at the beginning, an index that works well, and a glossary. There is a good cross-referencing system of footnotes signalled by asterisks in the text. A helpful single-page user guide explains the layout to child readers.

Children's assessments
'The things I like about it: I like the pictures because they are realistic. The writing is easy to understand. I think the size is a nice size, it's not too small and not too big.

The things I don't like about it: There are too many facts on one page. The front cover doesn't look exciting because to me it doesn't stand out. The print could be bigger, but I can read it.'

Other aspects
This is an informative and interesting book which is reasonably priced for a hardback volume of this size. It is also available as part of a combined volume: *The Usborne World of Knowledge Encyclopedia*. (see the section on general encyclopedias, later in this chapter).

National Curriculum test results
Geography
Coverage of total subject area: 21%
Coverage of topics broached: 39%
Science
Coverage of total subject area: 56%

Coverage of topics broached: 60%

The Usborne Science Encyclopedia. Usborne Publishing Ltd: 1988, re-issued 1993

ISBN: 0 7460 0192 4 hardback

Price: £10.99

Target age range: 7–11 yrs. Publisher's recommendation: 8–12 yrs

Coverage: There are sections dealing with: 'Counting and measuring'; 'Heat and energy'; 'Forces and machines'; 'Light and colour'; 'Sound and hearing'; 'Atoms and molecules'; 'Electricity and technology'. Additional tables list scientists and inventors, measurements, Solar System planets and so on.

Language, layout and images
The language is clear, quite simple and to the point. There is a glossary (words included are highlighted in bold in the text) to help the young reader. Each double-page spread covers a different topic, the title of which appears in bold, highlighted on a coloured band at the top of the page. Boxes are used to separate different subjects, but the layout is a little 'busy'. Unlike those of its companion volumes (*The Usborne Geography Encyclopedia* and the *Usborne Living World Encyclopedia*) the images drawn are rather cartoon-like and stereotypical in their representations of human faces.

Retrieval devices
Topics are thematically arranged, with a table of contents at the beginning and a comprehensive index. Sections are colour-coded, with a coloured band at the top of the page.

Children's assessments
Not chosen for review.

Other aspects
With 'Did you know' questions and practical experiments, this is again an interesting book. Also available as part of a combined volume: *The Usborne World of Knowledge Encyclopedia.*

National Curriculum test results
Science
Coverage of total subject area: 44%
Coverage of topics broached: 94%

[Usborne] *Where Things Come From and How Things are Made*, This is a combined volume which brings together: *Where Food Comes From*, by Janet Cook and Shirley Bond S.R.D. (ISBN 0 7460 0280 7 paperback, price £2.99); *How Things Are Made*, by Felicity Brooks (ISBN 0 7460 0276 9 paperback, price £2.75); *How Things Are Built*, by Helen Edom (ISBN 0 7460 0278 5 paperback, price £2.99). Usborne Publishing Ltd: 1989

ISBN: 0 7460 1111 3 paperback, 0 7460 0282 3 hardback

Price: £4.95 paperback, £5.50 hardback

Target age range: 7–11 yrs

Coverage: Sections follow the separate books which make up this combined volume. *Where Food Comes From* includes topics ranging from staple items such as bread to sugar and chocolate. *How Things Are Made* covers numerous items, including familiar domestic goods such as leather shoes, woollen sweaters and even bars of soap. *How Things Are Built* looks at a variety of constructions, from brick houses and skyscrapers to tunnels and offshore oil rigs. Additional features in each section include fact and date boxes and quizzes.

Language, layout and images
Although the book is clearly written and conveys simple information, there is a lot on each page. The resultant rather 'busy' layout could be confusing for younger readers. Information is presented in a mixture of text and illustrative material that verges on a comic-strip style.

Retrieval devices
A table of contents at the front of the book gives page references for the three sections. Individual sections then have their own contents lists. There is a full combined index for the whole book.

Children's assessments
'**The things I like about it:** making things in it is interesting. There are lots of pictures on the cover. It has lots of colours. The pictures are good.

The things I don't like about it: cutting trees down. The words are small, it is too thin. The print is too small.'

Other aspects
This is a 'chatty' and informal book that children who like this distinctive style would enjoy.

National Curriculum test results
Geography
Coverage of total subject area: 12%
Coverage of topics broached: 22%
Science
Coverage of total subject area: 19%
Coverage of topics broached: 22%

The Usborne Book of the Countryside, Usborne Publishing Ltd: 1993, first published in 1976. The material in this book is also published as three separate titles: *The Usborne NatureTrail Book of Birdwatching*, by M. Hart and M. Stephens (ISBN 0 7460 1169 5 paperback, price £3.99; 0 7460 1170 9 hardback, price £5.95); *The Usborne NatureTrail Book of Trees & Leaves*, by I. Selburg and M. Stephens (ISBN 0 7460 1267 5 paperback, price £3.95; 0 7460 1268 3 hardback, price £5.95); *The Usborne NatureTrail Book of Wild Flowers*, by S. Tarsky and M. Stephens (ISBN 0 7460 1167 9 paperback, price £3.95; 0 7460 1168 7 hardback, price £5.95).

ISBN: 0 7460 1636 0 paperback, 0 7460 1637 9 hardback

Price: £5.99 paperback, £7.99 hardback

Target age range: 9–12 yrs

Publications for Key Stage 2   73

Coverage: In addition to the general information on birds, trees and wild flowers there are ideas for things to make and do, such as growing a tree from a seedling and making a bird garden.

Language, layout and images
Written to involve the young reader with plenty of activities and ideas, the words and images integrate well and complement each other. The uncluttered layout uses unobtrusive arrows and numbered boxes to good effect to guide the reader through the subject matter. There are lots of attractive and colourful drawings and diagrams.

Retrieval devices
Contents are organized in sections which correspond to the individual books that make up the combined volume. Each section has its own contents list and a short, single-paragraph user guide; there is also a combined index at the back of the complete volume.

Children's assessments
Not chosen for review.

Other aspects
Redesigned, with new artwork and text, this is a well-presented and informative volume, which is likely to appeal to most Key Stage 2 nature lovers. An even larger (six books in one) omnibus edition: *The Usborne NatureTrail Omnibus* (ISBN 0 7460 0767 1, price £7.95 paperback) has additional sections covering insects and sea and pond life.

National Curriculum test results
Science
Coverage of total subject area: 17%
Coverage of topics broached: 100%

The Usborne Book of World History, by Dr Anne Millard and Patricia Vanags. Usborne Publishing Ltd: 1985. This combined volume is also published separately as: *The Children's Encyclopedia of History: First Civilisations to the Fall of Rome* (ISBN 0 7460 1018 4 paperback, price £6.99) and *The Children's Encyclopedia of History: Dark Ages to 1914* (ISBN 0 7460 1019 2 paperback, price £6.99).

ISBN: 0 7460 0555 5 paperback

Price: £9.99

Target age range: 7–11 yrs. Publisher's recommendation 8–12 yrs

Coverage: With material covered organized under these headings – 'The First Civilisations', 'Warriors & Seafarers', 'Empires & Barbarians', 'Crusaders', 'Aztecs', 'Samurai, Explorations and Discovery', 'The Age of Revolution' – the book offers a rather 'whistle-stop' survey of world history. There are, however, helpful key date boxes and chronological charts.

Language, layout and images
Written in child-friendly language, the book utilizes a comic-strip-style format, with well-integrated images and text. Overall the book has a slightly old-fashioned appearance.

Retrieval devices
There is a contents list at the front of the book, with page references for the various

sections. Each section then has its own contents lists for individual topics. An index covering the full combined volume is situated at the back of the book, but there is no glossary or user guide.

Children's assessments
Not chosen for review.

Other aspects
This is not particularly helpful for anyone studying British history; however, there are some interesting snippets of information and overall it is useful for setting civilizations in their chronological and spatial context.

National Curriculum test results
History
Coverage of total subject area: 49%
Coverage of topics broached: 49%

The Usborne Book of World Wildlife, Usborne Publishing Ltd: 1994. Another combined volume from Usborne, comprising the following separate publications: *Polar Wildlife*, by Kamini Khanduri; *Rainforest Wildlife*, by Antonia Cunningham; *Grassland Wildlife*, by Kamini Khanduri; *Mountain Wildlife* by Anna Claybourne and Antonia Cunningham.

ISBN: 0 7460 1982 3 paperback, 0 7460 1983 1 hardback

Price: £7.99 paperback, £9.99 hardback

Target age range: 8–12 yrs

Coverage: The book is organized in four sections, to correspond with the four publications it combines. In *Polar Wildlife*, topics move from a general discussion of Polar areas through the variety of polar wildlife to people in Polar lands. *Rainforest Wildlife* looks at rainforest plants, birds, animals, reptiles and insect life, concluding with information about the people who live in rainforest areas and consideration of these regions as threatened habitats. *Grassland Wildlife*, in similar vein, looks at plant-eaters, meat-eaters, changing seasons and people who inhabit the grasslands. Endangered habitats are also examined in *Mountain Wildlife*, which also looks at mountains of the world, wildlife, and people who live in mountainous regions of the world.

Language, layout and images
A mixture of straightforward text and attractive, colourful images illustrates the subject matter well. There are also a few lovely photographs (particularly in the *Polar Wildlife* section).

Retrieval devices
Contents are organized in sections which correspond to the individual books that make up the combined volume. Each section has its own contents list; there is also a combined index at the back of the complete volume.

Children's assessments
'The things I like about it: well it's easy to read, very interesting, good for 10-year-olds and it's got some animals in that I have never seen before. The pictures are very attractive. I think that the way that they have the pictures and the way they draw them is good.

The things I don't like about it: It's telling me some of the things that I have heard of before and when you get past a few of the pages it starts to get boring. The print is small.'

Other aspects
An appealing volume, covering a topic that is popular with children in this age-group, the paperback represents good value for money. Usborne also market a companion jigsaw puzzle (360 pieces) priced at £6.99 including VAT.

National Curriculum test results
Geography
Coverage of total subject area: 6%
Coverage of topics broached: 11%
Science
Coverage of total subject area: 11%
Coverage of topics broached: 50%

The Usborne First Guide to the Universe. Usborne Publishing Ltd: 1993, first published in 1982. Yet another combined volume from Usborne, this time comprising three books: *Our Earth*, by Jane Chisholm, illustrated by Martin Newton, Louise Nevett, Joseph McEwan and Guy Smith (ISBN 0 86020 582 7 paperback, price £2.75); *Rockets and Spaceflight*, by Lynn Myring, illustrated by Martin Newton, Louise Nevett and Philip Schramm (ISBN 0 86020 584 3 paperback, price £2.99); *Sun, Moon and Planets*, by Lynn Myring and Sheila Snowden, illustrated by Martin Newton, Louise Nevett and Philip Schramm (ISBN 0 86020 580 0 paperback, price £2.99).

ISBN: 0 7460 0556 3 paperback

Price: £5.99

Target age range: 7–9 yrs

Coverage: A range of space-related topics are discussed, grouped under sections which correspond to the individual publications which make up the combined volume. The section entitled *Our Earth* looks at the weather and diurnal and seasonal cycles, and takes a 'Journey to the centre of the earth'. In *Rockets and Spaceflight*, there is a 'Mission to the Moon' and a star travel fantasy, as well as a look at the space station 'Skylab'. The final section, *Sun, Moon and Planets*, looks at our solar system and the galaxies beyond.

Language, layout and images
Lots of bright and colourful images are used, together with 'line and blob' characters in a fairly well-spaced layout. Supporting text is written in child-friendly language.

Retrieval devices
There is a contents list at the front of the book with page references for the various sections. Each section then has its own contents list for individual topics, and also a glossary. An index at the back covers the full combined volume.

Children's assessments
Not chosen for review.

Other aspects
This will appeal to children who like a friendly picture-book format.

National Curriculum test results
Not tested.

[Usborne] *The Children's Encyclopedia of Our World*, by Jenny Tyler, Lisa Watts, Tessa Campbell, illustrated by Bob Hersey and Peter Mousdale (maps). Usborne Publishing Ltd: 1993, first published in 1976. A combined volume, the encyclopedia incorporates: *The Usborne Book of the Earth* (ISBN 0 86020 062 0); *The Usborne Book of the Seas* (ISBN 0 86020 064 7); *The Usborne Picture Atlas* (ISBN 0 7460 0113 4). These individual titles are all produced in paperback and are priced at £3.95 each.

ISBN: 0 7460 1845 2 paperback

Price: £6.95

Target age range: 8–11 yrs.

Coverage: Topics looked at include: rocks and fossils; seasons; how towns grow; ports and harbours; shaping of the land by the sea; whales and divers. There are also picture maps of the world.

Language, layout and images
Fairly child-friendly text, with a few stories included, makes this a book that is intentionally addressed to a child reader. However, the layout is rather old-fashioned, with bland colours, dated illustrations and unattractive paper, which will put a lot of young readers off.

Retrieval devices
There are contents lists for each section, and a full general index for the combined volume. An index for place names is also included; however, it is not easy to locate places on the maps from a simple page reference, and no supplementary grid lines or other referencing devices are offered.

Children's assessments
Not chosen for review.

Other aspects
This is not an inviting or appealing volume.

National Curriculum test results
Geography
Coverage of total subject area: 53%
Coverage of topics broached: 53%

General encyclopedias and books of facts

The general encyclopedias on offer for children in Key Stage 2 still struggle to balance information provision, child-appeal, size and price, to the detriment of at least one of these factors. There are only a few really comprehensive general encyclopedias on the market, and these do not compete well with single-subject volumes in terms of quality and quantity of illustration and of child-appeal. This may be due in part to the competition provided by multimedia products (see Chapter 6). There is more incentive for publishers to produce small, relatively inexpensive single-subject books, which purchasers can more easily afford, than to publish large single- or multi-volume sets in direct competition with CD-ROM encyclopedias. On a CD-ROM masses of information, including high quality images, can be included at a comparatively reasonable price (for homes with the necessary equipment); when printed in book form, this is much more costly (for example, the electronic version of the *Oxford Children's Encyclopedia* costs £59.99, compared with £125 for the seven-volume printed set).

The comments earlier in this chapter, p.64, relating to National Curriculum requirements and to the children's assessments also apply here.

A selection of general encyclopedias and books of facts

Children's Britannica, Encyclopaedia Britannica Inc.: 1988 (fourth edition), reprinted with revisions 1993 (a 1995 revised reprint is available)

ISBN: 0 85229 209 0 twenty-volume set (including index volume).

Price: £225 (quoted for the 1995 edition in October 1996)

Target age range: 9–12 yrs

Coverage: As might be expected, the encyclopedia offers a very wide range of topics in all subject areas. One noteworthy (and comparatively uncommon) inclusion is a quite lengthy section on Children's Literature. This offers a variety of book lists (including work by contemporary writers such as Alan Ahlberg, Gillian Avery, Sue Townsend and many others) under the headings: 'Picture Books for Younger Children'; 'Reading Aloud and Family Reading'; 'Reading Alone'; 'Fiction for Middle Readers'; 'Fiction for Older Readers'; 'Myth, Fairy Tale and Folklore'; 'Reading for Teenagers' (including Robert Cormier's *I am the Cheese* and Paul Zindel's *The Pigman*); 'History'; 'Poetry and Verse'; 'People'; 'Religions'; and 'A Miscellany of Interests'.

The set includes a world atlas and has over 4000 article titles and 30 000 subject entries.

Language, layout and images
The language used is comparatively straightforward; however, the text is organized in fairly long, unbroken blocks, requiring fluent readers. Some areas of text have a faintly patronizing tone which may not go down well with young people. For example, in the section on nutrition, the text advises: 'Mealtimes are an important part of the day. Food should be carefully prepared and attractive to look at when served, so that we are encouraged to eat it.' [p.73]

A 'traditional style' encyclopedia, it has quite a dense layout, and, although there are images on most pages, the emphasis is on lengthy written explanations rather than on the visual information offered by the wealth of diagrams and illustrations to be found in the majority of other reference works. A significant proportion of the illustrations are in black and white.

Retrieval devices
The encyclopedia is arranged alphabetically, with a comprehensive index volume to supply references for subjects that do not have a separate article. There is a very helpful six-page guide to using the index (the index is almost a dictionary in itself, having brief information about the topics covered as well as page references).

Children's assessments
Not available for review.

Other aspects
Unfortunately, many children will find this unappealing and will need to be encouraged to see that it does contain a wealth of information of interest to them. In view of the price tag it is worth observing children's reactions to it over time, using an edition in the local library, before contemplating paying such a large sum for a set that is unlikely to enthuse the majority of children in this age-group.

National Curriculum test results
Geography
Coverage of total subject area: 71%
Coverage of topics broached: 71%
History
Coverage of total subject area: 74%
Coverage of topics broached: 74%
Science
Coverage of total subject area: 97%
Coverage of topics broached: 97%

The Kingfisher Beano Book of Amazing Facts. Kingfisher (an imprint of Larousse plc): 1995

ISBN: 1 85697 477 4 hardback

Price: £6.99

Target age range: 7–11 yrs

Coverage: Characters from the Beano guide the reader through sections entitled: 'Journey into Space'; 'Planet Earth'; 'Living World'; 'Back in Time'; 'Discover Science'; 'On the Move'; 'Human Body'; 'Around the Globe'; 'Facts and Figures'.
   Coverage of some of the topics is rather superficial, but this is perhaps to be expected in such a slim volume. For example, the section on the body has a double-page spread showing various 'body' diagrams but little real explanatory text, and the remaining 'Human Body' pages cover sporting activities (bungee jumping, lacrosse on horseback (in Georgia), the Olympics and so on). 'Amazing Facts' boxes do offer interesting nuggets (such as: 'You shed a complete layer of skin about every 3 weeks. Most house dust is actually dead skin.'), but very little volume of information.
   The 'Discover Science' pages are slightly more informative, showing, for example, different types of energy in familiar objects such as a hairdryer: 'Energy is the world's greatest form-changer. It cannot be created or destroyed, but is constantly changing from one form to another. Hairdryers turn electrical energy into heat energy and kinetic energy. In other words they blow hot air!'.

Language, layout and images
This is an easily-read format, friendly and informal with good use of graphics. The younger reader will be encouraged by the cartoons and short stories involving Beano characters which are integrated into the factual material. This should at least be fun learning.

Retrieval devices
There is a contents list and an index.

Children's assessments
'The things I like about it: the pictures, because it is a mix of cartoon and real live pictures. The pictures are brilliant. You can read it because it has large print.
The things I don't like about it: none.'
Lyn Bentley comments: 'Several children initially wanted to review *The Kingfisher Beano Book of Amazing Facts*; however, in practice, it contains little information and was used very little.'

Other aspects
The amazing facts may stimulate further reading; and this is an imaginative way of encouraging younger children to develop a curiosity and thirst for knowledge. The Beano characters are a good choice for this enterprise; the Roehampton survey reveals that the majority of children questioned, in Key Stages 2, 3 and 4, name it as their favourite comic.

National Curriculum test results
Geography
Coverage of total subject area: 12%
Coverage of topics broached: 22%
History
Coverage of total subject area: 19%
Coverage of topics broached: 19%
Science
Coverage of total subject area: 22%
Coverage of topics broached: 36%

Also available in this series and aimed at the 7+ age group:

The Kingfisher Beano Book of Britain. (ISBN 0 7534 0086 3 hardback, price £7.99)

The Kingfisher Beano File: Ringbinder (ISBN 0 7534 0079 0 hardback, price £5.99) with the following insert titles – *Biggest, Tallest, Greatest, Bestest!* (0 7534 0078 2); *Little Horrors* (0 7534 0075 8), *School Rules* (0 7534 0077 4); *Brain Blasters* (0 7534 0076 6); *Pesky Pirates* (0 7534 0080 4); *Rhymes and Riddles* (0 7534 0081 2); *Dreadful Dinosaurs* (0 7534 0082 0); *Revolting Recipes* (0 7534 0083 9). The inserts are priced at £1.99 each.

Kingfisher Children's Encyclopedia, general editor: John Paton. Kingfisher (an imprint of Larousse plc): this edition 1995, first published in ten volumes in 1989, first published in this format in 1991

ISBN: 0 86272 696 4 hardback

Price: £25.00

Target age range: 9–12 yrs. Publisher's recommendation: 8–14 yrs

Coverage: With over 1300 A–Z entries, the encyclopedia covers 16 subject areas, which are listed as: 'Plants and Food'; 'The Arts'; 'Peoples and Government'; 'Language and Literature'; 'Sports and Pastimes'; 'Astronomy and Space'; 'Science'; 'Animals'; 'Machines and Mechanisms'; 'Travel and Transport'; 'Human Body'; 'Buildings'; 'Our Earth'; 'History'; 'Countries and Places'; 'Religion, Philosophy and Myth'. Each subject area is allocated a symbol; one or more of these then appears beside relevant A–Z entries. There are also more detailed special feature pages, 'See-for-yourself' guides to carrying out simple experiments, and summary fact panels with statistical data.

Language. layout and images
The book is well written, in simple, to-the-point language. The layout is enhanced by numerous diagrams which are clearly linked with and amplify the text. There are attractive illustrations and photographic images.

Retrieval devices
A useful and well-thought-out section at the front advises on use of the alphabetically organized encyclopedia. There is a general index and a subject index at the back. Topics are also cross-referenced from within the text.

Children's assessments
'**The things I like about it:** the text is a good size. It has lots of pictures, the pictures are very good. The print is a good size. I found everything I needed.

The things I don't like about it: This book is too big to carry around.'

Other aspects
This is a very useful extended dictionary for home reference. For those who find the size (and weight) of the single volume daunting, it is also available as a ten-volume set (ISBN 0 86272 467 8) priced at £79.99

National Curriculum test results
Geography
Coverage of total subject area: 35%
Coverage of topics broached: 67%
History
Coverage of total subject area: 40%
Coverage of topics broached: 40%
Science
Coverage of total subject area: 81%
Coverage of topics broached: 81%

The Oxford Children's Encyclopedia (seven-volume boxed set). Oxford University Press: 1992 (revised reprint, first published in 1991).

ISBN: 0 19 910151 5

Price: £125

Target age range: 8–13 yrs

Coverage: The encyclopedia boasts 700 000 words, 1500 articles and 650 biographies, and offers a solid foundation of knowledge in science, technology, history, geography and the arts. The entries are given good coverage – sometimes up to three pages – providing the reader with a good initial introduction to each topic. Additional facts and figures appear in the margins and there are also ideas for activities and experiments.

Language, layout and images
Our Education Adviser is concerned that this encyclopedia lacks 'child appeal', using rather unimaginative language with a lot of unbroken text. She also finds the layout rather dull and dated (though less so than that of *Children's Britannica*). On the other hand, our Science Adviser is impressed by the colourful illustrations, which he thinks are excellent and numerous, with lots of good photographs, drawings, sectional diagrams and maps in full colour.

Retrieval devices
Topics are arranged alphabetically with added cross-reference panels at the end of each article. Topic titles appear at the top of the page in a coloured panel. Each letter of the alphabet is featured in a different colour. There is also a contents list at the front of individual volumes plus a section advising readers on how to use the encyclopedia.

Children's assessments
'The things I like about it: There are good pictures and good sized writing.

The things I don't like about it: Some print is too small for younger children.'

Other aspects
It is also possible to purchase a boxed set of three science videos drawn from the encyclopedia: *Oxford Children's Encyclopedia of Science Video*. Video 1: *Acid to Evolution*; Video 2: *Fire to Metals*; Video 3: *Nuclear to X-rays* (ISBN 0 10 910161 2, priced at £25 including VAT).

This is more child-friendly and has a less patronizing tone than *Children's Britannica*; however, in view of the reservations expressed by our Education Adviser, it is worth trying this one out with children in the library before buying.

National Curriculum Test Results
Geography
Coverage of total subject area: 35%
Coverage of topics broached: 67%
History
Coverage of total subject area: 80%
Coverage of topics broached: 80%
Science
Coverage of total subject area: 97%
Coverage of topics broached: 97%

82   A Guide to Children's Reference Books

Sainsbury's Children's Encyclopedia, by John Farndon. HarperCollins Publishers Ltd: 1992 (published exclusively for J Sainsbury plc).

ISBN: This is not shown on the book

Price: The price is not marked on individual copies – thought to be under £10.

Target age range: 9–13 yrs

Coverage: Subjects covered are: 'The Living World'; 'The Human Body'; 'Animals with Backbones'; 'Animals without Backbones'; 'Plants'; 'Space'; 'The Earth'; 'The Ages of the Earth'; 'The Human Story'; 'History'; 'Science'; 'Technology'; 'Inventions & Discoveries'; 'Society'; 'Places'. There is a very useful supplementary section with famous people listed in chronological order under a variety of categories: for example, 'Thinkers' runs from Buddha to Jung; 'Politicians' from Richelieu to Gorbachev; 'Scientists' from Archimedes to Einstein. Of particular note are the writers: the list runs from Homer to Roald Dahl, taking in, unusually, a number of writers for children (such as A.A. Milne and Lewis Carroll).

Language, layout and images
This is in the format of a rather dense traditional encyclopedia with a comparatively high proportion of text, although the language used is fairly straightforward and reader-friendly. In the introduction readers are advised to use a dictionary to discover the meaning of the more complex terms which are italicized in the text – rather a novel way to get around the need to include a glossary! The illustrations are artistically drawn and relevant, but overall the volume rather lacks 'child appeal'.

Retrieval devices
Material is arranged in thematic order, with a contents list, index and user advice (the latter contained in the introduction).

Children's assessments
Not chosen for review.

Other aspects
This is a useful general reference book for those on a tight budget; however, children may need to be persuaded to use it.

National Curriculum test results
Geography
Coverage of total subject area: 18%
Coverage of topics broached: 33%
History
Coverage of total subject area: 33%
Coverage of topics broached: 33%
Science
Coverage of total subject area: 68%
Coverage of topics broached: 68%

The Usborne Children's Encyclopedia, by Jane Elliott and Colin King. Usborne Publishing Ltd: 1993, first published in 1986

ISBN: 0 7460 0031 6 hardback

Price: £10.99

Target age range: 7–9 yrs. Publisher's recommendation 8–12 yrs

Coverage: The subject areas covered are: 'Our Planet'; 'Natural Life'; 'History'; 'People'; and 'Science Around Us'. An added appendix looks at machines, inventions and new technology.

Language, layout and images
Simple language, organized in short paragraphs, is used throughout. There is rather a lot on each page, making the layout rather busy. The images, often small cartoon-like illustrations which are not that clear, support the text almost in the manner of a picture story.

Retrieval devices
The encyclopedia is organized in topic sections rather than alphabetically. There is a table of contents and an index.

Children's assessments
'The things I like about it: The thing I like about it is they keep it simple and have lots of pictures. I like the pictures because they are cartoons. The other pictures are O.K. but very simple and unrealistic. The print is the right size for children.

The things I don't like about it: it doesn't say much about each item.'
(this reviewer added that he thought the book was too expensive)

Other aspects
This is not a particularly wonderful book; however, there is quite a lot of fairly superficial information, packaged in comic-strip format, which may appeal to some readers.

National Curriculum test results
Geography
Coverage of total subject area: 6%
Coverage of topics broached: 11%
History
Coverage of total subject area: 18%
Coverage of topics broached: 18%
Science
Coverage of total subject area: 14%
Coverage of topics broached: 63%

The Usborne Book of Facts and Lists: Omnibus Edition. Usborne Publishing Ltd: 1987. This is a combined volume, featuring four books in one: *Earth Facts*, by Lynn Bresler; *Countries of the World Facts*, by Neil Champion; *Weather Facts*, by Anita Ganeri; *Space Facts*, by Struan Reid.

ISBN: 0 7460 0026 X paperback

Price: £6.99

Target age range: 8–12 yrs

Coverage: Material is organized under the headings of the four books which have been combined in this single volume. *Earth Facts* ranges from Earth's 'vital statistics' to the

Earth 'in a nutshell', and includes a look at icebergs, glaciers, grasslands and savannah land. *Countries of the World Facts* gives a variety of facts about countries of the world, including: capital city (the capital city of Nigeria is, incorrectly, still listed as Lagos and not Abuja); population; area (in square kilometres and square miles); other major cities; natural products; plus traditional food and drink in each country. *Weather Facts* has weather records and looks at such things as thunder and lightning; freak weather conditions; disasters; and even ancient weather gods. *Space Facts* looks at the Solar System, considering individual planets, and moves on to facts about galaxies and astronomy (early and modern).

Language, layout and images
Written in language that is clear and to the point, the book has quite an interesting and creative layout. There are facts in lists with pictures and charts; question and answer boxes; and an abundance of colourful images, ranging from diagrams and graphs to cartoon images, all of which help to bring the text to life.

Retrieval devices
Material is organized in the four subject areas. These are listed, with page references, at the front. Each former book then has a separate contents list, glossary, and index.

Children's assessments
'**The things I like about it:** The pictures in this book are really good because they are the cartoon kind. It's just the right size. You can understand the writing. The facts are very interesting. It's also very colourful. It's worth the money that you pay for it.

The things I don't like about it: The writing's a bit close together, it could be bigger.'

Other aspects
This is a portable little book, which is likely to appeal to children who enjoy a cartoon-style format and like to collect 'amazing facts'. The Roehampton survey shows that boys in particular tend to like 'snappy' facts and lists: 44% of the boys questioned at Key Stage 2 said that they like information in this format, compared with only 20% who said that they like encyclopedias. The format is less popular with girls, who prefer magazines and activity books.

National Curriculum test results
Geography
Coverage of total subject area: 23%
Coverage of topics broached: 44%
Science
Coverage of total subject area: 8%
Coverage of topics broached: 18%

The Usborne Book of Knowledge. Usborne Publishing Ltd: 1988, first published 1979. This volume combines five books in one; individual titles are: *How Animals Live*, by Anne Civardi and Cathy Kilpatrick, illustrated by George Thompson; *How Birds Live*, written by Tony Bremner; *How Machines Work*, by Christopher Rawson, illustrated by Colin King; *How Your Body Works*, by Judy Hindley and Christopher Rawson, illustrated by Colin King; *How Things Began*, by Mary Jean McNeil, illustrated by Colin King.

ISBN: 0 7460 0359 5 paperback

Price: £9.95

Target age range: 7–11 yrs

Language, layout and images
Clearly written for children in this age-group; the language and mode of address used attempt to involve the reader by presenting subject matter in a child-friendly manner. Words and images are well integrated, using a large format with clear arrows and boxes. There is a good relationship between the words and images, with lots of inventive (though not always wholly successful) diagrams. The human characters represented are drawn in a slightly stereotypical comic-strip style.

Retrieval devices
As with other combined Usborne volumes, the subject matter remains in clearly delineated sections; each of these has its own contents list and glossary. There is a combined index for all the books and also an additional picture index for 'How Things Began'.

Children's assessments
'The things I like about it: I like the animals on the cover. I like the pictures. They have good detail. It has lots of information. It has colours. It is the right size and a good price.

The things I don't like about it: I do not like the print.'

Other aspects
This is quite a reasonably priced compendium, although it is rather an arbitrary collection of subject matter.

National Curriculum test results
Science
Coverage of total subject area: 25%
Coverage of topics broached: 35%

The Usborne World of Knowledge Encyclopedia. Usborne Publishing Ltd.

ISBN: 0 7460 1843 6 hardback

Price: £17.95
This is a combined version of the three volumes: *The Usborne Geography Encyclopedia*, *The Usborne Living World Encyclopedia* and *The Usborne Science Encyclopedia*, which are discussed above in the section on subject encyclopedias.

Mini-libraries

National Curriculum requirements

Some very inviting series are now on offer for children in Key Stage 2. History books are in specially good supply, particularly with regard to coverage of British history. Pupils following the study units 'Romans, Anglo-Saxons and Vikings in Britain', 'Life in Tudor times', 'Victorian Britain' and 'Britain since 1930', laid down in the National Curriculum (History, Key Stage 2), should easily find relevant material if they have access to one or more of the series relating to history that are reviewed below.

Other subjects are not neglected, with coverage of science (particularly related to life processes and living things), geography and technology topics in multi-subject sets. Tempting material related to hobbies and other interest areas is also provided. The comments earlier in this chapter, p.64, relating to the children's assessments also apply here.

A selection of mini-libraries

Collins 'Faxfinder' series. HarperCollins Publishers Ltd: 1996
The series consists of a personal organizer, which includes some 'starter' facts such as 'History Firsts', and a range of 'Faxfinder' titles designed to fit into the ring binder.

ISBN: 0 00 197928 0 hardback binder with starter facts (see also individual 'infill' titles)

Price: £4.99 for the personal organizer, £1.99 each for individual titles

Target age range: 7–11 yrs

Language, layout and images
These are modern, slightly 'wacky' and are directly addressed to child readers. The range is colourful and well illustrated, with plenty of 'child appeal'.

Retrieval devices
There is an index in each section, and topics are colour-coded.

Children's assessments
'**The things I like about it:** it is a little interesting and it is very good. I like the size of the book. I like some of the pictures, they are the right size and very good to look at.

The things I don't like about it: I do not like to look at the pages, the shape of them. I do not like the price on it at all [the reviewer here suggested that the binder should be £1.00 cheaper]. I do not like some of the writing.'

National Curriculum test results (overall for series)
Science
Coverage of total subject area: 25%
Coverage of topics broached: 100%

Individual 'infill' titles are listed below.

Animal World

ISBN: 0 00 197906 X

Coverage: Topics ranging from 'The Animal Kingdom' to 'Animal Babies' are covered; there is even a look at 'Animal Courtship' and at camouflage, with additional 'Strange but True' facts about animals.

Publications for Key Stage 2

Body Facts

ISBN: 0 00 197907 8

Coverage: A fascinating collection of facts, ranging from 'Your Body Map' to 'Staying Healthy' and 'Vital Statistics', is included. There is even information on 'Brain Waves', 'Food Processing' and a look at human reproduction (from fertilization through to birth, but omitting mention of how egg cell and sperm cell meet).

Castles

ISBN: 0 00 197908 6

Coverage: Here topics include 'Castle Design'; 'Highlife'; and 'Lowlife'. There is also a useful cross-sectional diagram of castle living quarters, and a section called 'Gruesome' (featuring instruments of torture), plus castle 'Follies and Fantasies'.

Earth and Space

ISBN: 0 00 197917 5

Coverage: Information ranges from facts about our own solar system to a look at 'The Big Black Beyond' and 'Future World'. There are 'Cosmofacts' and facts about space exploration, including spacelabs.

Great Inventions

ISBN: 0 00 197915 9

Coverage: Details of inventions from the wheel to satellites are given, including mention of medical inventions and a look at machines both at work and in the home. Readers are invited to guess the function of a small number of pictured gadgets.

Major Disasters

ISBN: 0 00 197916 7

Coverage: A wide range of disasters are examined, under headings ranging from 'Flood Alert' to 'Nuclear Nightmares and Chemical Catastrophes'. There is quite a thoughtful look at the causes of famine, considering the effects of pests and crop diseases (such as that which caused the potato famine in Ireland) and the loss of cultivatable land due to tree-felling and subsequent soil erosion.

Unsolved Mysteries

ISBN: 0 00 197918 3

Coverage: Moving from 'Beasts from the Deep' via 'The Baffling Bermuda Triangle' to 'All in the Stars?', this collection also finds time to enquire whether these are 'All in the mind?'

World Facts

ISBN: 0 00 197909 4

Coverage: Facts given range from record-breakers (entitled 'Wow!' and featuring deepest rivers, highest mountains and so on) to 'Eco-facts'.

Heinemann 'History of Britain' Series. Hamlyn Children's Books (an imprint of Reed International Books Ltd): 1993–5

ISBN: various (see individual titles)

Price: £4.99 (paperback)

Target age range: 8–12 yrs
Although different books within the series are specifically coded ('KS2', 'KS3' or 'KS2 & 3'), this has more to do with the relevance of the subject matter to the particular National Curriculum programme of study than with any additional degree of difficulty in language or format in those texts designated for Key Stage 3.

Language, layout and images
The books use clear and uncomplicated language; unfamiliar terms are explained in a glossary. Very well laid out, they have clear bold print and plentiful illustrations, diagrams and photographic images. The images illustrate the text well.

Retrieval devices
There is a contents list, index and glossary in each volume. A helpful user guide at the start of each gives details 'About this book', and the first volume in the series, *Roman Britain 55 BC to AD 406*, explains BC and AD dating.

Children's assessments
Not chosen for review.

Other aspects
These volumes relate well to the requirements of the National Curriculum programme of study for history, although, being a 'History of Britain' series, they do not, of course, cover the requirement to study Ancient Greece and one non-European society. The inclusion of photographs of artefacts and archaeological 'digs' are particularly helpful, as are the time charts which set each volume in the appropriate period within a band stretching from 55 BC to the 1990s. Other noteworthy features include a map of Britain showing places mentioned in the text; a list of places to visit; a page giving famous people of the times (in alphabetical order); and details of rulers (in the later volumes in the form of a Royal Family Tree for the period in question).

National Curriculum test results (overall for series)
History
Coverage of total subject area: 90%
Coverage of topics broached: 97%

Individual titles are listed below, under the appropriate Key Stage. Some books have relevance for both Key Stages 2 and 3 and are therefore listed twice.
Key Stage 2:

Roman Britain 55 BC to AD 406, by Brenda Williams
ISBN: 0 600 58086 5

The Saxons & Vikings 406 to 1066, by Brenda Williams
ISBN: 0 600 58211 6

The Tudors 1485 to 1603, by Andrew Langley
ISBN: 0 600 58028 8

Victorian Britain 1837 to 1901, by Andrew Langley
ISBN: 0 600 58088 1

Modern Britain 1901 to the 1990s, by Andrew Langley
ISBN: 0 600 58213 2

Key Stage 3:

Medieval Britain 1066 to 1485, by Brenda Williams
ISBN: 0 600 58217 5

Georgian Britain 1714 to 1837, by Andrew Langley
ISBN: 0 600 58026 1

The Stuarts 1603 to 1714, by Andrew Langley
ISBN: 0 600 58215 9

[Ladybird] A 'History of Britain' series. Ladybird: these editions 1994–5.
ISBN: various (see individual titles)
Price: £3.50 each
Target age range: 7–9 yrs

Language, layout and images
Simple and direct language is used throughout. There is almost more information in the images than in the text. Nicely coloured pictures and diagrams are helpfully labelled to give further information. Some small photographic images are included, showing artefacts, period photographs or archaeological sites, where appropriate.

Retrieval devices
There is a contents list, an index and a glossary in each book.

Children's assessments
The series was not chosen for review; however, Lyn Bentley observes: 'The Ladybird book on the Victorians was used most [of all the reference books], having relevant information for local studies on the cholera epidemic in Leamington Spa.'

Other aspects
At the back of each book there is a helpful list of places to visit and an extremely useful 'timeline' guide to the time periods covered in the series (with both dates and a note of the duration of each). One of the 'Key Elements' of the National Curriculum programme of study for history at Key Stage 2 is the requirement that pupils be made aware of the *sources* of information relating to the periods they are studying. Of particular relevance to this is the double page spread, 'How we know', which is included in these Ladybird books. This discusses the evidence used by historians in piecing together the past and is enhanced by the inclusion of a photograph of an artefact for children to identify. The following titles are particularly useful as starter volumes for the Key Stage 2 programme of study for history: *The Romans, The Saxons and the Normans, The Tudors, The Victorians, Britain 1901–1945*.

National Curriculum test results (overall for series)
History
Coverage of total subject area: 90%
Coverage of topics broached: 97%

Individual titles are:

The Romans, by Tim Wood, illustrations by Peter Dennis
ISBN: 0 7214 3366 9

The Saxons and the Normans, by Tim Wood, illustrations by John Dillow
ISBN: 0 7214 3367 7

The Middle Ages, by Tim Wood, illustrations by John Dillow
ISBN: 0 7214 3368 5

The Tudors, by Tim Wood, illustrations by Peter Dennis
ISBN: 0 7214 3369 3

The Stuarts, by Tim Wood, illustrations by Peter Dennis.

ISBN: 0 7214 3370 7

The Georgians, by Tim Wood, illustrations by John Dillow.

ISBN: 0 7214 3371 5

The Victorians, by Tim Wood, illustrations by Peter Dennis.

ISBN: 0 7214 3359 6

Britain 1901–1945, by Tim Wood, illustrations by John Dillow.

ISBN: 0 7214 1792 2

Companion volumes to the above are:

Kings & Queens of England: Part 1 871–1485, by Louise Jones, illustrated by Robin Davies, and *Kings & Queens of England: Part 2 1485 to The Present Day*, by Louise Jones, illustrated by John Dillow. Ladybird: 1996

ISBN: Part 1 – 0 7214 1793 0, Part 2 – 0 7214 1794 9 (both paperback)

Price: £3.50 each

These are quite interesting and well-presented books for a child interested in the Monarchs of England. Fairly forthright, sometimes rather subjective views are expressed; for example, Elizabeth I could be 'fussy' (p.18), Edward VIII was 'charming' (p.42), George IV was 'pig-headed and selfish' (p.34). Each book has a foldout family tree.

Ladybird 'Discovery' Series. Ladybird Books Ltd: various

ISBN: various (see individual titles)

Price: £2.99 per volume

Target age range: 7–10 yrs

Coverage: The Ladybird Discovery Series consists of a range of titles grouped under the themes 'Astronomy', 'Beginning Biology', 'Lifestyles and Living' and 'Our Earth'. Each book has a common format which includes a unique eight-page foldout centre section summarizing some of the important aspects of the subject area covered. In addition, each book contains a page of *amazing facts* which adds to the overall interest, especially for young readers.

Language, layout and images
These books are attractively produced with clear, readily accessible text and excellent illustrations. Technical terms used in the text are highlighted in bold type to signify that further explanations can be found in the glossary. The layout is quite adventurous and attractive, with cleverly arranged foldout flaps. As there are slightly more images than text, even less fluent readers can get something from these books.

Retrieval devices
There is a comprehensive index and table of contents in each volume. Headings and subheadings are quite full, helping the reader to discover the required section easily.

Children's assessments
See individual titles.

Other aspects
A lovely series of little books at a very reasonable price, although the choice of topics is rather arbitrary. *Dinosaurs* (see below) won the 1996 TES Schoolbook Award for Science: Primary. In order to cover a wide subject range within the 30 to 40 pages available, with an above-average amount devoted to illustrations, the information has breadth rather than depth, but the reader will be enthused and encouraged to pursue the subject further. They are excellent starters.

National Curriculum test results (overall for series)
Geography
Coverage of total subject area: 18%
Coverage of topics broached: 33%
Science
Coverage of total subject area: 40%
Coverage of topics broached: 97%

The individual books are:

[Astronomy] *Planets*, written by Nigel Henbest, illustrated by Studio Boni/Galante and Lorenzo Cecchi. Ladybird: 1996

ISBN: 0 7214 1823 6 hardback

Coverage: In addition to information on planets, moons and comets, each section has details and a picture of the particular space probe that brought evidence about that planet or related body back to the Earth. The foldout diagram depicts our Solar System.

Children's assessments
'The things I like about it: the size is very good. The pictures are good. The print is good.

The things I don't like about it: None'

[Beginning biology] *Food*, written by Dene Schofield and Charlotte Evans, illustrated by Studio Boni/Galante. Ladybird: 1995

ISBN: 0 7214 1790 6 hardback

Coverage: This is a comprehensive look at food, with coverage of the growing, catching, farming, cooking and preserving of the food we eat. There is a look at diet and a page on amazing food facts.

Children's assessments

'**The things I like about it:** The size is great. It is not too big but it has got all the information you need.

The things I don't like about it: There are quite a few pictures in this book but they are not very realistic, they don't explain things and you don't understand them.'

[Beginning Biology] *Plants*, written by David Alderton, illustrated by Studio Boni/Galante and Ivan Stalio. Ladybird: 1996

ISBN: 0 7214 1819 8 hardback

Coverage: In addition to covering National Curriculum (Science) specified areas such as pollination, feeding and so on, the book also looks at: the way plants protect themselves (for example with thorns); the threat to plants from human cultivation; and interesting uses of plants (such as in perfumes and medicines).

Children's assessments
'The things I like about it: It is quite interesting. It only has a bit about what I want.

The things I don't like about it: I do not like the pictures. I like the rest.'

[Beginning Biology] *The Body*, written by David Alderton, illustrated by Studio Boni/Galante, Lorenzo Cecchi and Ivan Stalio. Ladybird: 1995

ISBN: 0 7214 1791 4 hardback

Coverage: The book has good body charts and makes useful comparisons with other species. There is, however, very little on human reproduction.

Children's assessments
'The things I like about it: I like the foldout page because it shows you everything clearly. The pictures are clear and good. The print is a reasonable size.

The things I don't like about it: I think the book could be bigger (the size is quite small so you could carry it around with you). The book could be a bit more interesting.'

[Lifestyles and Living] *Castles*, written by David Alderton, illustrated by Studio Boni/Galante, Susanna Addarro and Lorenzo Pieri. Ladybird: 1995.

ISBN: 0 7214 1741 8 hardback.

Coverage: A fascinating introduction to castles; the foldout section is very effective.

Children's assessments
'The things I like about it: the pictures are clear and realistic. I can understand the words.

The things I don't like about it: I think the print could be bigger. I think the size could be bigger.'
(second review)

'The things I like about it: the pictures are big and good and you can understand the writing.

The things I don't like about it: The letters could be a bit bigger.'

[Lifestyles and Living] *Clothes and Costume,* written by David Alderton and Dawn Stubbs, illustrated by Studio Boni/Galante. Ladybird: 1995

ISBN: 0 7214 1789 2 hardback

Coverage: An interesting and wide-ranging collection of information, which covers early civilizations and traditional costumes around the globe, and also looks at synthetic materials.

Children's assessments
'**The things I like about it:** There is a lovely picture that folds out and it's of an Elizabethan lady. They set out the index neatly. The pictures are good and there's lots of detail. The print is small and very clear.

The things I don't like about it: There's too many people that dress in bow and arrow clothes.'

[Lifestyles and Living] *Flight,* written by Fiona Campbell, illustrated by S. Boni/Galante, Ivan Stalio and Lorenzo Cecchi. Ladybird: 1996

ISBN: 0 7214 1748 5 hardback

Coverage: Bringing together topics as diverse as space travel, hot air balloons, flying squirrels and fruit bats, this is a fascinating volume.

Children's assessments
Not chosen for review.

[Natural Habitats] *Rainforest Animals,* written by D. Alderton, illustrated by Studio Boni and L.R. Galante. Ladybird: 1995

ISBN: 0 7214 1745 0 hardback

Coverage: In addition to looking at rainforests around the world and the strange creatures and plants that inhabit them, the book also examines the water cycle and climatic conditions.

Children's assessments
'**The things I like about it:** I like the foldout rainforest and I like the animals as well. I like the pictures because they are very detailed.

The things I don't like about it: I suppose the print is OK but I think it's a bit small.'
(second review)

'**The things I like about it:** The pictures because they help you understand the words. The pictures aren't that realistic so I like them. The print is just the right size but it's a bit faint.

The things I don't like about it: I don't understand a few of the words.'
[The reviewer went on to comment that the book is suitable for children aged between ten and twelve years 'because the words are too difficult for anyone... [younger] and people older would find it too easy and it would be boring.']

[Natural Habitats] *Polar Animals*, written by D. Harper, illustrated by S. Boni and L.R. Galante. Ladybird: 1995

ISBN: 0 7214 1747 7 hardback

Coverage: A look at the poles and their climatic conditions is followed by information on the animals that inhabit these regions and how they are adapted to survive in such conditions.

Children's assessments
Not chosen for review.

[Our Earth] *Thunder and Lightning*, written by Fiona Campbell and Don Harper, illustrated by Studio Boni/Galante and Ivan Stalio. Ladybird: 1995

ISBN: 0 7214 1749 3 hardback

Coverage: In addition to looking at thunder and lightning, this small but full book covers a comprehensive selection of weather topics ranging from windy weather (including hurricanes, typhoons and cyclones), clouds and rain, to Solar System storms, frost and snow, floods, and changing climates.

Children's assessments
'The things I like about it: I like the four page foldout because it's the only interesting part.

The things I don't like about it: I do not like the pictures they look nothing like real.'

[Our Earth] *Volcanoes and Earthquakes*, written by Don Harper, illustrated by S. Boni/Galante and Lorenzo Cecchi. Ladybird: 1995

ISBN: 0 7214 1744 2 hardback

Coverage: This volume includes information on volcanoes on other planets, such as Mount Olympus on Mars, and looks at earthquake and volcano disasters as well as giving cross-sectional diagrams which show Earth's layers, volcanoes and moving continents.

Children's assessments
'The things I like about it: it has lots of facts about earthquakes. The book is a good size. The pictures are good.

The things I don't like about it: all the writing is crowded onto a page. The print is small.'

[Wildlife] *Birds*, written by David Alderton, illustrated by L.R. Galante. Ladybird: 1996

ISBN: 0 7214 1820 1 hardback

Coverage: This volume looks at feeding habits, eggs and hatching, and bird behaviour; it also examines conservation issues.

Children's assessments
Not chosen for review.

[Wildlife] *Dinosaurs*, written by Dougal Dixon, illustrated by S. Boni and L.R. Galante. Ladybird: 1995

ISBN: 0 7214 1788 4 hardback

Coverage: Winner of the 1996 TES 'Schoolbook Award for Science: Primary', this volume gives a fascinating account of dinosaurs, with a chart showing the relevant geological timescale and a discussion of fossilized evidence. Judges commenting on the book admired its accuracy, enthusiasm and imaginative diagrams, summarizing their views with the words 'it's a winner' (TES2 March 8 1996).

Children's assessments
'The things I like about it: The pictures are good. The print is good.

The things I don't like about it: There are too many pictures'

[Wildlife] *Quest for New Animals*, written by David Alderton, illustrated by Studio Boni/Galante and Ivan Stalio. Ladybird: 1996

ISBN: 0 7214 1821 X hardback

Coverage: An interesting and unusual account of rare, recently discovered or rediscovered animals, birds and reptiles; the book may encourage budding young zoologists and explorers.

Children's assessments
'The things I like about it: It's got some interesting facts in and the writing's the right size. I used it for my presentation. It's worth the money.

The things I don't like about it: I don't like the pictures because they're not life like.'

[Wildlife] *Sharks*, written by M. Oakley, illustrated by Studio Boni and L.R. Galante. Ladybird: 1995

ISBN: 0 7214 1746 9 hardback

Coverage: An interesting look at sharks, this volume examines, amongst other things, their movement, growth, and how they reproduce.

Children's assessments
'The things I like about it: This book is very interesting. It has well illustrated pictures. This book says everything about sharks, like inside sharks and what they eat, and lots more. I like the foldout pictures.

The things I don't like about it: The pages are a bit too crowded.'

[Wildlife] *Whales and Dolphins*, written by Mark Oakley, illustrated by Studio Boni/Galante and Lorenzo Pieri. Ladybird: 1995

ISBN: 0 7214 1743 4 hardback

Coverage: In addition to looking at the biology of whales and dolphins, the book also considers the effects of hunting by man, and the products derived from the slaughter of whales.

Children's assessments
'**The things I like about it:** I like it. It's got some interesting facts about them. I like the way they've done the foldout bit in the middle. The print is not too small or too big. The size is O.K. Its good for its price.

'**The things I don't like about it:** I don't like the pictures because they don't look like them.'

(second review)

'**The things I like about it:** It shows you lots of sea creatures in and the pictures are very colourful. It shows you one of my favourite species a whale.

The things I don't like about it: I don't like the writing because it looks like you can't read so they do big writing.'

Other titles recently published or due to be published shortly are:

Computers (ISBN 0 7214 1845 7)

Religions of the World (ISBN 0 7214 1843 0)

Scientists and Inventors (ISBN 0 7214 1840 6)

The Sea (ISBN 0 7214 1750 7)

Threatened Planet (ISBN 0 7214 1841 4)

A mini-library set considered with publications for Key Stage 1 which would also be suitable for the early years of Key Stage 2 is the **Usborne 'Starting Point Science'** series. These books are marketed for children of six years and upwards. Although they are broadly suitable for children of six, seven and eight years, teachers of Key Stage 1 children reported that the books only appealed to those who had very good reading skills. (See Chapter 3 for full review.)

Editor's personal selection

At Key Stage 2, it is necessary to make a major purchasing decision. Is it better to invest in one of the large and expensive general encyclopedia sets, in which case there will be less need for ancillary single-subject texts, or is it preferable to build up a comprehensive collection of the latter instead? Also, as a result of the wide age range encompassed, the same books are not necessarily appropriate for children for the whole of their time in this Key Stage. For this reason selections have been divided into two age ranges: year groups three and four (children aged between seven and nine) and year groups five and six (children aged between nine and 11). It is in the second of these age-groups that the choices divide into two: (1) the general encyclopedia route; and (2) the single-subject encyclopedia route.

A selection from the publications reviewed for year groups 3 and 4

It is not really necessary to rush to purchase a new atlas for children in this age-group. The *Ladybird Picture Atlas* (see Key Stage 1) should last for most of this time, and this can be supplemented with a general geography reference book, such as *The Usborne Geography Encyclopedia*. A good first choice of dictionary is *The Oxford Primary School Dictionary*, with its attendant activity book. With regard to other reference works, even if it is the intention to purchase a full general encyclopedia when the child reaches the age of about nine, it is still worth adding another mini-library set, such as the Ladybird 'Discovery' series, to the Usborne 'Starting Point Science' volumes purchased at the end of Key Stage 1. It is not necessary to buy all available titles; a selection can include some books which are of particular interest to the child recipient (perhaps the book about dinosaurs or the one on whales and dolphins) and some (such as *Plants* and *Planets*) which relate to science. Similarly, titles from a set of history books, such as the Ladybird 'History of Britain' series, are worth collecting. *The Romans*, *The Saxons and the Normans*, *The Tudors*, *The Victorians* and *Britain 1901-1945* are recommended.

		£
The Usborne Geography Encyclopedia (hardback)		9.95
The Oxford Primary School Dictionary (hardback)		5.99
Using the Oxford Primary School Dictionary (paperback)		3.00
Ladybird 'Discovery' series (hardback)	4@ £2.99	11.96
Ladybird 'History of Britain' series (paperback)	5@ £3.50	17.50
TOTAL		48.40

If extra funds are available, additional volumes can be added to the Ladybird 'Discovery' collection, or purchasers could choose the combined *Usborne World of Knowledge Encyclopedia*, (priced at £17.95 hardback), instead of purchasing *The Usborne Geography Encyclopedia* separately. *Kings and Queens of England* (parts 1 and 2) could also be added to the Ladybird history collection.

A selection from the publications reviewed for year groups 5 and 6: Route 1

Both *The Oxford Children's Encyclopedia* and the *Children's Britannica* offer excellent coverage of National Curriculum material, together with information on an amazing range of topics. It really is a case of choosing whichever of these best suits the child for whom they are intended. *The Oxford Children's Encyclopedia* is perhaps the more child-friendly of the two and certainly has better illustrations, so this is the one that has been included in the costings below. Whichever is chosen, the outlay is large and purchasers really need to be sure that such expensive purchases will not merely sit on the shelves unused and unappreciated. Another problem is the speed with which material becomes outdated; revised reprints and even new editions become available every two or three years, and purchasers are then faced with the daunting question of whether to purchase yet another expensive set of books.

Children at this age also need portable reference books to carry around in their satchels or school bags. *The Usborne Pocket Dictionary*, *The Mini Oxford School Speller* and the Kingfisher *Pocket Atlas* (the *Pocket Atlas* is reviewed in Chapter 5) are good texts to carry around. This is also the time to capitalize on children's enthusiasm, purchasing extra interest books such as *The Usborne Book of the Countryside* and *The Usborne Book of World Wildlife*, and perhaps starting a collection of Collins 'Faxfinders', with a few infill titles on topics of particular interest.

		£
The Oxford Children's Encyclopedia (7-volume set)		125.00
The Usborne Pocket Dictionary (paperback)		4.99
The Mini Oxford School Speller (vinyl)		2.99
Kingfisher *Pocket Atlas* (paperback)		4.99
The Usborne Book of the Countryside (paperback)		5.99
The Usborne Book of World Wildlife (paperback)		7.99
Collins 'Faxfinders' binder with 'starter facts'		4.99
Collins 'Faxfinders' infill titles	4@ £1.99	7.96
TOTAL		164.90

A selection from the publications reviewed for year groups 5 and 6: Route 2 (the preferred route)

If not buying a multi-volume general encyclopedia, the following single-subject and mini-library texts are recommended: the *Kingfisher Visual Encyclopedia of Science* and the Heinemann 'History of Britain' series (this assumes that children are still enjoying *The Usborne Geography Encyclopedia*, purchased earlier). *The Chambers Children's Illustrated Dictionary*, which is part dictionary, part encyclopedia (with interesting biographical entries and topic boxes), would also be a valuable acquisition.

The additional texts recommended in route 1 (above) would also be useful additions to this collection; see the paragraph commencing: 'Children at this age also need portable reference books ... p.99.'

		£
Kingfisher Visual Encyclopedia of Science (hardback)		17.99
Heinemann 'History of Britain' series (paperback)	5 @ £4.99	24.95
The Chambers Children's Illustrated Dictionary (hardback)		19.99
The Usborne Pocket Dictionary (paperback)		4.99
The Mini Oxford School Speller (vinyl)		2.99
Kingfisher *Pocket Atlas* (paperback)		4.99
The Usborne Book of the Countryside (paperback)		5.99
The Usborne Book of World Wildlife (paperback)		7.99
Collins 'Faxfinders' binder with 'starter facts'		4.99
Collins 'Faxfinders' infill titles	4 @ £1.99	7.96
TOTAL		102.83

5 Publications for Key Stage 3 (children aged between 11 years and 14 years, in year groups seven to nine)

Availability and suitability: the issues at Key Stage 3

Changing priorities

As children enter Key Stage 3, thoughts inevitably begin to turn to the examinations that will take place toward the end of their secondary education. Publications are again plentiful, with concise single-subject revision guides coming to the forefront for obvious reasons. The children themselves (see the 'Children's assessments' sections in each review), although still impressed by design features and the quality of illustrative material, are even more conscious of the significance of the information given: is it of relevance to their studies? is it presented in a way that makes it accessible and comprehensible?

The Roehampton survey shows that the majority of girls in this age group read non-fiction primarily to help with their homework (at Key Stage 2 the majority of children, both boys and girls, read non-fiction because they want to find things out for themselves). For boys, reading non-fiction to help with homework now figures alongside reading for pleasure and reading to find things out for themselves. For pleasure, boys favour reading about their hobbies and about sport. Girls also opt for hobbies, but still like reading about animals and plants.

The 'Children's assessments' Panel

The Key Stage 3 reference books were reviewed by pupils from Aylesford School, under the guidance of Graham Tyrer, who is Head of English and Curriculum Coordinator for Communications, with the kind permission of Headteacher Lesley King. Graham Tyrer writes:

> Aylesford School is a thriving and growing fully comprehensive school on the outskirts of Warwick: we accept the full range of ability and this is represented here. Our students are keen to read and take work very seriously. They were really pleased to

be allowed to read the books I issued and this excitement is obvious in the liveliness of their comments. Personally I continue to find it reassuring that students still find books an adventure.

The texts we looked at all seem to have taken account of the need to appeal to students' growing multi-literacy: young people are becoming increasingly skilled at reading images and print and responding to the impact these forms have on each other.

So, here [see the 'Children's assessments' section in each review] are the reactions of students aged 12–14. You will see that some have chosen to add a star rating. We agreed that if they did, five would be high.

The market place

At Key Stage 3 the market is very well supplied with reference works, particularly single-subject dictionaries, encyclopedias and atlases. Many of the books on offer will be of interest to the whole family, and the quality of the production of some of these makes them irresistible. The significance of mini-libraries decreases in this sector; however, a number of publishers offer a comprehensive range of single-subject encyclopedias that can be collected over time and which build up into a coherent and comprehensive multi-volume set of reference material.

Atlases

In contrast to those on offer at Key Stage 2, some excellent atlases are published for this age-group. The atlas format is also extended to include books which relate to subject areas other than geography. These subject atlases help to set topics (such as history topics) into a global context.

National Curriculum requirements

In geography lessons at school, pupils are building on the skills which they acquired at Key Stage 2. For example, their map-reading abilities are now extended to include the use of six-figure grid references. Comparative work on localities continues, with a country from list A: Australia and New Zealand, Europe, Japan, North America or the Russian Federation, and a country from list B: Africa, Asia (excluding Japan) or South and Central America (including the Caribbean) being studied in depth. Geographical themes investigated are: 'Tectonic processes'; 'Geomorphological processes'; 'Weather and climate'; 'Ecosystems'; 'Population'; 'Settlement'; 'Economic activities'; and 'Development' (Geography, Key Stage 3). As at Key Stage 2, pupils ideally need access to information on geographical themes (usually found in encyclopedias) as well as to map-based atlases.

A selection of general atlases

[Dorling Kindersley] *Eyewitness Atlas of the World*. Dorling Kindersley: 1996 – new revised edition, first published in 1994

ISBN: 0 7513 6015 5 hardback

Price: £16.99

Target age range: teenagers and upwards

Coverage: At the front of the atlas, a section on the world as a whole considers 'The Earth in Space', including a look at the Solar System and at Earth's orbit, discussing the resultant patterns of day and night, seasonal cycles, global wind directions and ocean currents. Subsequent pages also examine: 'The Earth's Structure' (continental drift, earthquakes and volcanoes); 'Shaping the Landscape' (with diagrams and information on glacial action, coastal and river erosion and the formation of desert dunes); 'Climate and Vegetation' and 'People and Planet' (which considers population growth with a chart showing figures from 1500 to the present day and forecast figures up to the year 2020).

The remainder of the book is organized by continent: North America; Central and South America; Europe; Africa; North and West Asia; South and East Asia; Oceania. Each section opens with a double-page spread introducing the physical geography of that region. Following pages divide the continent by country or group of countries, dealing with human geography and supplementing detailed maps with photographs, illustrations and landscape models.

'Continent' spreads have locator maps, keys to symbols used (natural vegetation and so on), tiny pictures of threatened species and symbols to show where they may be found (see 'Language, layout and images' below) and a cross-sectional 'slice' through the Earth. 'Country' spreads also have locator maps, key boxes for symbols and a compass point, and include flags and population figures for the countries shown. There are photographs and paragraphs relating to relevant industries, crops, arts and crafts, and festivals.

Language, layout and images

The text is straightforward and readable; the maps and illustrations, particularly cross-sectional diagrams, are superbly executed. Despite the volume of information, the layout does not have a 'cluttered' feel, largely because the bulk of the information supplied is in picture, diagram and symbol form with only comparatively short chunks of written text. The print, although quite small by the time individual labels are reached, is clear and distinct. Some of the photographs are, however, rather too small to give any real 'feel' for what they convey. Particularly problematic are the coloured boxes which are intended to show natural vegetation and used to indicate the habitat of endangered species on the accompanying maps. These minute boxes are printed on a purple-coloured background in the key, but on a white background alongside the animal picture; it is extremely difficult to distinguish between some of the colours and even harder to relate these correctly to their appearance elsewhere.

Retrieval devices

A contents page at the front locates the different sections of the book. There is also an extremely helpful user guide, located after the global section on pages 18 and 19. This has a key to the general symbols and abbreviations used on the maps and shows sample pages with features labelled and explained. Details of how the atlas was made, using innovative computer technology and the latest cartographic data, are also included. At the back of the book there is a short glossary (the appearance of a word in the glossary is not signalled from the text) and an index. Prefaced with brief information on using the simple letter/number grid referencing system for locating places listed, the index also includes interesting fact boxes for countries. These give information (where available) on: language spoken, currency, population density, average life expectancy, price of 1 dozen hen's eggs, literacy, number of TVs per 1000 people, number of people per doctor, whether the death penalty still operates, percentage of urban-based population and average number of calories consumed daily per person (very useful for pupils learning how to assess the level of development in countries they are studying).

Children's assessments
'The layout in this book is good; the pictures are very colourful but some of them are too small. On most pages in the book there is large writing so you can read about the main parts of the country, ocean, planet or whatever. There is a lot of small writing on the pages so you need to look hard to read some of it.

The front cover is nice and bold and there is lots of colour. Also there is a bright silver border.

Overall, I enjoyed reading it and would recommend it to someone my age.'
Ben Dunnell (aged 12)

Other aspects
The atlas is sumptuously produced, in the style that one has come to expect from Dorling Kindersley. For those who assimilate information most easily from sectional diagrams and charts the format is good. However, the information may be just a little *too* compressed; excellent eyesight is certainly a prerequisite for anyone attempting to decipher the smallest symbols used. This is more of a 'coffee table' book than one which could be easily transported to school and back.

National Curriculum test result: 91%

[Kingfisher] *Pocket Atlas*, by Jill and David Wright. Kingfisher Books (then Grisewood & Dempsey Ltd): revised edition 1993, first published in paperback in 1987 and in hardback in 1983

ISBN: 0 86272 276 4 paperback

Price: £4.99

Target age range: 9–13 yrs

Coverage: At the front of the atlas there is a section on the world; this looks at the Earth as a planet (with a diagram of the Solar System) and goes on to cover 'Climate and Vegetation', 'World Facts and Figures', 'The World's Population' 'East, West, North, South' (an interesting and thought-provoking look at contrasts between developed, developing and least developed nations) and 'Countries of the World'. There is also a useful section on the making of maps, covering aspects such as latitude and longitude and earth time.

The detailed sections on countries are grouped by continent: Europe; Asia; Africa; North America; South America; Australasia; Antarctica and the Arctic. Following a physical map and information about the relevant continent, the area is broken down into individual countries or small groups of countries which are then considered in more detail. For example Europe is broken down as follows: 'Scandinavia and Finland'; 'Netherlands, Belgium and Luxembourg'; 'The British Isles'; 'Germany'; 'Switzerland, Austria and Liechtenstein'; 'France'; 'Spain and Portugal'; 'Italy and its neighbours'; 'Central Europe'; 'The Balkans and Romania'; 'Russia and its Neighbours'. Small locator maps appear on each new page of maps; these highlight the relevant area, with continents shown on a spherical globe-style map and regions/individual countries on a 'flat' map of the relevant continent and its immediate surrounding area. Maps show physical features, political boundaries and principal towns and cities. There are 'Facts and Figures' boxes, offering such details as: language, area, population, capital city (Lagos is, incorrectly, still shown as the capital of Nigeria), highest point, currency and main exports. Other interesting fact boxes offer information on climate, agricultural and industrial products, style of government, and items of particular interest relating to the area under consideration. For example, the section on 'Scandinavia and Finland' has fact boxes about the Lapps and the Vikings, plus a cross-sectional diagram showing an Icelandic geothermal power station, located near a volcano, utilizing heat from hot rocks in the Earth's crust.

Language, layout and images
Despite its pocket size, the atlas is well laid out, with plenty of space and print of a reasonable size and clarity. Economies of scale are made by putting as much information as possible in 'fact bites' rather than in lengthy wording. The language used is reader-friendly, with more complex technical terms italicized and then explained in a glossary. Numerous photographs and diagrams illustrate the text well.

Retrieval devices
There are a contents list and a helpful user guide at the front of the book. At the back there is quite a lengthy glossary and both a map and a topic index. There are, however, no grid references (see the start of this section on atlases). The sections on each continent are colour-coded, having a stripe at the start and similarly coloured 'thumbprints' near the top of those following pages that relate to the same continent. It would have been useful if the designers had colour-coded the contents list entries as well; however, even without this 'extra', this is still a helpful device.

Children's assessments
'The layout of the book is good. After saying about the Earth it tells you about the climates and vegetation then it tells you facts about all the different continents.

The pictures and photographs are very good. They fit in with what is being said. Everything is very clear and bright.

The language in the book is also very clear. If you don't understand any of the words, they would most probably be in the glossary at the back. The language is sort of in between formal and informal and I think it is aimed at 12 plus year olds.

The content of the book is very interesting so long as you enjoy Geography and from that point of view it is a very good book to buy.'
Samantha Vale (aged 12)

Other aspects
This is an easily accessible format which enables the reader to find out significant data on each country or group of countries. As well as being a good source of information, it is a handy, portable revision guide and fact-finder which will appeal to pupils both primary and secondary. The atlas is competitively priced.

National Curriculum test result: 77%

The New Oxford School Atlas, editorial adviser Patrick Wiegand. Oxford University Press: 1995 (reprinted with corrections), first published in 1990

ISBN: 0 19 831682 8 hardback, 0 19 831667 4 paperback

Price: £8.99 hardback, £7.50 paperback

Target age range: 11 yrs and upwards

Coverage: Like the atlases reviewed above, this is broadly organized by continent: Europe; Asia; Australasia; Africa; North America; South America; Oceans and Poles, with a section at the front on 'Latitude and longitude', 'World maps' and 'Understanding atlas maps'.

Unlike the others reviewed so far, this atlas also has 42 pages devoted to the British Isles. These pages are grouped into two sections: 'Thematic' (with map-based information on topics as diverse as 'Solid Geology', 'Sport and Recreation' and 'Extractive Industries') and 'Topographic and Economic' (which has maps covering regions from 'South East England and East Anglia' to 'Glasgow and Edinburgh' and 'Ireland, Belfast and Dublin').

There is also a fairly substantial 'World' section at the end of the book. This looks at physical and human features, including topics such as 'Natural Hazards', 'Plate Tectonics', 'Cities and Urbanization', 'Energy' and 'Environmental Damage'.

Language, layout and images
At first sight the atlas is similar in format to many others on the market. However, the rather drab formal cover belies the contents which are well laid out and colourful, with a clarity that should appeal to all users. The colouring of maps is of an almost jewel-bright quality, ensuring that even minute areas of population, climate, land height and the like can be easily spotted and linked to the relevant key boxes. Judicious use of satellite images, diagrams, graphs and charts adds further interest to the pages of excellent cartography. This is a truly map-based atlas and has very little in the way of text.

Retrieval devices
At the front of the book is a comprehensive contents list and a user guide which includes a key to the symbols used throughout. The gazetteer at the end is much more sophisticated than those in the atlases reviewed above, giving page number, number/letter grid code and latitude and longitude (see above regarding the National Curriculum requirement that children are taught to use map referencing as demanding as this). A separate page at the start of the gazetteer explains, in words and with diagrammatic examples, how such a referencing system operates. Abbreviations used are listed at the back of the book; there is also a short glossary which gives English language translations for the unfamiliar foreign terms used for various overseas geographical features.

Children's assessments
'*The New Oxford School Atlas* is the best atlas I have ever picked up. It stands out from all the others I have seen because it presents a vast amount of information in a way that is easy to both find and understand by using colour and pictures.

The last 22 pages are devoted to statistics and general geography about the world. The front focuses on Great Britain and each separate country. Throughout the book each section of countries provides both a political and physical map and interesting infor-

mation. Each continent is made a spectacle of and offers a variety of facts. I think this book is brilliant for my age range. It lists the countries in the top corner which makes it quick and easy to use. I have not got a bad word to say for this book. Both the illustrations and text appeal. It would definitely be worth having. Personally I would love one.'
Star rating: *****
Abigail Marshall (aged 12 years)

Other aspects
Up-to-date maps are well supported by keys, statistics, industrial and manufacturing information, agricultural and climatic data. It is also easy to access details about energy supply and consumption and mineral resources. This is an excellent reference atlas and a winner of the 'TES Senior Information Book Award'.

National Curriculum test result: 100%

The Oxford Practical Atlas: Oxford University Press: 1986 limp edition, 1992 cased edition

ISBN: 0 19 831691 7 cased (hardback), 0 19 831658 5 limp (paperback)

Price: £5.99 hardback, £5.00 paperback

Target age range: 10–13 yrs

Coverage: Smaller than *The New Oxford School Atlas*, this volume still has substantial coverage of the British Isles (eighteen pages), and goes on to look at continents and topics, such as population and climates, relating to the world as a whole. Geared to a slightly younger age-group, this atlas does not feature more complex topics such as plate tectonics (other than a brief paragraph and diagram) or maps showing the solid geology of the British Isles. On the other hand it does include a look at the 'Earth in Space' with diagrams of the Earth's orbit and information on the atmosphere.

The section on 'Continents, Countries and Capitals' shows that the atlas has not been fully updated recently; it still lists Czechoslovakia as a single country (the political map of Europe is similarly in error) and gives Lagos, rather than Abuja, as the capital of Nigeria.

Language, layout and images
Although this atlas is similar in format to *The New Oxford School Atlas* the colouring on some of the regional maps of the British Isles is far less successful and there are no satellite images. This is again a map-based book, with very little text.

Retrieval devices
A contents page is situated at the front and supplemented by maps showing page-numbered segments. The printing of headings in red is not very successful, making them less distinct than summaries of the topics covered, which are printed in black underneath. The page numbering for individual topics is slightly cramped and confusing – not very well set out at all. The gazetteers (one for the British Isles and one for the rest of the world) have page numbers and latitude and longitude (there is no supplementary grid system), but do not offer any explanation of how to use the latitude and longitude references. A page labelled 'Maps', not listed on the contents page, is actually the user guide. Here mention is made of the reference system, and use of symbols and scale is also discussed.

108   A Guide to Children's Reference Books

Children's assessments
'The layout of the book is designed for easy learning; every page is bright and colourful. Every page is set up with boxes containing information about each map.

Different pages have different information on world wide countries and continents, like the communications systems and history of that particular country.

The book has sections on how the earth moves round the sun and movements of other planets and moons. There are sections on the atmosphere and cloud formations.

The pictures and maps in the atlas are simple enough to understand but have the right amount of information for any aged child to follow.

The atlas is full of information and jam packed with geographical knowledge.'
Star rating: *****
Robert Langley (aged 14)

Other aspects
This is not nearly such a good atlas as *The New Oxford School Atlas*, but perhaps that volume is a particularly hard act to follow.

National Curriculum test result: 64%

A selection of subject atlases

[Dorling Kindersley] *The Oceans Atlas*, by Anita Ganeri, illustrated by Luciano Corbella. Dorling Kindersley: 1994

ISBN: 0 7513 5114 8 hardback

Price: £12.00

Target age range: teenagers and upwards

Coverage: The atlas moves from images of the 'Earth Exposed' (the globe minus its water covering) through topics such as 'Moving Plates', 'Exploration' (a history of deep-sea exploration and present day developments), and 'The Web of Life' (which explores the food chain) to maps of each of the ocean beds. There is coverage of 'Continental Margins', 'Abyssal Plains', 'Deep Sea Trenches', 'Black Smokers' and much, much more. Issues such as the water cycle, changing sea levels, fishing, oil and gas extraction, pollution and future management of ocean resources are also explored.

Language, layout and images
With an excellent layout and beautiful images, which almost give more information than the text, this is a spectacular book. There is so much to intrigue and interest the reader that it is really difficult to put down; particularly fascinating are the maps of the oceans, minus their water covering.

The language is quite reader-friendly, although not particularly child-oriented. Diagrams are utilized to full advantage in exploring such things as hydrothermal vents, volcanic islands, continental drift, wind, waves and currents.

Retrieval devices
There is a well-set-out contents list at the front of the book and a comprehensive index at the back. Although there is no glossary, most complex words or terms are explained in small fact boxes or paragraphs on the way through.

Children's assessments
'The layout of the book is fairly well done. Each little bit has its own heading which I like. If I was looking for something in particular I would be able to find it immediately.

The pictures have been nicely drawn and have been labelled which I also like. The labels show what it is what it does and what happens to it. They are also very clear.

The language of the book is formal. I could understand it and it made me see things in a different perspective. This will help me use formal language more.

The content is interesting and stimulates the brain cells and makes you think about different things. It tells you about things that you don't expect to be in there, like oil and gas. It also tells you how they extract the oil and gas.

I would definitely recommend people to buy this book as it has a fascinating collection of information about the oceans of the world.'

Star rating: *****

Kelly Beck (aged 12)

Other aspects
With its large format and lavish illustrations this could be seen as a 'coffee table' book; however, it is full of information and very-up-to date, and the sumptuous presentation invites readers to pick it up.

National Curriculum test result
Not tested

[Dorling Kindersley] *The Space Atlas,* by Heather Couper and Nigel Henbest. Dorling Kindersley: 1992

ISBN: 0 86318 829 X hardback

Price: £12.00

Target age range: teenagers and upwards

Coverage: The atlas looks in detail at the Solar System, covering such aspects as the structure, atmosphere, and size of each of the planets (including a view from space). There is also information on our moon and sun, and on the stars (with star maps and an absolutely fabulous diagram of the galaxies). Space probes, satellites, optical observatories and radio telescopes are also examined. Practical activities are suggested for budding astronomers, who are, for example, encouraged to look for the Andromeda Galaxy, using star maps and binoculars.

Language, layout and images
Like the other books in this series, the atlas has a superb layout – clear and spacious with fantastic images. As with other Dorling Kindersley productions aimed at a mixed audience, the language is reader-friendly, with the emphasis on images rather than text.

Retrieval devices
As with *The Oceans Atlas* there is a well-set-out contents list at the front of the book and a comprehensive index at the back. Although there is no glossary, most complex words or terms are explained in small fact boxes or paragraphs on the way through.

Children's assessments
'The layout of the book is really superb and it has all of the information that you might

want. At the start it tells you where all the launch stations are and at the back it tells you about aliens and the unknown which I thought was fascinating.

The pictures just seem to pop out of the page at you. They are truly magnificent and they must have spent a lot of time on them.

The language in this book is good and it explains any queries you might have. It explains things well but you need to be a good reader to understand some things.

The content of the book is very varied: there are all sorts of things about space. The most interesting thing to me was the section about the stars because there is so much information about them.

This book is really enjoyable to read and the pictures really enhance this. I would recommend this to anyone even if they were not interested in space: after reading this book you can be sure they will be.'
Phillip Lee (aged 12)

Other aspects
Although this is not a volume to be transported about in a school satchel, it is certainly a book to enjoy at home.

National Curriculum test results: 100% (for coverage of Physical Processes: 4. 'The Earth and beyond' only)

Other books offered by Dorling Kindersley in this range are:

The Animal Atlas, by Barbara Taylor, illustrated by Kenneth Lilly.
ISBN 0 86318 769 2 hardback
The Atlas of Ancient Worlds, by Dr Anne Millard, illustrated by Russell Barnett.
ISBN 0 7513 5115 6 hardback
School copy reviewed:
'I am not usually interested in history or geography books but this one tries and succeeds in making information understandable and interesting.

One thing I found happened as I read the book was that, despite it being an atlas, it didn't seem to be just about maps, so crammed was it with useful information and helpful illustrations.

If I had to improve the book I would put in more 'Did you know...?' because these were very interesting, being about unusual subjects.

The glossary at the back is a good place to look for all the highlighted words throughout the book. It explained the words clearly and understandably.

I liked the book. The price is very reasonable.'
Star rating: ***
Nicola Ladwiniec (aged 14)

The Bird Atlas, by Barbara Taylor, illustrated by Richard Orr.
ISBN 0 7513 5068 0 hardback
The Earth Atlas, by Susanna van Rose, illustrated by Richard Bonson.
ISBN 0 7513 5211 X hardback
The Great Dinosaur Atlas, by William Lindsay, illustrated by Giuliano Fornari.
ISBN 0 86318 628 9 hardback
The Great Atlas of Discovery, by Neil Grant, illustrated by Peter Morter.
ISBN 0 86318 830 3 hardback

The Usborne Illustrated Atlas of World History, by Lisa Miles. Usborne Publishing Ltd: 1995

ISBN: 0 7460 1728 6 hardback, 0 7460 1727 8 paperback

Price: £10.99 hardback, £8.99 paperback

Target age range: 12–14 yrs

Coverage: The atlas gives whistle-stop coverage to 38 topics, ranging from 'The Earth Begins' through 'Ancient Cities' and 'Feudal Europe' to the two World Wars and 'The 20th Century Ends'. Additional features include a helpful world time chart showing: Africa; the Americas; Asia; Australasia; Europe; this has key dates and events from prehistory to the present day.

Language, layout and images
The language used is clear and to the point; words and images are skilfully linked, maximizing the information given. Overall the book is well illustrated, with the maps helping to point out historical developments. The layout is uncluttered and the print is of a reasonable size.

Retrieval devices
The book is thematically arranged in roughly chronological order with a contents list, map index and general index to make information retrieval relatively straightforward. The map index includes alternative names through history: for example there is an entry for 'Edo (now Tokyo), Japan 52'. A two-page glossary covers the more complex terms used, cross-referenced within by the use of bold print. Useful boxes, labelled 'FIND OUT MORE', have topic cross-references and advise the reader: 'Turn to the above pages for more information'.

Children's assessments
'The pages are appealing with lots of pictures and maps to help the description. It is very interesting with an informative layout.
 The text is clear and easy to follow, with numerous pictures that help greatly with understanding the information. The language is in chunks which makes it both accessible and easy to read.
 The book gives a good start and general impression of a topic. It has four pages on each main theme.
 I wanted to keep on reading the book till I had finished. It is well worth taking a look at.'
Star rating: *****
Ben Harvey (aged 14 years)

Other aspects
Posters, paintings and photographs that are contemporary with the period under discussion are used illustratively; unfortunately these are not clearly labelled as such, which would have been useful for students learning to evaluate such items as source material for historical studies. Nevertheless this is a useful book that would be a good starting point for students.

National Curriculum test result: 50%

Dictionaries and related texts

By the time children reach Key Stage 3, parents and carers may begin to question the necessity of purchasing dictionaries specially designed for children, wondering whether a good family dictionary might be just as suitable. However, there is quite a 'leap' to be made from the child-friendly (often illustrated) dictionaries in use at Key Stage 2 to the formal adult dictionaries found on family bookshelves. At the beginning of Key Stage 3, the majority of children still need the added help which can be offered by a version specifically designed for pupils at this stage in their school life. The sample definitions which follow, taken from the dictionaries reviewed later in this section, show that these can be both helpful and readable for Key Stage 3 pupils.

Collins Shorter School Dictionary

media
(plural noun) You can refer to the TV, radio and newspapers as the media.
[Latin *medius* = middle]
species (pronounced **spee**-sheez)
(noun) a class of plants, animals, birds, insects, etc., e.g. *a species of butterfly*

era, eras (pronounced **ear**-a)
(noun) a period of time, usually several years, marked by a particular feature, e.g. *The post-war era was noted for things being in short supply.*
[Latin *aera* = copper counters used for counting, hence for counting time]

Similar words: period, age

The Oxford School Dictionary

media *plural* of **medium** *noun*

the media newspapers, radio and television, which convey information and ideas to the public. (See *medium²* 2.).

USAGE: This word is a plural. Say *The media are* (not 'is') *very influential*. It is incorrect to speak of one of them (e.g. television) as 'this media'.

species (*say* **spee**-shiz) *noun* (*plural* **species**)

1 a group of animals or plants that are very similar. 2 a kind or sort, *a species of sledge*.
[Latin, = appearance]
era (*say* **Eer**-a) *noun*
a period of history.

The Mini Oxford School Dictionary

('mini' version, with the complete text of the *Oxford School Dictionary*, see above)

The Oxford Study Dictionary

media (meed-iă) *plural noun* see medium.   the media newspapers and broadcasting, by which information is conveyed to the general public.
   This word is the plural of *medium* and should have a plural verb, e.g. *the media are* (not is) *influential*. It is incorrect to refer to one of these services (e.g. television) as *a media* or *the media*, or to several of them as *medias*

species (spee-shiz) *noun* (*plural* species) 1 a group of animals or plants within a genus, differing only in minor details from the others. 2 a kind or sort, *a species of sledge*. [Latin, = appearance]

era- (eer-ă) *noun* 1 a period of history; *the Christian era*, the period reckoned from the birth of Christ. 2 a major division of geological development.

As the above examples show, there is helpful extra guidance (such as advice on common errors) in dictionaries designed for this age-group. The definitions given concentrate on the sense (or senses) in which pupils are most likely to encounter the particular word being defined, rather than attempting an exhaustive list of possible definitions which could be confusing for children in this age range.

A selection of dictionaries

Collins Shorter School Dictionary, editorial consultant John McIlwain BA PGCE, with additional material by Tony Bisson BA LGSM. HarperCollins Publishers Ltd: 1995, first published in 1989 as *Collins School Dictionary*, second edition in 1992 as *Collins Concise School Dictionary*

ISBN: 0 00 196479 8 hardback

Price: £5.99

Entries: 10 000 headwords

Target age range: 11–14 yrs

Language, coverage and layout
The language is more formal than that found in comparable Key Stage 2 dictionaries, nevertheless it is still fairly child-friendly, and definitions are clear and to the point. The print is larger and less 'off-putting' than in an adult dictionary. Each headword is accompanied by the relevant part of speech (written in full), definition (or numbered definitions) and plurals, verb endings and other derived forms (where appropriate). Wherever necessary there is a pronunciation guide and/or example sentence. Some word origins and synonyms are given.

Retrieval devices
The first and last word on each page are printed again at the top, in the format: 'unreal to until' (p.396). A contents list gives page references for the user guide and appendices.

Children's assessments
'I thought this was brilliant. Words were really easy to find and each one had a detailed explanation which was easy to understand. You are also given an example of how to use

the word, what type of word it is, its history and related words. I would recommend it to school children from year 5 upwards.'
Tammy Lyons (aged 14 years)

Other aspects
There is a user guide, with activities and tests (these are generally designed for full class participation and are not geared to home users; suggestions such as: 'Write a brief account, with examples, of the information to be found in this dictionary' are certainly neither fun nor enticing), and prefaced with a few words to the teacher. A supplementary snippet of information or a quotation appears on each page in an unnumbered footnote at the base: for example, 'Poetry – the best words in the best order. (Samuel Taylor Coleridge)' (p.275). Additional features include lists of: basic words to learn; words to help with 'creative writing'; words with interesting origins; and words that are often mispronounced (no pronunciation guide is given with the list; readers who consult the main body of the dictionary in order to discover what the pronunciation should be will find it infuriating to discover that not all the words (for example 'aerate') are there!). More helpfully, there is a section on finding books in a library.

National Curriculum test result: Overall score: 57% (third place)

The Mini Oxford School Dictionary, compiled by Joyce M. Hawkins. Oxford University Press: 1994, first published as *The Oxford School Dictionary* in 1990, first published in Mini format in 1992

ISBN: 0 19 910333 X vinyl

Price: £3.50
A true 'mini' (tiny, but with fairly distinct print) which contains the entire text from *The Oxford School Dictionary* (see full review below), missing only one appendix (weights and measures).

The Oxford School Dictionary, edited by Joyce M Hawkins. Oxford University Press: 1994 (redesigned edition), first published as *The New Oxford School Dictionary* in 1990

ISBN: 0 19 910314 3 hardback

Price: £6.99

Entries: 35 000 headwords

Target age range: 11–14 yrs

Language, coverage and layout
A good range of headwords is given, each accompanied by the relevant part of speech (written in full) and definition (or numbered definitions). Plurals, verb endings and other derived forms are also appropriately supplied. Wherever necessary there is a pronunciation guide and/or example sentence. Some of the definitions are very short; however, they are generally clear and helpful. An uncluttered layout (with a space between each entry, headwords printed in slightly larger bold print, and indented definitions) makes it easy to find words.

Retrieval devices
The first and last words on each page are reproduced at the top of the page. A contents list gives page references for the added features and appendices; a three-page user guide is also included.

Children's assessments
'*The Oxford School Dictionary* is a very useful book. It has large print which enables you to find whatever you want in moments. It gives a detailed description of the meaning of any word.

The dictionary also comes with a user guide [this is a separate purchase]. The guide is fun and an interesting way to learn to use the book: there are lots of little puzzles for you to try and work out. This dictionary is well worth the price and I would definitely recommend it.'
Louise Smith (aged 14 years)
'This dictionary is very large and you would find almost everything you would want to know. It is made especially for school and it is easier than most dictionaries. Sometimes it tells you how to say the word as well as what the spelling is. It is so useful I would give it five stars.'
Star rating: *****
'*Using the Oxford School Dictionary* is a very useful book for people who are not sure how to use a dictionary. It is easy to understand and has lots of quizzes to help you. It is easy to read and is helpfully illustrated.'
Star rating: ****
Nigel Villiers (aged 14 years)

Other aspects
Information on word origins is included in this volume, with 8000 etymologies given. There is also an introduction to the history of the English language and notes on English usage and grammar, including common grammatical mistakes and words that are easily confused. Appendices containing prefixes and suffixes, foreign words and phrases, countries and weights and measures are also supplied.

As with other Oxford dictionaries in this series, an accompanying book: *Using the Oxford School Dictionary* (ISBN 0 19 910325 9 paperback, price £3.50) offers a range of exercises and games designed to stimulate readers to make the most of their dictionaries. Amusing black-and white illustrations help to make these activities look fun to do.

National Curriculum test results: Overall score: 79% (second place)

The Oxford Study Dictionary. Oxford University Press: redesigned impression 1994, first published in 1991

ISBN: 0 19 910311 9 hardback, 0 19 910312 7 paperback

Price: £7.00 hardback, £5.50 paperback

Entries: 45 000 headwords

Target age range: 14 yrs and upwards

Language, coverage and layout
This has a very good range of words and scored best in the test on National Curriculum coverage (see the end of this section). The language is fairly formal, although definitions

are still clear and precise. Parts of speech are included (written in full), as are irregular derived forms. Helpful guides to word usage and to pronunciation are given, together with example sentences, wherever these are thought to be useful. The layout is denser than that of *The Oxford School Dictionary*. However, bold headwords and indented definitions make it comparatively easy to find entries.

Retrieval devices
The first and last word of each page are reproduced at the top. There is a contents list giving page references for the introductory guide and appendices.

Children's assessments
'*The Oxford Study Dictionary* has a wide variety of words and a strong vocabulary. The sentences on the words explain the meaning of the word clearly.

The fact that it has the common mistakes in is very good, as it may help children or foreigners. It uses plurals and punctuation which is also good. It mentions the periodic table and the chemical elements which again is good. It also mentions countries.

The Oxford Study Thesaurus being the same make as the dictionary is also good quality. It is also good in that it uses alphabetical order.'
Star rating: ****
Luke Maddison (aged 12 years)

Other aspects
In addition to etymologies (over 10 000 word origins are given), there are appendices with lists of countries, counties of the United Kingdom, chemical elements, and weights and measures. This is a good solid dictionary for a teenager or young adult; ideal for pupils preparing for examinations.

National Curriculum test result: Overall score: 97% (first place)

A word on the National Curriculum test results:

The Oxford Study Dictionary, as might be expected since it is aimed at an older age-group, has a much wider coverage than the other two dictionaries. By the end of Key Stage 3 this is the sort of dictionary that pupils preparing for examinations need to have available (although the test did throw up one error: 'adjectivally' is listed as a noun instead of an adverb – *The Oxford School Dictionary*, however, gets it right). Of the other two, *The Oxford School Dictionary* scored better than the *Collins Shorter School Dictionary*; however, some of the definitions in the former are rather more abbreviated (compare for example the definition of 'era' at the start of this section) than in the latter, which needs to be borne in mind. The reviewer from Aylesford School who looked at the *Collins Shorter School Dictionary* commented particularly on the quality of the definitions which she found 'detailed' and 'easy to understand'.

A selection of related texts

The Mini Oxford School Thesaurus. Oxford University Press: 1994, first published in Mini format in 1992

ISBN: 0 19 910334 8 vinyl

Price: £3.50

Another full volume in a 'mini' format, this contains the entire text of *The Oxford Study Thesaurus* (see review below). The typeface is clear, although very tiny.

The Oxford Study Thesaurus. Oxford University Press: 1994

ISBN: 0 19 910315 1 hardback, 0 19 910316 X paperback.

Price: £6.50 hardback, £4.99 paperback

Entries: 20 000 headwords, 150 000 similar and related words

Target age range: 14 yrs and upwards

Language, coverage and layout
Many example sentences help pupils use synonyms effectively and precisely. Some word-families are also given (for example, under the entry for 'sweets' is a list of 24 sweets, ranging from 'acid drop' to 'Turkish delight'). Notes on etymology are provided for some entries, separated from surrounding text by horizontal lines. Some antonyms are also supplied. The layout is well spaced, making it easy to find entries. Headwords are in bold print.

Retrieval devices
The thesaurus utilizes an A-Z sequence for easy access. The first and last word on each page are reproduced at the top, and a helpful user guide is provided.

Children's assessments
See joint assessment with *The Oxford Study Dictionary* reviewed above.

Other aspects
Another useful tool for English language students from Oxford University Press, this is well worth including on the book shelf.

The Oxford School A-Z of English, by John Ayto. Oxford University Press: 1995

ISBN: 0 19 910308 9 hardback, 0 19 910361 5 paperback

Price: £5.99 hardback, £3.99 paperback

Target age range: 10 yrs and upwards

Language, coverage and layout
This useful little book offers clear guidance on spoken and written English. It answers questions on confused and misused words; spelling; usage; pronunciation; grammar; punctuation; and British and American English, using straightforward and child-friendly language. An interesting range of topics is covered, including sexist language, standard written and spoken English, language change, and races and peoples. Example sentences are taken from contemporary texts and readings of spoken language. The layout is uncluttered; the print is well defined and comparatively large.

Retrieval devices
Entries are arranged alphabetically, with cross-references to indicate related sections. The

relevant letter of the alphabet is highlighted on the side of each page. First and last entries on each double-page spread are reprinted at the top.

Children's assessments
'This is a useful guide to the English language. It is in alphabetical order so it's easy to find the word. The essential guide tells you the meaning of the word and what part of speech it is.'
Star rating: ****
Jagdeep Sangha (aged 14 years)

Other aspects
This is a very helpful guide to English language usage for Key Stage 3 pupils. The paperback edition is quite reasonably priced, making it a 'must' for home and school reference.

Subject dictionaries and encyclopedias

A wealth of subject dictionaries and encyclopedias are marketed for pupils in Key Stage 3. Many of them are of a high standard and choosing between them is a difficult task. Unfortunately the quality of most of the highly illustrated books makes them comparatively expensive to acquire (see the end of this chapter for recommended 'best buys'.)

National Curriculum requirements

Many of the volumes reviewed here are geared to coverage of aspects of the National Curriculum, with dedicated geography, history and, particularly, science texts much in evidence. History topics to look out for at this stage are: 'Medieval realms: Britain 1066–1500'; 'The making of the United Kingdom: crowns, parliaments and peoples 1500–1750'; 'Britain 1750-circa 1900'; 'The twentieth-century world'; 'An era or turning point in European history before 1914'; 'A past non-European society' (History, Key Stage 3). As with geography (see the section on atlases near the beginning of this chapter), the National Curriculum programme of study for science builds on work done at Key Stage 2, going on to look in greater depth at the topics introduced there. For example, whereas at Key Stage 2 children learned, in simple terms, that 'plant growth is affected by the availability of light and water, and by temperature' (Science, Key Stage 2), at Key Stage 3 they are taught that 'photosynthesis produces biomass and oxygen' and learn about other elements such as nitrogen that are required for plant growth (Science, Key Stage 3). At the end of each review there is an analysis of coverage of National Curriculum subject matter.

A selection of subject dictionaries and encyclopedias

[Dorling Kindersley] *The Body Atlas*, by Steve Parker, illustrated by Giuliano Fornari. Dorling Kindersley: 1993

ISBN: 0 7513 5004 4 hardback

Price: £12.00

Target age range: teenage and upwards

Coverage: The atlas is divided into sections that deal with the major regions of the body: the head and neck, the upper torso, the arm and hand and so on. Useful diagrams locate the region discussed by highlighting it on a drawing of the torso. There are interesting supplementary fact boxes on most pages: one, for example, shows the height a human being would need to be if the intestines were straight and not coiled; another demonstrates eye movement in a series of diagrams.

Language, layout and images
Well laid out, in the usual Dorling Kindersley style, the latest technology (including computer-enhanced, colour-coded x-rays) is employed to make the images both spectacular and informative. Layered cross-sectional diagrams are used to particularly good effect; however, the text is rather fragmented, being broken up into comparatively short, one-or two-paragraph segments on a range of sub-topics.

Retrieval devices
The book is thematically organized, with a contents list and an index to assist with locating specific information. At the front, a section on 'Mapping the Human Body' explains how the book is laid out and includes a helpful box with a selection of relevant Latin terms and their meanings.

Children's assessments
'I found this a very interesting book, especially the pictures. They are fascinating because they are drawn with lots of details. It was the pictures that attracted me to the book. Also, the pictures made me want to know more, which got me to read the book. Additionally, the book contains quite a few pictures of the body which can't be seen with the naked eye. For this, they have used a new technology.

The text is interesting but I don't think there is enough in it. I like the layout of the text.

The book contains the basic facts which is good for students to use in school. I think this book is suitable for 12–16 year olds. Overall it is a good educational book for the school library.'

Josie Ling (aged 14 years)

Other aspects
A 'coffee table' production rather than a portable satchel book; the book works best with those who enjoy pictorially-presented information.

National Curriculum test results

Science
Coverage of total subject area: 9%
Coverage of topics broached: 50%

[Dorling Kindersley] *Dictionary of Nature*, by David Burnie. Dorling Kindersley: 1994
ISBN: 0 7513 5125 3 hardback
Price: £12.99

Target age range: 11 yrs and upwards

Coverage: The bulk of the book is divided into 14 main sections: 'What is Nature?'; 'The Science of Life'; 'Cells'; 'The Chemistry of Life'; 'Inheritance and Genetics'; 'Evolution'; 'Classifying Living Things'; 'Microorganisms'; 'Plants'; 'Fungi'; 'Plant Biology'; 'Animals'; 'Animal Biology'; 'Ecology'. There is also a supplementary alphabetically-organized section giving brief details of more than 150 of the world's greatest biologists.

Language, layout and images
The layout is brilliant, packing masses of information (2000 key words, 400 illustrations) into a comparatively small and portable volume, yet never looking cluttered or anything but clear and spacious. The images, photographic and diagrammatic, are superb and perfectly chosen to illustrate and amplify the well-written text.

Retrieval devices
A user guide with sample pages explains clearly and concisely how to use this thematically-organized book. The contents list is simply and sensibly organized; page references for each of the main sections are given, together with a one-line summary of the contents of each, and individual topics are then listed beneath, with their own page references. More than usual thought has been given to making the alphabetically-organized index reader-friendly: for example, sub-entries are helpfully accompanied by the name of the main entry in brackets, as well as the page reference. 'See also' boxes in the text show related topics and give the relevant page references.

Children's assessments
'When I saw the front cover I thought it looked quite interesting. The idea of having a few large pictures on the front was a good idea because it makes it stand out more. It shows that it ranges from a skeleton to a kangaroo. Just inside the front cover there is a passage of questions about nature. It makes you want to turn the page.

To start off with there is a section on how to use the book which is very useful for children who are not used to non-fiction books. Although it is called a dictionary, it is not in alphabetical order but there is an excellent index at the back.

The book is laid out very clearly and it is easy to find out what you're looking for. There is the basic information to get you started so that you can go and look in other books for more in-depth information. The pictures are brilliant. They are big and bold. They make you want to learn about the thing.

The language is easy to understand so it would be great for younger children. This is definitely a seller.'
Star rating: *****
Emily Onions (aged 14 years)

National Curriculum test results
The *Dictionary of Nature* and the *Dictionary of Science* were considered jointly as a single set.
Science
Coverage of total subject area: 86%
Coverage of topics broached: 86%

Publications for Key Stage 3   121

[Dorling Kindersley] *Dictionary of Science* by Neil Ardley. Dorling Kindersley: 1994

ISBN: 0 7513 5112 1 hardback

Price: £12.99

Target age range: 11 yrs and upwards

Coverage: There are 18 main sections in the dictionary: 'What is Science?'; 'Matter'; 'Atoms'; 'Time and Space'; 'Force, Motion, & Machines'; 'Transport'; 'Energy'; 'Light'; 'Heat'; 'Sound'; 'Magnetism & Electricity'; 'Electronics & Computing'; 'Communications'; 'Elements & Molecules'; 'Chemical Changes'; 'Chemical Compounds'; 'Chemical Industry'; 'Mathematics'. There is also a supplementary, alphabetically-organized section giving brief details of more than 150 of the world's greatest scientists, and an A-Z table of scientific abbreviations.

Language, layout and images
The layout and images are again brilliant, organized in an easily portable format similar to that of the *Dictionary of Nature* reviewed above.

Retrieval devices
See the *Dictionary of Nature* above.

Children's assessments
'This book is packed full of facts and inventions. It ranges from the making of a car to the flying of a bird. It is also illustrated which I think helps a lot.

It covers all sorts of inventions and touches on physics and chemistry. This is a very good book, if you want to know about scientific things and even if you know a lot already it is very helpful.

I would definitely recommend this book given that it is so helpful and informative. The only real drawback is the price of £12.99. Nevertheless this reference guide answers all your questions about the ever changing world of science.'
Star rating: *****
Dean Coulson (aged 14 years)

Other aspects
Dorling Kindersley plan a further addition to this range: the *Dictionary of the Earth* – well worth looking out for!

National Curriculum test results
The *Dictionary of Nature* and the *Dictionary of Science* were considered jointly as a single set.
Science
Coverage of total subject area: 86%
Coverage of topics broached: 86%

[Dorling Kindersley] *Illustrated Book of Myths: Tales & Legends of the World*, retold by Neil Philip and illustrated by Nilosh Mistry. Dorling Kindersley: 1995

ISBN: 0 7513 5317 5

Price: £14.99

Target age range: 9–12 yrs

Coverage: This is an interesting and informative look at myths from around the world. A very wide range of ethnic groups are represented, with, amongst others, African, Polynesian, Iranian, Native American, Serbian, and Sumerian legends recorded. There is also an alphabetically-organized 'Who's Who in Mythology' at the back of the book, with short paragraphs on various mythological figures (including some pictorial representations) and inset boxes showing 'The Greek Pantheon' and 'The Norse Pantheon'.

Language, layout and images
The illustrations accompanying the myths are beautiful; there are also photographs of places and artefacts relating to the part of the world where each story originated. Explanatory paragraphs are in straightforward child-friendly text. The language used to recount the myths and legends is fairly simple, yet expressive, following the word-patterning that tends to be associated with the telling of this kind of story in English.

Retrieval devices
The book is organized thematically, grouping together creation myths, fertility myths and so on. The contents list gives page references for individual myths; these are listed by name, under their relevant grouping, with an accompanying note of the country of origin. There is also a comprehensive index at the back of the book.

Children's assessments
'The book has a well thought out and interesting layout. On the outside of the pages there is a theory of inspiration that the original author of the myth might have had.

Pictures are scattered about all over the pages and are well drawn and considered. The drawings explain the queries or thoughts the reader might have had. There are photographs in the book showing objects that might prove the myth to be true.

The text is quite formal and is nice to read and easy enough to understand. The author uses very descriptive words that just seem to open up a picture in front of you. I would say the age-group is about ten-year-olds who can read well for their age, up to any age.

The book is very interesting and pulls the reader in; it is amazing to see what people thought of the world and its creation a long time ago.

I would not buy this book because of its fifteen pound price tag but if I saw it in a library I wouldn't hesitate to borrow it.'
Star rating: ****
Daniel Braithwaite (aged 12)

National Curriculum test results
Not tested

[Dorling Kindersley] *A Young Person's Guide to Music*, by Neil Ardley and Poul Ruders. Dorling Kindersley Ltd: 1995

ISBN: 0 7513 5320 5 hardback

Price: £16.99

Target age range: 11 yrs and upwards

Coverage: The book is divided into two sections: 'Making Music', which looks at the orchestra, conductor, composer, instruments (stringed, woodwind, brass, percussion and keyboard) and chamber music; and 'The History of Music', which moves from ancient music, through medieval, baroque, classical, romantic and national music to revolutionary and modern music. A specially-commissioned CD accompanies the book, allowing the reader to hear as well as read about the music. The CD features the *Concerto in Pieces* by Poul Ruders: a set of variations on the *Witches' Chorus* from Purcell's opera *Dido and Aeneas*, performed by the BBC Symphony Orchestra, conducted by Andrew Davies. Each of the ten variations highlights different groups of instruments; these are then discussed at the end of the CD (by Andrew Davies) and within the text of the book.

Language, layout and images
The layout is excellent, with photographs, diagrams, and reproductions of relevant period paintings, drawings and photographs. Straightforward, reader-friendly text is used, well supported by the images used, and with unfamiliar terms explained in the glossary. The print, although in some places rather small in size, is well-defined and clear.

Retrieval devices
The thematically-organized contents are referenced via a contents list and an index; difficult terms are explained in an alphabetical glossary. Further alphabetical reference sections give information on 81 composers (from 'Adams, John' to 'Weill, Kurt') and 40 musical terms (from 'Anthem' to 'Waltz or Valse'). A track index for the *Concerto in Pieces*, on the accompanying CD, is also included. This is cross-referenced so that individual tracks, featuring each of the various instruments used, can be easily identified. The invaluable user guide, with sample pages, explains the format used in each of the sections and offers advice on accessing the CD tracks.

Children's assessments
'This was very informative and told me everything from the parts of a violin to how to conduct the BBC Symphony Orchestra.

The layout was varied throughout and made it interesting for the reader. The book has lots of diagrams of different instruments and these were clearly labelled and easy to understand. At the beginning of each new section in the book, there was a small introduction which briefly explained the contents of each section.

The language used in the book is both simple to understand and descriptive. It tells the reader what he needs to know but so that he or she can understand it.

The book contains information and pictures, even excerpts of music on compact disc.

I would recommend this book to anybody who is interested in or wants to know more about music.'
Star rating: ****
James Wing (aged 14 years)

Other aspects
The book itself is full of information and the CD adds a new and important dimension, really bringing the music alive.

National Curriculum test results

Music
Coverage of total subject area: 75%
Coverage of topics broached: 75%

The Kingfisher Encyclopedia of Lands and Peoples, general editor Sue Grabham. Kingfisher (an imprint of Larousse plc): 1995

ISBN: 1 85697 292 5

Price: £25.00

Target age range: 10–14 yrs. Publisher's recommendation: 8–14 yrs

Coverage: Over 180 independent countries are included in this comprehensive look at the lands and peoples of the world. There is also a list, with details, of dependencies. Coverage ranges from one or two pages on countries such as Kazakhstan and Zambia to as many as ten pages on the United Kingdom, France and other developed nations. For each country a relief map, locator globe map (with the relevant country indicated by a red arrow), national flag (and emblem) and facts and figures box (detailing capital city, area, population, other major cities, highest point, official language, main religions, currency, main exports, type of government and per capita GNP) complement the information on human and physical features conveyed by the written text, photographic images and illustrations. The wide-ranging information given includes details of the geography of the country; its peoples and their culture; its history (often including images showing artefacts with dates and details); and economy. For example, the pages on Zaire include the information that 'Zaire is a world leader in the production of copper, cobalt and industrial diamonds. . . .' (p.212) and also that the 'Zairean style of guitar playing, with singing in French or Lingala language, has become world famous.' (*ibid*) Brief, fairly up-to-date background information on areas of human conflict, such as the tragic events in Rwanda and Bosnia-Herzegovina, is also provided. Additional features include language scrolls, giving 'hello' and 'goodbye' in the official language of the country (together with a pronunciation guide); a small box with details and picture of a national dish; and information on an endangered species (with beautiful illustration) from the region being discussed.

In addition to coverage of individual countries there are sections on the oceans; the earth as a planet (including discussion on how it is thought to have come into being); map projections; and pages on population, religion, environment, government, conflict and the UN. An interesting historical time line (by continent) is also included.

Language, layout and images

The language is comparatively reader-friendly, although better suited to Key Stage 3 pupils than to children at the start of the publisher's recommended age range. Overall, the text is well written (with atmospheric sentences such as: 'From west to east, the country of Kazakhstan stretches from the salty Caspian Sea to the soaring Altai Mountains.' (p.406) and tries to bring the countries discussed 'alive' for the reader. The attractive layout creates an excellent relationship between text and images, with lots of colourful illustrations and photographic images to enhance and amplify the written sections.

Retrieval devices

The material, which is mainly arranged by continent, with supplementary features located in a reference section at the back, is accessed via a contents list (for some reason this does not give page references for the introductory guide to using the encyclopedia and the maps) and a comprehensive index (with letter/number grid references for the relief maps). The introductory section gives details of the various features included, using a sample page to illustrate these. There is also a useful page entitled 'Using the Maps' which has a key to map symbols, with information on the representation of scale, grid references and on lines of latitude and longitude. A five-page glossary is supplied, although words defined in the glossary are not highlighted in any way in the main text.

Children's assessments

'There is a good introduction and it is easy to use the contents pages, glossary and index. The book is aimed at seven to sixteen year olds mainly with photographs, pictures and maps, all coloured. In addition, there are figures, facts and dates of important events in each country and the language they speak, their history and religions. It features the animals that live in the countries, including endangered species, what kind of food the people eat and what kind of land they live in.

Overall this is a fascinating encyclopedia about people and their cultures, well worth reading. A fun and enjoyable book.'
Holly Hiatt (aged 12 years)

Other aspects

This is an interesting and inviting book, a useful first point of reference which will appeal to most readers.

National Curriculum test results

Geography
Coverage of total subject area: 38%
Coverage of topics broached: 38%

The Kingfisher Encyclopedia of Lands and Peoples is also available in a ten-volume set, priced at £79.99 (ISBN 1 85697 420 0)

The Kingfisher History Encyclopedia, general editor Charlotte Evans (with a foreword by Magnus Magnusson KBE). Kingfisher (an imprint of Larousse plc): 1995 revised edition, first published by Kingfisher in 1992 as *The Kingfisher Illustrated History of the World*

ISBN: 1 85697 413 8 hardback

Price: £25.00

Target age range: 10–14 yrs. Publisher's recommendation: 8–14 yrs

Coverage: There are over 800 pages, with 250 essays covering major historical events. Material is grouped under the following main section headings: 'The Ancient World'; 'The Classical World'; 'The Early Middle Ages'; 'The Middle Ages'; 'The Renaissance'; 'Trade and Empire'; 'Revolution and Independence'; 'Unification and Colonization'; 'The World at War'; 'The Modern World'. Themes followed throughout are arts and crafts; communication and transportation; food and farming; people; religion; society and government; science and technology; trade and money; war and weapons. A continuous 'timeline', located in a coloured strip at the side of many pages, shows the chronological sequence of events discussed. Summaries, each with six columns ('The Americas'; 'Europe'; 'Africa'; 'Near East'; 'Asia and the Far East'; 'Australasia and Pacific'), located near the start of each section, help to set events into a global context. A thought-provoking section, appropriately located right at the beginning of the book, asks 'What is History?', going on to look at historical evidence and the work of the historian, and concluding with a page of advice on researching local history. At the end of the book there are ready-reference tables with information ranging from lists of Ancient Egyptian Dynasties to rulers and political leaders in Great Britain, Germany, France, Spain, Japan, Russia, United States of America, Canada, Australia, New Zealand, Italy and India. Lists of major wars (dates, names and warring parties) and explorers (who, where, when and what was achieved) are also provided.

Language, layout and images
Clearly-written text is supported throughout by a wealth of colourful illustrations, with maps, diagrams and some photographic images. The layout is attractive and 'uncluttered', with images and supplementary boxes skilfully arranged around the written essays.

Retrieval devices
The contents list is rather unhelpful, only giving page references for the main sections. Page references for the articles listed under these headings would have speeded up information retrieval on major topics. However, the comprehensive index at the back, which occupies just over 33 pages, is much more helpful, and cross-references are also given in the main body of the book. There is a user guide at the front, with sample pages reproduced to illustrate some of the added, colour-coded features, such as fact boxes, biography boxes, and special feature boxes (which give snippets of information about the arts, sciences, and people and homes: for example, on the pages about 17th-century Africa, a box entitled 'The Gold Coast' mentions – and illustrates – the work of skilled Asante goldsmiths and the significance of gold as a symbol of power in the Asante empire).

Children's assessments
'This book is very good. It is laid out in a time line from 40 000 BC to 1994 AD. The pages are set out in a very good way with illustrations and photographs spread around the page and write-ups scattered in between, giving a thorough explanation of what's happening in the pictures/photos. Also there is a strip down one side of the pages showing some of the other important things that happened about the same time with the year next to the event. There is a ready-reference section which lists all the rulers, presidents or prime ministers of the book's time frame, listing dates of rule next to the name and under the country.

The index is set in a simple alphabetical order with the page number next to the place, word or person you are looking for. I think this book is very understandable for people my age and under. It is a good reference and easy to use.'
Star rating: *****
Christopher Stevens (aged 12)

Other aspects
A useful point of first reference for topics in world history, the encyclopedia still manages to include a reasonable coverage of British history. The thematic essays ensure that time periods are examined from a variety of relevant perspectives, whilst timelines, summaries of key events by continent, and locator maps help to give a chronological and spatial context to the topics discussed.

National Curriculum test results

History
Coverage of total subject area: 91%
Coverage of topics broached: 91%

The Kingfisher History Encyclopedia is also available in a ten-volume set, priced at £79.99 (ISBN 1 85697 467 7)

The Kingfisher Science Encyclopedia, general editor Catherine Headlam. Kingfisher (an imprint of Larousse plc): reprinted with revisions 1995, first published in 1991

ISBN: a puzzle! 0 86272 697 2 is given inside the book, 0 86272 850 9 on the back cover. The catalogue lists the first of these numbers, giving the second as the number for the ten-volume boxed set.

Price: £25.00

Target age range: 10–13 yrs. Publisher's recommendation: 8–14 yrs

Coverage: This book of almost 800 pages attempts to be the most comprehensive science encyclopedia and contains around a thousand main entries, plus simple projects and home experiments as well as scientist biography boxes. Eight subject areas are represented: astronomy; chemistry; earth sciences; electronics; life sciences; mathematics; physics; technology.

Language, layout and images
The encyclopedia has a colourful format with several photographs, drawings and diagrams on every page. The language used is fairly simple, but somewhat formal in phrasing. The print is of a reasonable size, clear, with large bold headings.

Retrieval devices
The contents are alphabetically arranged, with subject codes to indicate which area (or areas) of interest each entry falls into. In addition to the general index at the back, which has main entries in bold and page numbers for illustrations in italics, there is also a subject index and a special features index. The last two do not have page references, but give the word as it appears in the main alphabetical body of the book. A user guide at the front of the book and an explanatory paragraph at the top of the general index assist the reader in accessing information. Cross-referencing is achieved by printing words with a separate entry in small capitals.

Children's assessments
'The layout of this encyclopedia is very good; it was really easy to find the articles that I wanted to look at. It is set out in alphabetical order which also helps. The pictures are very good as well. The cross-sections are well labelled and clear. They weren't very imaginative which I thought was a bit on the down side.

The type of language they used is OK but in a few years it will be too easy for thirteen year olds. It is quite formal.

The content of the encyclopedia was good. It wasn't that interesting but it was still useful.

I would buy the encyclopedia because it would be helpful in exams.'
Star rating ****
Charlotte Dent (aged 13)

Other aspects
Given the task, the authors have managed to cover most of the questions which might be asked by the layman or parent struggling to understand schoolwork and homework. There are drawbacks, however, in trying to cover so much in one volume. Inevitably some

entries leave many questions unanswered and are unable in the space available to do full justice to the scientific principles and concepts involved. Many of the entries will need further back-up by the teacher or by reference to more specialist texts before the reader can fully appreciate the science. It is, therefore, a cross between a reference book and a dictionary and, as such, could be a valuable addition to any library.

National Curriculum test results

Science
Coverage of total subject area: 89%
Coverage of topics broached: 89%

The Kingfisher Science Encyclopedia is also available in a ten-volume set, priced at £79.99 (ISBN: 0 86272 850 9 – see above)

The Usborne Illustrated Handbook of Invention & Discovery, by Struan Reid. Usborne Publishing Ltd: 1986

ISBN: 0 86020 956 3 paperback

Price: £5.95

Target age range: 11–14 yrs. Publisher's recommendation 12–16 yrs

Coverage: Inventions and discoveries are listed under nine section headings: 'Energy and power'; 'Tools, machines and building'; 'Transport'; 'Farming and food'; 'Communication'; 'Domestic appliances'; 'Scientific instruments'; 'Medicine, chemistry and biology'; 'Warfare'. There is also a consolidated chronological list of inventions and discoveries and an A-Z of inventors.

Language, layout and images
Lots of little snippets of information are conveyed by interlinked images (mainly small, colourful diagrams) and text. Overall the layout is fairly well spaced out. Bold text highlights headings. Individual topics within sections are separated by coloured lines. The print is fairly small, but quite strong and dark.

Retrieval devices
Contents are thematically organized in sections and subsections. The small, individual topic boxes that make up the subsections follow chronological order. Sections are colour-coded, with the section colour appearing in a small triangle at the base of each page and used to colour the topic dividing lines. There is a key to the colours used at the front of the book; repeat colours are far enough apart not to cause problems. A major flaw in the arrangement is that the contents list only gives subsection page references; section headings are not even mentioned, let alone colour-coded. So, for example, the reader must guess that the topic labelled 'Astronomy' comes in the section on 'Scientific instruments', if using the colour-coding system. True, there is a page reference, but if this is used instead what is the point of the colour-coding?

There is no index or contents list for the headings of individual topic boxes; the reader must find a related word in the index at the back of the book. A small glossary of unfamiliar terms also appears at the back, although there is nothing in the text to indicate that the word is explained there. Cross-referencing of related topics is achieved by printing the relevant word in bold and adding an asterisk; a cross-reference then appears in small print at the bottom of the page.

Children's assessments
'The whole of this book is great fun to read. The pictures are excellent, they show you what happened in great detail. The language is very easy to understand. I would say that it is worth its price because it would be very valuable in History or Science lessons.'
Star rating: *****
Graham Lee (aged 14)

Other aspects
This is an interesting little book but rather let down by being jumbled together. The referencing system is not as well thought out as it might have been.

National Curriculum test results
Not tested

The Usborne Book of the Earth. Usborne Publishing Ltd: 1992
This is a combined volume, bringing together the following individual titles: *Planet Earth*, by Fiona Watt, illustrated by Kuo Kang Chen, Chris Shields and Aziz Khan; *Ecology*, by Richard Spurgeon, illustrated by Kuo Kang Chen, Brin Edwards and Caroline Ewan; *Energy & Power*, by Richard Spurgeon and Mike Flood, illustrated by Kuo Kang Chen, and Joseph McEwan; *Weather & Climate*, by Fiona Watt and Francis Wilson (Television Weatherman), illustrated by Kuo Kang Chen, Peter Dennis and Denise Finney.

ISBN: 0 7460 1454 6 paperback

Price: £9.95

Target age range: 10–14 yrs. Publisher's recommendation 10–16 yrs

Coverage: A wide variety of topics, too numerous to list, are discussed within sections which correspond to the individual book titles detailed above. There is some slight overlap of material; for example, the topic 'Weather' appears in *Planet Earth* and in *Weather & Climate*; however, these tend to be complementary rather than too repetitive. Readers are encouraged to get involved in the many simple projects and activities that are suggested. They can, for example, learn how to build a bird table, test for carbonates, and make a wind-measuring device, a battery and recycled paper. Useful addresses such as museums (in the UK, USA, Canada, Australia and New Zealand) and international organisations (the World Wide Fund for Nature and Greenpeace International amongst others) are given for those readers who want to become more involved in any of the subject areas covered.

Language, layout and images
The text is written in a style which aims to involve young readers and to relate the subject to them. Words and images integrate well, with bold labelling arrows to guide the reader. Lots of clear, colourful diagrams are used to good effect in illustrating the topics covered.

Retrieval devices
Thematically organized, the book has a short contents list at the front, giving page references for the individual books that comprise it. Each individual section then has a more detailed contents list of its own. There is a combined index at the back of the book,

although this is not quite as comprehensive as it should be: for example, the entry for 'weather' sends the reader to coverage of that topic in *Weather & Climate*, but not to the similarly-named section in *Planet Earth*. Each title has its own glossary (no indication in the text that a word is to be explained there) and helpful user guide.

Children's assessments

'This book is very well presented with its beautiful cover and well written subjects. The book is split up into four chapters which are: 'Planet Earth', 'Ecology', 'Energy and Power' and 'Weather and Climate'.

The first chapter shows you what planets exist in space and describes them thoroughly. It tells you about volcanoes and weather and about experiments you can do. It gives many facts and tells you how you can help the earth in the future.

Next, 'Ecology' tells you about the environment and is full of descriptions and details. It has useful addresses and contact numbers if you want to help the environment.

'Energy and Power' is about nuclear, wind, coal and gas power. It is very informative on what energy is used where and how.

'Weather and Climate' takes you through the varied climate conditions in a range of countries and even on other planets

I would definitely recommend this book – it would be brilliant for schools.'
Adam Crump (aged 14)

National Curriculum test results

Geography
Coverage of total subject area: 50%
Coverage of topics broached: 60%

The Usborne Book of World Religions, by Susan Meredith, illustrated by Nicholas Hewetson, map illustrations by Jeremy Gower. Usborne Publishing Ltd: 1995

ISBN: 0 7460 1750 2 paperback, 0 7460 1751 0 hardback

Price: £6.99 paperback, £8.99 hardback

Target age range: 10 yrs and upwards

Coverage: Six full pages are devoted to each of the following religions: Hinduism, Judaism, Buddhism, Christianity, Islam and Sikhism. The book also takes a shorter look at other less well-known faiths, such as Shinto and Zoroastrianism. There is a section on religions of the past, and an interesting map showing the current main religions of different parts of the world. An excellent time chart of religions is included.

Language, layout and images
The language used is more sophisticated than that employed in others of *The Usborne Book of...* series. It is organised in small, one-, two- or three-paragraph segments under topic subheadings. The book has a good, uncluttered layout, with well-executed diagrams and illustrations. Words and images integrate well and the print is clear and of a good size, with headings and subheadings in large, bold print.

There are some photographic images showing, for example, religious buildings such as St Basil's Cathedral in Moscow. Paintings and drawing from the relevant time period are also used illustratively and clearly labelled as such: for example, there is a portrayal of the Last Supper, bearing the caption 'The Last Supper, as shown in a 15th-century Italian painting'.

Retrieval devices
Thematically-organized material is indexed via a contents list and index. Difficult terms are mentioned in the text with a note referring the reader to the glossary at the end of the book.

Children's assessments
'The cover is jammed with lots of images of holy places, religious items and lots more. The contents are straightforward and to the point. If you're looking for where the religion is found, it clearly states what you want in bold lettering.

You sometimes find the information seems to jump around but there is always a picture to help the understanding.

The book describes every possible religion. I found the religion time chart very handy to use: it really sticks in the mind.

If you're looking for a certain religious fact then this is definitely the book.'
Star rating: ****
Craig Heritage (aged 14)

Other aspects
Clearly the subject-matter cannot be covered in any great depth in one comparatively slim volume; however, this is an excellent introductory book, with lots of interesting details about the beliefs, history and customs of all the major world religions (much more than would be found in the average multi-subject volume).

National Curriculum test results
Not tested

The Usborne Computer Dictionary for Beginners, by Anna Claybourne, illustrated by Andy Burton. Usborne Publishing Ltd: 1995

ISBN: 0 7460 1986 6 paperback, 0 7460 1987 4 hardback

Price: £5.99 paperback, £7.99 hardback

Target age range: 10 yrs and upwards (this is still a useful dictionary for adult beginners!)

Coverage: Topics covered range from a look at 'Essential computer words' to sections on various types of hardware and software, a look at the Internet, and sections on the history of the computer and possible future developments in the field. There is a supplementary glossary of computer slang and a quick guide to computer acronyms. A short introductory section guides the reader through the format used.

Language, layout and images
The language is reader-friendly, integrating and explaining computer jargon for the beginner. A clear layout, with excellent photographic images, brings the subject matter 'alive'. There is a good relationship between images and text, with images used to good effect in explaining the topic under discussion.

Retrieval devices
The material is organized by subject, with sections accessed from the well-set-out contents list (complete with computer-style icons). There is also a full index at the back of the

book. Cross-referencing within the body of the book is achieved by printing the relevant word in italics, with an asterisk; page numbers for the cross-reference are then printed in small type at the bottom of each page.

Children's assessments
'The layout of the book is very good: it is different to most books, being set out in columns instead of long sentences. There are pictures on every page and lots of clear explanations. The pictures are very interesting to look at and tell you a lot of what you need to know about a computer.

The language is very straightforward and makes interesting reading. The only real criticism is that it does not have much about the CD-ROM which was a bit disappointing as these will be in every school in Britain soon.

It is priced reasonably for a computer book and I would recommend it to every school.'
Star rating: *****
Andrew Reeves (aged 14 years)

National Curriculum test results
Not tested

The Usborne History of the Twentieth Century, by Christina Hopkinson, illustrated by Peter Dennis. Usborne Publishing Ltd: 1993

ISBN: 0 7460 0701 9 paperback

Price: £6.99

Target age range: 11–14 yrs. Publisher's recommendation 11 yrs and upwards.

Coverage: Two-page spreads are allotted to each of 38 main topics, ranging from 'The world in 1900' to 'Facing the future'. As might be anticipated, considerable coverage is given to the two World Wars: the Second World War, for example, is dealt with in sections entitled: 'The Second World War, From Pearl Harbor to Hiroshima'; 'Aspects of war 1939–1945'; and 'Problems of the post-war world'. This is very much an international history, with coverage of areas such as 'The Russian Revolution' and 'China and Japan 1900–1945'. There are also various sections on technological and scientific advances, on decolonization (covering both Africa and Asia) and a little about the Arts (including popular music and films). There is a useful date chart at the end of the book, organized in columns covering: 'International Politics'; 'Domestic Politics'; 'Science and Invention'; 'Arts'; and 'Sports and general'. An A-Z 'Who's who of 20th century people' covers a wide range of people (102 in all: 89 men and 13 women, with 48 political figures included) from 'Ali, Mohammad' to 'Zapata, Emiliano'.

Language, layout and images
Relevant, to-the-point language is used, with less familiar terms explained in the glossary. The book is well laid out, with clear images set in the text to bring it 'alive'.

Retrieval devices
The thematically-organized contents are well-supplied with a full contents list and index headings that are clear and give good guidance.

Children's assessments

'This book is good if you are looking for something important. The pages are set out in columns so you can easily read them and titles are very clear and obvious.

There is a good selection of pictures some of which are really quite attractive. The language used is simple and very effective. I don't think this book is supposed to be merely entertaining: it is very specific and down to earth. I think this book would be very useful for history and I would buy it.'
Emily Beaglehole (aged 14)

National Curriculum test results

History
Coverage of total subject area: 23%
Coverage of topics broached: 100%

[Usborne] *Essential Science*. Usborne Publishing Ltd: 1992

ISBN: 0 7460 1011 7 paperback

Price: £8.99

Target age range: 12–16 yrs (particularly helpful as a revision guide for GCSE students)

Coverage: The book is a concise aid to reference and revision, dealing, in separate sections, with Physics, Chemistry and Biology. Within each section an impressively wide range of topics is covered, with one or two pages devoted to each. Particularly useful in terms of revision are the sample questions and answers, equations, guide to laboratory apparatus (including a section on drawing and labelling apparatus), sections on the classification of organisms and biological keys and appendices listing crystals, common acids, metal compounds and alloys.

Language, layout and images
The language used is clear, to-the-point and adult in tone. A small glossary of scientific jargon is included in each section.

Although the print is quite small (necessary in order to cram as much information as possible into the portable, satchel-size format), it is clear and distinct. The layout is varied, using devices such as boxes and arrows to enhance clarity. With excellent illustrations, including diagrams which link well with the text, this colourful book really brings the subject matter 'alive'.

Retrieval devices
There is a clear table of contents for each section and a comprehensive index; also included is a section on how to use the book. Sections are colour-coded with a band at the top of the page; unfortunately this does not extend to the contents list, so is of minimal use in information retrieval.

Children's assessments
'The first thing I noticed when I opened the book was the amazing amount of colour. This was to continue all through the book.

The book is laid out in a very easy style which makes taking in all the information very easy. It is divided into three separate parts: 'Essential Physics' 'Essential Biology' and 'Essential Chemistry'. I think that this is a very good idea as it splits the different aspects of science into their traditional sections.

At the beginning of each section there is a very competent contents page which gives the separate ideas covered such as sound, forces and magnetism, just to name a few. When you turn to the page you want, the overall title of the section is in a coloured band at the top. The book describes quite simply what each subject is about and uses very accessible English which does not patronize. It still uses the appropriate scientific jargon.

Pictures are also well used to support the descriptions. These are all brightly coloured and give you an added sense of what they are trying to tell you.

Getting around the book is very easy.

An added extra I especially liked in this book that I had not seen before, was that if they mentioned specific new words in descriptions, they would put an asterisk by them and at the bottom of the page they would tell you where you could find out more.

The index is very efficient; it has many different subjects and they are all easily found.

Another point I liked was that at the end of each module there was a series of pages that told you how to do the experiments mentioned earlier. It also gives all the equations for the chemicals used which is useful for exams.

The book is of sturdy construction and is of just the right size to carry around with you in your bag without it getting too dog-eared.

I would definitely buy this book: it covers everything in brilliant detail from Year 6 science wanting to know simple things to Year 9 science wanting to know more of the mechanics. I think this book is excellent and well worth the money.'

Star rating: *****

Simon Legge (aged 14 years)

Other aspects

An interesting, compact and useful book; it is better value than *The Usborne Illustrated Dictionary of Science* reviewed below.

This is a combination volume which is also available separately as *Essential Physics*, by Philippa Wingate, illustrated by Sean Wilkinson and Robert Walster (ISBN 0 7460 0703 5 paperback, price £3.50, 0 7460 0704 3 hardback, price £5.50); *Essential Chemistry*, by Clive Gifford, illustrated by Sean Wilkinson and Robert Walster (ISBN 0 7460 0727 2 paperback, price £3.95, 0 7460 0728 0 hardback, price £5.95); and *Essential Biology*, by Rebecca Treays et al, illustrated by Sean Wilkinson and Robert Walster (ISBN 0 7460 0743 4 paperback, price £3.95, 0 7460 0744 2 hardback, price £5.95).

National Curriculum test results

Science
Coverage of total subject area: 87%
Coverage of topics broached: 87%

***The Usborne Illustrated Dictionary of Science*,** by Corinne Stockley, Chris Oxlade and Jane Wertheim. Usborne Publishing Ltd: 1988

ISBN: 0 86020 989 X paperback, 0 86020 990 3 hardback

Price: £9.99 paperback, £12.99 hardback

Target age range: 12–16 yrs

Coverage: A good first reference book for science, the dictionary is divided into physics, chemistry, and biology colour-coded sections. These in turn are divided into other categories such as heat, electricity and magnetism, waves and atomic physics. It can serve as a secondary revision guide as well as a general reference book.

Language, layout and images
The layout is very dense, but uses excellent colour graphics to make the items more accessible and interesting.

Retrieval devices
Each section has its own contents list, and there is an index to the complete volume at the end. The colour-coding is handled better in this volume, with the colour-coded sections tied in to headings used in the contents list.

Children's assessments
'This book was interesting with colourful illustrations that described everything. The text is bold and bright to keep your attention, but I think it could have been a bit bigger. The price is reasonable for this bright clear book. I liked it, overall, because the layout makes it easy to find your way around and it was a good read.'
Jessica Rudge (aged 14 years)

Other aspects
In terms of content, the [Usborne] *Essential Science* guide is a better buy.

This is a combination volume which is also available separately as *The Usborne Illustrated Dictionary of Physics* (ISBN 0 86020 987 3 paperback, price £5.95); *The Usborne Illustrated Dictionary of Chemistry* (ISBN 0 86020 821 4 paperback, price £5.95); *The Usborne Illustrated Dictionary of Biology* (ISBN 0 86020 819 2 paperback, price £5.95).

National Curriculum test results

Science
Coverage of total subject area: 75%
Coverage of topics broached: 75%

General encyclopedias and books of facts and lists

The Dorling Kindersley Illustrated Factopedia. Dorling Kindersley: 1995

ISBN: 0 7513 5236 5 hardback

Price: £25.00

Target age range: 11 yrs and upwards

Coverage: Over 50 000 facts are covered in 456 pages. These are organized into the following general subject areas: 'Universe and Space'; 'Earth'; 'Living World'; 'Human Body'; 'Beliefs, Customs and Society'; 'Arts and the Media'; 'Sports'; 'Science and Technology'; 'Transport, Communications and Industry'; 'International World'; 'History'. The book has an amazing range and is filled with fantastic facts that children would love to read about.

Language, layout and images
The language is accessible, bearing in mind the wide age range covered. Some more complex words are defined in brackets. The book is well laid out and filled with excellent

charts, diagrams, maps, photographs and illustrations. A very good complementary relationship exists between the words and images. The volume of material included means that the print and the graphics tend to be rather small; however, they are very clear, and the quality of the graphics seems to 'lift' them off the page.

Retrieval devices
Thematically organized, the encyclopedia has a contents list at the front, plus a full index at the back. An informative section at the beginning advises on how to use the book.

Children's assessments
'This book was laid out with lots of subtitles with short paragraphs under each one. Almost every one had an illustration next to it.

The pictures were more like detailed diagrams and everything was explained. They ranged from detailed drawings to intricate cross-sections. Some pictures were photographs.

The language was complex but was mostly understandable. Some words which they didn't expect you to understand were explained in brackets.

The book has something written down about almost every title under the sun!

At the beginning there is a double page explaining about the book and how to use it. There is a nine-page contents at the front and a 28-page index at the back.

Overall I thought the book was very interesting and helpful. I would recommend it to a school library as a reference book.'
Dean Whyte (aged 14 years)
'The interesting and attractive layout of this book makes looking up facts extremely interesting and fun.

The book is packed with interesting facts and lives up to its expensive price tag. It is wonderfully illustrated with thousands of full colour pictures and photos.

The interesting layout does not make the book confusing to read and instead, makes learning from the book fun and amusing. Overall an interesting, fun book, for absolutely anyone wanting to learn something new.'
Star rating: *****
Peter Carvell (aged 14 years)
'I thought this was brilliant. Words were really easy to find and each one had a detailed explanation which was easy to understand. You are also given an example of how to use the word, what type of word it is, its history and related words. I would recommend it to school children from year 5 upwards.'
Tammy Lyons (aged 14 years)

Other aspects
This is an excellent first point of reference and a very good resource.

National Curriculum test results

Art
Coverage of total subject area: 73%
Coverage of topics broached: 73%

Geography
Coverage of total subject area: 49%
Coverage of topics broached: 49%

History
Coverage of total subject area: 41%
Coverage of topics broached: 41%

Music
Coverage of total subject area: 58%
Coverage of topics broached: 58%

Science
Coverage of total subject area: 63%
Coverage of topics broached: 63%

A range of other encyclopedias, reviewed with the publications for Key Stage 2, would also be suitable for children in the early years of Key Stage 3.

Children's Britannica, Encyclopaedia Britannica Inc.: 1988 (fourth edition), reprinted with revisions 1993 (this is the set examined; a 1995 revised reprint is available)

ISBN: 0 85229 209 0 twenty-volume set (including index volume)

Price: £225 (quoted for the 1995 edition in October 1996)

Target age range: 9–12 yrs
(for a full review see Chapter 4.)

Kingfisher Children's Encyclopedia, general editor: John Paton. Kingfisher (an imprint of Larousse plc): this edition 1995, first published in ten volumes in 1989, first published in this format in 1991

ISBN: 0 86272 696 4 hardback

Price: £25.00

Target age range: 9–12 yrs. Publisher's recommendation: 8–14 yrs (for a full review see Chapter 4.)

The Oxford Children's Encyclopedia (seven-volume boxed set). Oxford University Press: 1992 (revised reprint, first published in 1991)

ISBN: 0 19 910151 5

Price: £125

Target age range: 8–13 yrs
(for a full review see Chapter 4.)

Sainsbury's Children's Encyclopedia, by John Farndon. HarperCollins Publishers Ltd: 1992 (published exclusively for J Sainsbury plc)

ISBN: This is not shown on the book

Price: The price is not marked on individual copies – thought to be under £10.

Target age range: 9 yrs and upwards
(for a full review see Chapter 4.)

Mini-libraries

There are comparatively few of these for Key Stage 3; those that exist are mainly continuations of those that are available for children in Key Stage 2.

[Heinemann] 'History of Britain' series

ISBN: See individual titles

Price: £4.99 each paperback.

Target age range: 8–12 yrs

Language, layout and images
Topics are explained in straightforward language, supplemented with maps, photographic images and illustrations. The layout is clear and well spaced with good-size print and helpful arrows to guide the reader to the relevant picture from the small explanatory paragraphs which caption each illustration. Coverage is organized in two-page mini-chapters; each deals with a different theme of relevance to the period covered.

Retrieval devices
A clear, columnar contents list (with picture symbols) and an index appear in each volume of thematically-organized topics. There is a glossary for unfamiliar words and terms, but no indication in the text that a word will be explained in this section. A user guide at the front of each book does however mention that there is a glossary of unfamiliar terms, and gives the page reference. Each user guide also has a chronological bar chart of the periods covered by volumes in the full series, so that the time period for that particular volume can be set into the overall context of British history from 55BC to the 1990s.

Children's assessments
'I especially like the layout of these books because of the numerous pictures used. Most pages contain one big picture with a few smaller ones around. These pictures are very useful to visually explain things. All the pictures are labelled with good explanations. Most importantly the text is easy to read and not too small. The index is also adequate for the purpose it serves. The selection of books comes with an interesting poster showing British Kings and Queens [a special offer from a book club].

I feel the layout of the book is very user-friendly; substantial effort has obviously been put into it.

The language used is reasonably simple and any complicated words are covered in the small yet useful glossary. The language manages to give a good picture of what it is describing. It isn't challenging to anyone at KS3, but it isn't meant to be.

The contents of the book are varied. A considerable number of topics are covered.

I would definitely recommend this to any KS3 teachers looking for a well-laid out and easy-to-follow book about British history.

At £4.99, these books are a must and very good too. Definitely a good buy.'
Mark Brenig-Jones (aged 14 years)

Other aspects
A useful section at the end of each volume offers suggestions for places to visit. These range from museums to period houses, churches, cathedrals and castles.

National Curriculum test results

History
Coverage of total subject area: 62%
Coverage of topics broached: 62%

Individual titles:
Medieval Britain: 1066 to 1485, by Brenda Williams. Hamlyn Children's Books (an imprint of Reed Children's Books): 1994

ISBN: 0 600 58217 5 paperback, 0 600 58216 7 hardback

Coverage: Topics covered range from the Norman Conquest to the Hundred Years' War and the Wars of the Roses. In addition to looking at rulers and lords, everyday life is featured in mini-chapters such as those on 'Towns and Houses', 'Guilds and Crafts' and 'Markets and Fairs'. There is also coverage of 'The Black Death' and 'Revolt and Rebellion'.

Children's assessments
'This book is one of a series of books about historic Britain.

I enjoyed this book a lot and I have learned a great deal. My favourite part was The Hundred Years' War between the English and the French and I also learned a lot about The Wars of The Roses.

I would recommend this book to a teacher to get for children below 13 years because it tells you the essentials and shows you pictures as well.'
Star rating: ****
Andrew Wilkinson (aged 12)

The Tudors: 1485 to 1603, by Andrew Langley. Hamlyn Children's Books (an imprint of Reed Children's Books): 1993

ISBN: 0 600 58028 8 paperback, 0 600 58029 6 hardback

Coverage: The text moves from Henry VII to the last years of the reign of Elizabeth I. In addition to looking at the monarchy over this time-period, attention is also paid to the day-to-day life of ordinary people, with mini-chapters such as: 'Town and Country Life'; 'Food and Drink'; 'Towns, Trade and Transport'. Special areas of interest in the period, such as: 'Shakespeare and the Theatre'; 'Education and Science'; and 'Explorers and Pirates' are also covered.

Children's assessments
Not reviewed individually.

140   A Guide to Children's Reference Books

The Stuarts: 1603 to 1714, by Andrew Langley. Hamlyn Children's Books (an imprint of Reed Children's Books): 1993

ISBN: 0 600 58026 1 paperback, 0 600 58027 X hardback

Coverage: Mini-chapters look at a range of themes, from the reign of James I to 'Marlborough and War' and 'Scientific Discoveries'. Power struggles, particularly the disputes between King and Parliament which culminated in the Civil War, feature prominently in this period; however, there is still coverage of topics such as 'People and their Homes' and 'Trade and Transport'.

Children's assessments
Not reviewed individually.

Georgian Britain: 1714 to 1837 by Andrew Langley. Hamlyn Children's Books (an imprint of Reed Children's Books): 1994

ISBN: 0 600 58215 9 paperback, 0 600 58214 0 hardback

Coverage: Topics range from 'The Britain of Walpole' to 'Social Reform 1800–1837'. As with the other books, attention is paid to everyday life as well as to war (the Napoleonic wars) and revolution (the American Revolution). Industrial development is of course prominently covered, with mini-chapters on 'The Rise of Cotton', 'Steam, Iron and Coal', 'Life in the Factories' and 'Roads and Canals'.

Children's assessments
Not reviewed individually.

Also published in this series are the following titles, which are reviewed with the Key Stage 2 publications: *Roman Britain 55BC to AD406*, *The Saxons and Vikings 406 to 1066*, *Victorian Britain 1837 to 1901*, *Modern Britain 1901 to the 1990s*.

The Kingfisher 'Historical Atlas' series. Kingfisher Books ([then] Grisewood & Dempsey Ltd): 1991 paperback, first published in hardback in 1990. [Kingfisher] Books is now an imprint of Larousse plc)

ISBN: see individual titles

Price: see individual titles

Target age range: 8–13 yrs

Coverage: The four volumes in this series give an extremely readable overview of significant facets of human development over the last 30 000 years. They cover such diverse themes as political and religious changes, the development of agriculture and of the written word, the growth and decline of civilizations, the great migrations and explorations, and the impact of technologies ancient and modern. A time chart identifies the important happenings of the period covered, not only in Europe but throughout the world.

Language, layout and images
Black-and-white photographs, colour photographs, maps and drawings are used to illustrate the easily-read text which is broken up into readily-managed sections. Each volume contains a glossary of the more significant terms.

Publications for Key Stage 3 141

Retrieval devices
The contents of each book are organized thematically, with a slightly confusing arrangement of boxes giving page references for the various topics covered. A short but helpful introduction advises the reader on the way the book is organized and indicates that terms highlighted in bold are explained in the glossary. An index at the back gives text and picture page references (references to illustrations are written in italics).

Children's assessments
See individual titles.

Other aspects
To attempt such coverage in four slim volumes totalling some 180 pages is formidable, but the authors have managed to select material with which to enthuse the reader and provide pointers to more in-depth studies.

National Curriculum test results
History
Coverage of total subject area: 71%
Coverage of topics broached: 71%

[Kingfisher] *Historical Atlas. Ancient World: From the Earliest Civilizations to the Roman Empire, 30,000BC–AD456*, by John Briquebec.

ISBN: 0 86272 756 1

Price: £3.99

Coverage: The topics covered by this volume are divided into the following sections: 'The Earth is Peopled 30,000–8000BC'; 'The Fertile Crescent and its Neighbours 8000–300BC'; 'Civilizations of Eastern and Southern Asia 3500BC–AD200'; 'Civilizations of Europe and the Mediterranean 2000BC–AD456'; 'Peoples of the West and South 40,000BC–AD456'.

Children's assessments
Not chosen for review.

[Kingfisher] *Historical Atlas. Trade & Religion: Barbarian Invasions, Empires around the World & Medieval Europe, AD456–1450*, by Simon Adams & Ann Kramer

ISBN: 0 86272 758 8 paperback

Price: £3.95

Coverage: The topics covered are grouped under the following headings: 'The World in 450 and After 450–750'; 'The Religious World 450–750'; 'Empires and Invasions 750–1200'; 'Empires beyond Europe 450–1450'; 'The Growth of Trade 1200–1450'.

Children's assessments
'The writing in the book is big and bold. The pictures are detailed and there are clear maps to show where things happened. The pages sort of pulled you into the book to read on. On each page there isn't much writing but what there was contained lots of facts. The pictures made you read the text to find out more information.

The texts were easy to understand and readable. It didn't have many hard words to read. But if there was a word you found difficult you could look in the glossary.

The price isn't bad for what it is.

Overall this book is very interesting. It is about empires, invasions, religions, and the growth of trade. The quality of the written words and the pictures is very good. It is fun to read for fourteen-year-olds.'

Hazel McIntyre (aged 14 years)

[Kingfisher] *Historical Atlas. Exploration & Empire: Empire-builders, European Expansion & the Development of Science, 1450–1760*, by Simon Adams & Ann Kramer

ISBN: 0 86272 757 X paperback

Price: £3.99

Coverage: Here the coverage is of 'Old and New Horizons 1450–1500'; 'Exploration and the Scramble for Riches 1450–1650'; 'Religions and Change 1520–1650'; 'Slavery and the "New World" 1535–1760'; 'Struggles for Power 1648–1760'.

Children's assessments
'This book is for a School History Department or a child with an interest in history. The book shows how we have developed science and how empires are created. The contents of the book are wide-ranging.

I particularly enjoyed reading the chapter called 'Struggles for Power' which described a great many features in detail and with plenty of thought given to what might interest people my age. Overall I enjoyed reading the book and I felt I learned a lot from it. I would like to use it in school and I think it would go down well in a class of people my age.

It would help the lessons seem more interesting.'

Gavin Jones (aged 14)

[Kingfisher] *Historical Atlas. Revolution & Technology: Rapid Change and the Growth of the Modern World, 1760 – to the Present Day*, by Simon Adams & Ann Kramer

ISBN: 0 86272 759 6

Price: £3.95

Coverage: The contents are organized into these sections: 'The World in 1760 and After 1760–1815'; 'The Impact of Revolution 1815–1880'; 'Imperialism and Empire 1880–1914'; 'The World at War 1914–1945'; 'A Troubled World 1945–'.

Children's assessments
'I found this book interesting and inviting from the first page to the last. With the help of pictures, the book tells how the world grew in revolution and technology.

The book was fairly easy to understand and to read although children under the age of about ten may find it a little difficult.

The book keeps you interested throughout and I think it would make a good History book because it describes things so clearly and in so much detail.'

Star rating: * * * * *

Edward Hutchinson (aged 14 years)

Other aspects
Although coverage is good up until the 1990s, modern analyses are coloured by the fact that they were written before the break up of the Soviet Union.

Editor's personal selection

At Key Stage 3 there are so many almost irresistible publications to choose from, it is really difficult to know where to draw the line. Starting with atlases, *The New Oxford School Atlas* is a must for maps, adding *The Kingfisher Encyclopedia of Lands and Peoples* for more in-depth coverage of individual countries and their inhabitants and *The Usborne Book of the Earth* for more information on geographical themes such as weather and climate.

At the beginning of Key Stage 3, *The Mini Oxford School Dictionary* and *The Mini Oxford School Thesaurus* are helpful as 'satchel books'. *The Oxford School A–Z of English* is also very useful, with *The Oxford Study Dictionary* the dictionary to buy as pupils reach the age of 14 years.

It is almost impossible to choose between the science volumes on offer, so at the risk of duplicating material, two sets (comprising three books) are recommended here. *The Dorling Kindersley Dictionary of Nature* and its companion volume *The Dorling Kindersley Dictionary of Science* are recommended as hardback books for the home, with incredible illustrations that can surely not be bettered. For the satchel, with revision in mind, Usborne's *Essential Science* guide is a compact and fact-filled paperback.

The *Kingfisher History Encyclopedia* is probably the best single history text; however, those collecting the Heinemann 'History of Britain' books may wish to buy the remaining volumes in the series for children at the start of Key Stage 3.

The *Dorling Kindersley Illustrated Factopedia* offers concise coverage of most subject areas, with information on music, art and literature as well as some duplication of material covered in the single subject books recommended above.

For those with additional money to spend, the following are also highly recommended: *The Oceans Atlas*, *The Space Atlas* and *A Young Person's Guide to Music* (these books, all from Dorling Kindersley, can spark great enthusiasm for the subjects they cover). The *Illustrated Book of Myths* (also from Dorling Kindersley) and *The Usborne Book of World Religions* are also attractive and informative additions to any library. *The Usborne Computer Dictionary for Beginners* is a very useful text to own (for adult beginners as well as children).

	£
The New Oxford School Atlas (paperback)	7.50
The Kingfisher Encyclopedia of Lands and Peoples (hardback)	25.00
The Usborne Book of the Earth (paperback)	9.95
The Mini Oxford School Dictionary (vinyl)	3.50
The Mini Oxford School Thesaurus (vinyl)	3.50
The Oxford Study Dictionary (paperback)	5.50
The Oxford School A-Z of English (paperback)	3.99
Dorling Kindersley *Dictionary of Nature* (hardback)	12.99
Dorling Kindersley *Dictionary of Science* (hardback)	12.99
Usborne *Essential Science* (paperback)	8.99
The Kingfisher History Encyclopedia (hardback)	25.00
The Dorling Kindersley Illustrated Factopedia (hardback)	25.00
TOTAL	143.91

6 Information playgrounds: children's reference and multimedia

Limitations and expansions: the scope of this chapter

The goal of this chapter is to provide an introduction to the types of children's reference and informative multimedia available on CD-ROM,[1] and to suggest guidelines for purchasing such software; it is impossible to base purchasing decisions on the extravagant claims printed on its over-sized packaging. One of the most exciting aspects of the multimedia market is its magnificent range, which appeals to a heterogeneous audience of individuals with divergent tastes. Accordingly, the tone of this profile is objective and descriptive, enabling readers to make their own informed choices. Naturally, opinions are offered, though these largely relate to quality of production and performance.

It must be stressed that this is only an *introductory* guide; a limitation necessitated by two primary factors. Firstly, the advance of technology is unceasing; products are continually updated, improved or superseded and, as a result, many titles have a relatively short shelf-life. This makes a comprehensive analysis of the market virtually impossible; any commentary will quickly become dated and is therefore only able to serve as a preliminary guide. For example, even as I write, *Encarta 97* (£49.99) is due for release, outdating the review of the '96' version below (though previews indicate that changes mostly relate to its Internet links, suggesting that my comments remain substantially relevant). Secondly, the vast quantity of products available makes it impossible to discuss them all; it seems more useful to indicate the different categories of CD-ROM because multimedia has altered the boundaries of what is customarily regarded as 'reference'. Multimedia is an inherently malleable medium; its various audio-visual components allow developers to experiment with a diverse range of structural formats and, as a result, information can be presented in an almost infinite number of ways.

It is increasingly difficult to classify CD-ROMs in conventional terms due to the developmental advances of multimedia; 'straight' works of reference such as encyclopedias or dictionaries are multi-dimensional and usually involve games of some sort (whether specifically intended for children or not). The following definition exemplifies the inadequacy of current classifications:

> Reference book: *noun* 1. A book, such as a dictionary or an encyclopedia, to which one can refer for authoritative information.[2]

Ironically, this is taken from the electronic dictionary on *Microsoft Bookshelf 95*, where a book is: 'A set of written, printed or blank pages fastened along one side and encased between protective covers'. *Microsoft Bookshelf* appears to deny its own existence; there is no suggestion that works of reference exist in alternative forms. By definition, multimedia is polysemic and defies singular interpretation, which allows for the very loose set of criteria by which software has been selected for inclusion in this chapter. I have included any product which might be considered a reference resource, even if only marginally, in order to demonstrate the fluidity of boundaries and to explore the diversity of learning methods open to children, parents and teachers.

At first sight, the array of available multimedia titles is daunting; it is often difficult to distinguish between computer games, electronic fiction, interactive reference and 'edutainment' or 'infotainment' (see next section). In fact, numerous titles are a mixture of several genres because they make optimum use of the options offered by multimedia. However, the multimedia market is not entirely chaotic; it is possible to divide products into general categories and subject areas, facilitating discussion and selection (though it must be stressed that titles are not necessarily sold within these categories). Therefore, the central survey of software has been divided into two sections (general reference and single-subject reference), each containing its own sub-categories.

General reference is divided into the following sub-categories: encyclopedias, dictionaries and atlases. In each instance, an overview of the current market is provided, plus the detailed discussion of a featured product, followed by a range of alternative reference materials. Criteria for the selection of featured products are relatively loose; all of these products have received critical acclaim and are particularly suited to young users of multimedia. Single-subject reference is divided into the four core subjects of geography, history, science and the arts. For each subject, a general survey of available products is followed by brief but detailed reviews of various titles, and examples of the best and worst multimedia titles are provided.

Finally, details of price and publisher are provided for every title mentioned in this chapter, but it should be emphasized that, since the multimedia market is so fast-moving, both are subject to change. Price (RRP), in particular, should be regarded as approximate, because prices alter with an almost unnerving rapidity. I have tried to show cost inclusive of VAT, though it is possible that there are some exceptions. Also, there is often some confusion as to the intended age range of products; only on use is it possible to judge such areas as complexity of language or accessibility, accuracy and presentation of information. Consequently, all reviews evaluate the appropriate age range of featured products: where a title already signals age range, its accuracy will be indicated; where products fail to specify age, an approximate range is estimated (expressed thus: ~ 9+).

A meeting of minds: past and future united

> For truly it is to be noted, that children's plays are not sports, and should be deemed as their most serious actions. (Michel de Montaigne)[3]

In this famous aside, taken from his 1575 essay 'On Custom', Montaigne recognizes the formative influence of leisure activities on child development; he urges parents and teachers not to underestimate the potency of play. Accordingly note has been taken, for the effects of Montaigne's pedagogical prescriptions are far-reaching; they stretch from Rousseau to Random House, from Blake to Broderbund, from Freud to Flagtower. Random House, Broderbund and Flagtower are, of course, all publishers of educational software and, though their motivation is largely fiscal as opposed to philosophical, they are all, like Montaigne, keen to stress the potential of playtime for furthering education. However, where Montaigne's intended readership was undoubtedly adult, software publishers are aware that children of the 1990s exert an influence on sales equal to, if not greater than, that of their elders. As a result, a multiple audience or 'readership' must be targeted, attracting children, parents and teachers alike. This then presents a dilemma: should products be labelled as educational and informative, or as entertaining and fun? This difficulty has been resolved through the creation of lexical hybrids which implement the multiple address required by publishers. Edutainment is now a familiar term in the software industry, describing a product, usually for young children, which literally educates while it entertains. Correspondingly, infotainment describes a product for young people and adults which entertains while it informs. Nevertheless, despite the assurances explicit in such equations as, 'Fun School = Learning + Excitement',[4] many parents and teachers remain suspicious of multimedia and the claims of publishers producing it. Several factors contribute to these misgivings, two of which are expressed by a mother featured in *Parents & Computers*:

> Sue equated a multimedia computer with a MegaDrive and saw it as nothing more than a games machine for the children.... One of Sue's main worries was that a powerful computer would take over from books. 'I'm very keen on the children reading. Richard has just discovered Enid Blyton's *Famous Five* but as soon as the computers came along he stopped reading, or so I thought. But actually it was just the novelty and he soon started to get the balance right...'[5]

Conventional books are frequently endowed with the status of endangered species in the face of multimedia; a status which, as Sue discovered, is inappropriate. However, when Sue mentions books, she is really talking about storybooks (as distinct from informative reference), as evidenced by her allusion to Blyton. The reading of fiction is a different process from that of the acquisition of facts; put simply, these activities involve two different 'modes of thought,' as identified by Jerome Bruner:

> There are two different modes of cognitive functioning, two modes of thought, each providing distinctive ways of ordering experience, of constructing reality. The two

(though complementary) are irreducible to one another. Efforts to reduce one mode to the other or to ignore one at the expense of the other inevitably fail to capture the rich diversity of thought.... A good story and a well formed argument are different natural kinds.⁶

The narrative mode (manifest in stories or drama) and the paradigmatic mode (manifest in logical arguments, descriptions or explanations) are modes of thinking which are employed in both the production of and the reception of stories or arguments. Of course, it is not always possible to separate these two modes as clinically as Bruner suggests; scientific arguments often employ anecdotal narrative in their construction, for example. However, Bruner's classifications are useful when considering the relative success and failure of electronic reference and fiction. Multimedia struggles with the development of narrative; electronic fiction consistently receives a 'bad press' and is largely rejected by the young readers recently surveyed by the Roehampton Institute.⁷ This is, perhaps, because the imaginative process of reading a conventional book is violated by the audio-visual dimensions of multimedia; a violation which developers are currently unable to overcome. It seems that, as yet, the 'multimedia revolution' has made no significant impact on the world of children's fiction. Conversely, judging by the success of educational or informative titles, the paradigmatic mode of thinking is complemented, even stimulated, by electronic media. Nevertheless, it is still reductive to place electronic reference automatically in direct competition with its printed counterpart (though there are instances where one format supersedes the other). Reference multimedia is a learning tool which can be used to complement the skills acquired through reading conventional texts; it is defeatist to suggest that one medium should be favoured at the expense of another.

Sue also seems to underestimate the educational potential of 'games', in which, ironically, as Tim Norris points out, children are frequently robbed of the fun that is typically regarded as an inherent aspect of gaming:

> Most of the educational stuff puts education at the top of the list of priorities and relies on the notion that 'computers are fun and kids love to play with computers'. *I M Mean* is a game that plays superbly well and has its educational element hidden away subtly inside so your children will scarcely notice being taught.⁸

Fortunately, since Norris made this observation in 1995 many more balanced titles have appeared. On this basis, it appears that educational titles now frequently involve both modes of thinking mentioned above; facts, theories and lessons are often presented in narrative/imaginative contexts, involving complex cognitive juggling on the part of the reader/user. For example, *Peter Rabbit's Number Garden* (Mindscape: £29.99) invokes a familiar story which allows the interactive creation of a garden; this creation involves the narrative mode because the garden forms a kind of storyboard through which children can invent their own tales. However, the paradigmatic mode of thinking comes into play as children are asked to solve various mathematical equations. Children are, then, required to move between two cognitive levels in negotiating this product. This also suggests that multimedia is able 'to capture the rich diversity of thought' alluded to by Bruner. The producers of multimedia recognize that bare facts do not sell; after all, few contemporary parents or pedagogues would subscribe to the Gradgrindian philosophy that 'You can only form the minds of reasoning animals upon Facts: nothing else will ever be of any service to them'.[9] In actuality, the primary reason for parental diffidence is not the anxiety that children will overly enjoy themselves, but their own ignorance of computer technology, of a form of literacy absent from their own schooldays. As Margaret Meek observes:

> With this important new literacy I am, in several senses, out of my depth. But I know that anyone who takes being literate seriously has to attend to the consequences of computers. My children seem to be computer literate.... I often wonder how they communicate ordinarily with computer semi-literates, like me. They are sure that their own children, at three and a half can 'get the machine running' to print their names and addresses...[10]

Significantly, Meek recognizes that children are often more comfortable with emerging technologies than their parents. Accordingly, adults must strive to accommodate these technologies, in recognition that they are irretrievably bound up with the future of contemporary children.

Ironically, though multimedia and CD-ROMs are often associated with futuristic systems of knowledge, it has been suggested that the multimedia CD-ROM is actually a dying breed. The primary reason for this is the time it has taken for the multimedia revolution to take place; long heralded in the computing world, it has had little effect on the general public until very recently. Inevitably, doubts began to form, such as those quashed by Matthew Richards, editor of *CD-ROM Today*:

> So will the disc become obsolete, trampled underfoot by some new technology, before it has ever hit the dizzy heights many (us included) have been prophesying? Well, at the risk of repeating myself, I reckon that finally and at long last, 1996 really will be the year of the disc. So far, multimedia has lacked mass appeal for one simple reason. It's been too expensive. But that's changed. Many new discs from companies like Microsoft and Dorling Kindersley are being launched at half of last year's prices and the cost of older, but extremely good discs has been slashed in many cases.[11]

The veracity of this prediction is manifest in the increasing presence of multimedia in schools, high-street retailers and homes. The market is also less limited than it might appear; publishers do exist aside from the multimedia giants Microsoft and Dorling Kindersley (though the sophistication of their products is undisputed). Many publishers, including Flagtower, YITM, Broderbund and News Multimedia, have produced innovative titles which deserve similar attention. Additionally, designers continually attempt to attract new audiences, increasing the versatility of the market. A rather amusing example of this is manifest in Funsoft's imminent launch of multimedia Barbie™, *Barbie Fashion Designer* (£39.99) 'lets girls use their computers to design clothes for their dolls'.[12] This is a transparent attempt, revelling in the perpetuation of gender stereotypes, to encourage a larger female audience (the recent survey, *Young*

People's Reading at the End of the Century, reveals that girls are relatively reluctant PC users).[13]

More recently, however, the CD-ROM has faced the predatory threat of the Internet and, once again, insiders are predicting its decline; or at least the decline of its current format. In a recent *Telegraph* article, Sean Geer suggests that children's titles are the only CDs which sell, while observing that: 'the medium's promise – that it would create a new multimedia art form – has signally failed to become a reality. The book it seems is safe'.[14] Geer insists on perpetuating the hostilities between book and CD-ROM; an approach which has already been shown to be negativistic. He also fails to recognize the significance of the healthy children's market; today's children are destined to shape the future of our culture and, in so doing, are likely to utilize the formative literacies of their childhood. Indeed, if Montaigne is to be believed, that to which we are accustomed in childhood will 'grow to strength, and come to perfection,' in our adult years.[15] However, Geer is correct in signalling the importance of the Internet in furthering the development of multimedia. Multimedia is expensive to develop on CD-ROM, while the medium of the Web cuts these costs dramatically. However, video, sound and graphics are impossibly slow to download from the Internet, while CD-ROM is able to hold vast amounts of such digitized information. Consequently, as Geer explains:

> ... a new breed of multimedia title is emerging – a hybrid of CD-ROM and Web technologies that is just another intermediate solution of the problem but which offers some interesting possibilities. Microsoft was among the first to adopt this hybrid approach. . . . Two of its biggest selling titles, the Encarta encyclopedia and the Music Central guide to music, have links to the Web that allow users to download up-to-date information and store it on the hard disk.[16]

Perhaps the future is to be found in the fast lanes of the 'Information Super-Highway', but future potentialities are merely imprecise flickers on the screen. The past, however, can be revisited; Montaigne now lives quite comfortably at http://swift.eng.ox.ac.UK/jdr/monta.htm (a Web site providing biographical and critical information on Montaigne). As far as the present is concerned, there is an abundance of innovative and exciting multimedia titles to be discussed.

Of course, since multimedia is a relatively recent phenomenon it is not always used to its full potential, and many publishers still have far to go in developmental terms. The following list of 'pros and cons' provides a general idea of the best and worst that this electronic environment has to offer:

Advantages of multimedia

- Interactive Presentation: Numerous audio-visual components make the acquisition of information an exciting and appealing experience.
- Hypertext: Hot words or spots which, if clicked on, will activate hidden

animations or transport the user to related text/information; cross-referencing becomes almost intuitive as a result of this device.
- Concentration of information: CD-ROMs contain vast amounts of information, negating the problem of storage space (which might be caused by printed encyclopedias).
- Back-tracking: Many products include this option, allowing the user to return to articles or sections previously accessed in the same session; many encyclopedic discs provide lists of every section opened by the user. This is invaluable for research purposes.
- Games: Many reference titles involve games which are designed to aid the retention of information (as well as being great fun to play).
- Functional options: The option to print or download text and images into other documents is particularly beneficial for essays and project work. Notebooks are another common function, enabling the user to make notes while searching the disc.

Disadvantages of multimedia

- High Expense: The price of hardware and software makes multimedia inaccessible to many schools and families. However, the cost of PCs[17] and CD-ROMs continues to fall rapidly as the market grows.
- Americanization: Much of the software available in the UK originates in the USA, resulting in a bias evident in both subjects covered and vocabulary; language differences are especially problematic for British schoolchildren. However, many publishers, recognizing this problem, have started to release localized versions of their products.
- Brevity of Shelf-Life: Frequent technological advances mean that hardware and software are constantly updated; it is extremely infuriating to discover that your PC will not run the latest multimedia releases or that the disc you bought last month has just been updated. Nonetheless, many publishers/retailers offer various part-exchange deals.
- Design faults: A poorly designed interface can lead to user disorientation, making the information virtually inaccessible. Programs which continually crash are also aggravating and are probably the result of poor design or simply a lack of testing during development. Obviously, this type of fault is only discovered on use (which makes a little pre-purchase research a necessity).

The electronic reference library: encyclopedias

In both printed and electronic format, the encyclopedia is the most comprehensive form of reference available. However, if any type of software is likely to oust its printed counterpart it is the encyclopedia. An indication that this might be true can be found in the results of the Roehampton Survey. Children asked to choose between various formats for retrieving information, are less inclined to look at a conventional encyclopedia than they are at CD-ROMs; in fact the standard encyclopedia is found to be 'the least popular form of non-fiction reading'.[18] Consequently, it is not so much a case of the CD-ROM 'killing' the printed encyclopedia, as of it replacing an already defunct genre. The comprehensive nature of the encyclopedia is perhaps its downfall; in printed form it is both bulky and expensive, making it an impractical choice for most families. Multimedia changes this though, for, as Matthew Richards says in *CD-ROM Today*, 'encyclopedias... are, of course, the epitome of CD-ROM – masses of text, pictures, sound, animation and video clips all conveniently squashed onto one plastic-coated piece of tinfoil';[19] electronic encyclopedias are much cheaper to produce and inherently compact. More significantly, though, from an educational perspective, the optimum CD-ROM can be a much more effective and immediate learning tool; on-line dictionaries, cross-referencing tools and attractive audio-visual displays all contribute to this. Multimedia encyclopedias are produced principally for the family market, which renders problematic the existence of those designed specifically for children. A family is, by definition, inclusive of children, suggesting that 'family encyclopedias' (such as the *Encarta* or *Grolier* versions mentioned below) are suitable for adults and children alike. Should not the existence of family encyclopedias then negate the need for specifically child-orientated products? In reality, however, 'family' versions are often too linguistically complex for young children, opening the market for more suitable products. There are a number of encyclopedias sold specifically for children. They range from those which rely heavily on edutainment (an example of which is featured below), to more serious products, like the forthcoming *Oxford Children's Encyclopedia*, which resemble such 'grown-up' titles as *Encarta* (again featured later).

Featured product

Title: *Discovery Tree*

Publisher: Random House UK New Media

RRP: £29.99

Age Range: 4–8

Reputation
This is a localized version of a product which was first released in the USA under the title *My First Encyclopedia*. The British version is part of the new 'Jump Ahead' series launched by Random House. It is fully endorsed by PIN (Parents Information Network), which says:

> PIN is taking the important step of working with those software publishers committed to offering real support to the many parents who want to get involved with and help their children's learning using quality software titles. The Jump Ahead™ series provides a really extensive range of enjoyable learning activities, and most importantly through the parent support materials offers parents a useful guide to understanding and working with the products.[20]

Profile

Discovery Tree is not a conventional encyclopedia, even by electronic standards, relying on pictures and the spoken word, instead of written text, to convey information; it is undoubtedly 'edutaining'. The structural design of the program centres on the metaphor of tree-climbing; movement up or down the tree provides access to various areas of knowledge. The home screen shows a tree occupied by various children, beasts and objects. The most immediate way of obtaining information is to click on these objects or creatures (hot spots), evoking a spoken description of the subject. However, most information is held 'behind the scenes' in various rooms; the children act as guides to these 'learning rooms', accessed on different parts of the tree. There are ten learning rooms, covering the following subjects: Geology, Animals, Food, Transportation, Jobs & Sport, Buildings & Towns, Arts, Anatomy & Medicine, Geography and Astronomy. Each room offers a range of games, puzzles and hot spots relevant to the subject, and a question and answer section. This package contains an excellent parent's guide, which suggests ways of working with children and furthering the educational benefits of *Discovery Tree*. However, since explanations and layouts are extremely clear, children can easily work and play alone. This product is designed to accelerate the evolution of general knowledge in young children. Additionally, the audio-visual presentation of *Discovery Tree* recognizes that literacy cannot simply be defined as the ability to decipher written text; children are able to learn through 'reading' pictures and interpreting sounds. The colourful design of the *Discovery Tree* lends a light-hearted tone to this learning adventure; lessons really are fun when conducted up a tree! The suggested age range seems realistic, since children beyond 8 years old are likely to lose patience with this jocular approach.

Educational features

Localization

[✓] The American version used vocabulary which might have proved problematic for British children. In this localized version various terminologies have changed; for example, Autumn replaces Fall. However, in such subject areas as sport, emphasis is still undeniably American.

[x] American pronunciation has been dubbed out and British children can now be heard on the soundtrack. The dubbing is terrible, rendering the presenters more amusing than they are intended to be. I am not convinced that this was a necessary change.

The guides

[✓] That this product is designed for children is confirmed by the use of real children as guides; video clips reveal child presenters addressing child users. In this way it avoids being patronizing or dictatorial.

Hot spots

[✓] Early vocabulary skills are developed through the use of hot spots; clicking on an object reveals its title in large letters and provides clear pronunciation of the word prior to a more detailed definition.

Games

[✓] Logical reasoning, problem-solving and spatial-visualisation skills are developed through the numerous activities and games in each learning room.

Index

[✓] The index teaches the alphabet through letters presented on a sliding rule. It scrolls through a series of words beginning with A, B, C, etc., all of which are used at some point on the disc. Each entry is illustrated through sound and picture; clicking on the picture takes you to the relevant place on the tree. This teaches the child to associate specific words with certain subject areas.

[x] *The Discovery Tree* bases its approach on the inquisitive nature of young children, therefore emphasis is on discovery through random exploration. However, the parent's guide appears to deny this spontaneity, suggesting that it is possible to find answers to particular questions:

> The contents page is presented as a set of pictures which represent different rooms. Each room has a different theme. To find something more specific your child may need to use the index. Understanding how to find information in these ways is an important skill for children to develop....[21]

The intentions here are admirable, but are not achieved in practice. The contents page does perform as suggested, but the 'index' does not operate as indicated. There is actually no way of selecting a specific word or subject, beyond knowledge of its initial letter; even then it is unclear whether the word is indexed until the entire audio-selection has been heard for a given letter; a written list would have been invaluable here. Elsewhere, subjects are also discussed in an unnecessarily haphazard fashion. For example, the 'animal album' provides snapshots and descriptions of different animals in an entirely random sequence. It is impossible to know which animals are covered without listening to the complete album: a problem which simple alphabetic arrangement would have avoided. Also, the sorting of words would have complemented the interest in teaching the alphabet evidenced by the basic presence of the index.

Alternative children's encyclopedias

Kingfisher Children's Micropedia '96' (ESM) £45.00

Electronic version of *Kingfisher Children's Encyclopedia*. Features two levels (KS 1&2) of information and 'Read To Me' buttons, which allow for graduated reading development. Features include: sounds and sample animations, a 'Did you know?' section and topic choices.

Oxford Children's Encyclopedia £59.99

Electronic version of the printed edition with the advantages of multimedia. Designed for and tested by 8–13-year-old children, supporting UK National Curriculum requirements (KS 2&3). Cross-refers to the *Oxford Primary School Dictionary*. Features include: notebook, detailed maps and 'edutaining' game

Random House Kid's Encyclopedia £44.95

Companion to *Discovery Tree*, this is intended for an older audience. However, this is a move sideways rather than a graduation in educational terms. The main screen is based on a shopping mall, split between the worlds of reference, cinema and games; information is text based. Presentation is frenetic and glitzy (it has not been localized).

Featured product

Title: *Encarta 96 Encyclopedia: World English Edition*

Publisher: Microsoft

RRP: £49.99

Age Range: ~ 9+

Reputation

The *Microsoft Encarta Encyclopedia* led the British market for several years despite, like most of its competitors, catering primarily for the lucrative American market. Now, with the release of the 'World English Edition', it appears to have reached perfection, at least according to the reverent reviews it has elicited from almost every PC or CD-ROM journal.

Profile

Encarta boasts 27 000 articles, 125 videos and animations, 9 hours of sound, 8 000 pictures or illustrations and more than 800 atlas maps, all of which are easy to access and presented through a sleek, sophisticated interface. The package includes a user's guide, a quick-reference card (both printed) and a home screen which introduces the main sections of the encyclopedia, providing useful hints on how to move around. Simply clicking the 'find' button lists every article, while more specific searches are available by clicking on various icons or on the features bar. In addition to this, *Encarta 96* has been updated in several ways, two of which are of particular significance to British schoolchildren. It contains over 3 500 new localized entries and there is now access to *The Concise Oxford Dictionary*. A novel feature of *Encarta 96* is the Yearbook Builder, providing access to current events which can be downloaded free (for the first 12 months) from the Internet. However, Internet access and modems are pre-requisites for this feature.

It is often suggested that *Encarta 96* is for 'all ages', a claim which is simply untrue. Admittedly, the vast range of interactive tools allows children to grow with the encyclopedia, making it difficult to pinpoint an age range. Certainly it does not entirely exclude children, and it has won several awards including the *Children's Software Review* 'All Star Award' (1994 and 1995). However, I would not expect the encyclopedia to hold the interest of children under eight or nine for any length of time; they would certainly not be able to use it alone in any constructive manner. The text is lucid, but relatively advanced in terms of vocabulary and subject matter, as illustrated by the following excerpt from the entry on children's literature: 'With the development of vernacular literature, particularly after the invention of printing, more children's books appeared'.[22] How many five-year-olds would shriek with excitement over that revelation? Nonetheless, the correct age-group is likely to enjoy *Encarta's* riches, as evidenced by the experience of this father (of two children, aged nine and ten years), who compares Microsoft's electronic encyclopedia with the printed *Encyclopedia Britannica*:

> Now if I can sit down in front of Encarta I can keep their interest much longer, and that excites me because I know they are learning through what they believe to be a play medium. But the information is going in and once they actually use it themselves to acquire information I'll get an incredible buzz from it.[23]

Parental guidance is perhaps necessary for installation and introductory purposes; though once various functions have been explained, independent use should be possible.

Educational features

Guided tour
[✓] Tours are comprised of pre-selected articles on common topics, providing a basic introduction to research methods; they might serve as templates for trial essays/projects.
[x] There is only a very limited selection of tours.

Hypertext
[✓] Hot words teach basic cross-referencing skills; browsing is simple and enjoyable. An excellent back-tracking system, with the option to review articles which have already been displayed, takes optimum advantage of hot words.
[x] Reliance on this function can be misleading. For example, hypertext in the entry on children's literature leads to relevant literary biographies. The assumption is that all possible cross-references have been made, and since there is no mention of Enid Blyton, either as a related article or hot word, it should be safe to assume that there is no entry. However, a new search reveals that there is an article on Blyton, but unconnected to other entries. Why is it not linked to children's literature?

Games
[✓] The matching games in 'Interactivities' provide an excellent introduction to the encyclopedia for younger children; they are based on famous paintings, natural wonders and world music, and are compulsively entertaining. *Encarta* also has its own version of *Trivial Pursuit* called the Mind Maze; correct answers allow progression through the maze of a medieval castle, while inquisitive players are able to access relevant articles.
[x] The Mind Maze will only be of interest to older children with a thirst for general knowledge, since the castle trappings soon become tiresome.

Timeline/atlas
[✓] These features broaden the focus of specific articles, placing information in a geographical and historical context.
[x] When moving from these features to related articles or images, it is not always clear how to return to your place on the atlas/timeline once the article has been read.

Notemarks
[✓] They allow students to flag useful articles or to make their own notes. These can be listed or copied into word-processing programs for inclusion in essays or projects.
[x] A relatively complex tool to use; limited to older children, parents and teachers.

Dictionary
[✓] Any word is immediately defined by a simple double click on the relevant word; words can also be looked up separately via the dictionary located on the tool bar.

Media gallery
[✓] The gallery adds a dimension to the learning process which engages attention and aids the memorizing of information.
[x] Selecting a related article throws you out of the gallery without the option of returning.

Alternative family encyclopedias

British Multimedia Encyclopedia (GSP)	£19.99

This is actually a previous incarnation (1995 ed.) of the electronic *Hutchinson Encyclopedia* in disguise (though this is not revealed on the box). It cannot compete with *Encarta/Grolier* in terms of design. The Article Trail feature is limited, only recording searches within certain parameters.

Compton's Interactive Encyclopedia (Softkey)	£29.99

Awarded 'Best Buy' by *What PC & Software?* magazine, on the basis of ease of use and value for money.

Grolier Multimedia Encyclopedia 1996	£45.00

Similar in size to *Encarta*. Maps have better physical definition and timelines are clearer; it's easier to move between functions and related entries, though there's no list of articles visited. Main downfall is American emphasis, which is evident in Pathfinders & Yearbook sections. Lacks appeal for younger children – no games.

Hutchinson Encyclopedia 1996 (Attica & Helicon)	£49.99

Truly British, but contains only a fraction of the information in *Encarta* and *Grolier*. (The 1997 version is due for release and, like *Encarta*, is now linked to the Internet for on-line updates; it is priced at £39.99.)

Webster's World Encyclopedia (Ransom)	£34.99

Not yet released, but promises to compete seriously with *Encarta*. Includes full text of the *Cambridge U.P. Encyclopedia*, general interest word-game, plus such typical features as maps and timeline.

Dictionaries and language reference

Unlike encyclopedias, the contrast between child and adult electronic dictionaries is clear. The age range for children's dictionaries usually has a 'ceiling' of about 12 or 13 years old; at this point young people must graduate to adult editions, suggesting that a brief synopsis of the adult market would be advantageous. Adult dictionaries are available in several forms and, since the emphasis is on practicality, they make minimal use of the visual wizardry of multimedia. Basic dictionaries and thesauri are integrated into most word-processing packages, though often the dictionaries are limited to spell-check systems and must be used in combination with more thorough texts. Many encyclopedias also incorporate dictionaries; for example, the 'World English Edition' of *Encarta 96* includes the *Concise Oxford Dictionary*, although, in this context, it is limited to the provision of definitions. These dictionaries are really tools to be used in conjunction with specific programs and cannot compete with printed texts. Conversely, comprehensive electronic dictionaries offer several advantages over their printed counterparts, such as: options to print and download information, various search techniques, cross-referencing tools, spoken pronunciation, hyperlinks to thesauri and anagram finders. However, I am yet to be persuaded that my dog-eared, cloth-bound companion is 'past its heyday'; electronic dictionaries simply are not as practical. Dictionaries can be purchased as stand-alone products, but are often published as part of a 'reference library'. A reference library consists of several works bundled onto one CD-ROM; it might include a dictionary, thesaurus, atlas, almanac or a book of quotations. Language reference can be extremely expensive, but the topmost end of the range reflects titles suitable for intensive research rather than for schoolwork. The following table provides an indication of titles currently available.

Title	Publisher	RRP£
Collins COBUILD on CD-ROM	HarperCollins	47.00
Collins COBUILD Student's Dictionary	HarperCollins	34.08
Collins Electronic Dictionary & Thesaurus	HarperCollins	29.99
Corel Super Ten Reference Pack	Corel	46.99
Infopedia UK 96': (8 books)	Softkey	39.99
Microsoft Bookshelf 95: (7 USA-based books)	Microsoft	75.00
Microsoft Bookshelf: British Reference Collection	Microsoft	49.99
Oxford Compendium: (Concise Ox. Dictionary, Thesaurus, Dic of Quot. & Mod Quot.	OUP	79.99
Concise Oxford Dictionary (9th Ed.)	OUP	19.99
Oxford Reference Shelf: (16 books)	OUP	79.99
Oxford Thesaurus	OUP	49.99
Oxford Dictionary Of Quotations & Modern Quotations	OUP	49.99
Oxford English Dictionary	OUP	293.75
New Shorter Oxford English Dictionary	OUP	79.99
Penguin Hutchinson Reference Library (7 books)	Koch Media	39.99

There are very few electronic dictionaries available for children, but the fact that two are published by Dorling Kindersley makes this of less consequence than it might be. This dearth of titles is perhaps explained by the vast quantity of edutainment produced for young children. Such products as *Fisher Price ABCs* (ABLAC: £29.00) or *Great Word Adventure* (7th Level: £34.99) are intended to develop reading skills, focusing on basic vocabulary and grammar; and, consequently, their function begins to overlap that of 'early learning' dictionaries.

Featured product

Title: *The Dorling Kindersley Children's Dictionary*

Publisher: Dorling Kindersley

RRP: £29.99

Age Range: 7–12

Reputation

Dorling Kindersley is a 'force to be reckoned with' in the field of children's multimedia, producing titles which are internationally praised. The success of their range of printed books has been repeated by their CD-ROMs; as Conor McNicholas points out in *CD-ROM Magazine*:

> Combine good multimedia with the right subject and you're on to a winner. DK, as an independent developer/publisher, has had phenomenal success because it already knows its market intimately from book sales.[24]

Nonetheless, the value of direct transfer of books onto CD-ROM must be questioned; there seems little point in simply altering the format of a text. It has been suggested that the DK style is becoming a little staid, as the design of DK publications is unmistakable whether of book, video or CD-ROM. However, the *Children's Dictionary* does actually break from the traditional white simplicity of the DK interface, resulting in a colourful cocktail of alphabetic exploration. Like most DK titles, the *Children's Dictionary* has received enthusiastic reviews and is rated 11th in *CD ROM Today's* top 100 children's discs.[25]

Profile

Simply, this is edutainment at its best. The *Children's Dictionary* is a powerful learning tool, yet is highly entertaining; DK have judged the balance perfectly here. This dictionary, or 'Magical Word Machine', succeeds in making words interesting for the apathetic, while the etymologist (even a grown-up one) is likely to be thrown into paroxysms of delight! Seriously though, this is a 'proper' dictionary, containing 45 000 definitions and 14 500 headwords with pronunciations. There is no user manual, which might be regarded as a drawback; however, the help option provides a clear, concise introduction to moving around the Word Machine. The most conventional way of using the dictionary is through the Word Finder; merely type in a word and it appears, complete with definition, pronunciation, applicable parts of speech, syllabification, plural forms, verb forms or adjectival and adverbial endings. Words can also be accessed through the Alphabet Park or Alphabet Bar, which reveal the animated screens introducing each letter of the alphabet. These screens are beautifully presented and are brimming with hot spots which literally bring words to life; the Letter World for 'K' includes a spinning koala, a kilt-clad dancer and a lingering kiss. As each animation is triggered, the relevant word appears in the bar at the top of the main screen; clicking on the word accesses the main dictionary. There is also an opportunity to select words at random for those of a purely curious disposition. Functional options include a marker which tags up to six pages, printing the current page; and a back-tracking tool which allows you to revisit pages. Finally, there are three word-related games, Charades, Hangman and Spelling, which add to the overall fun of this package. The suggested age range is accurate; though all ages will potentially find it entertaining, if not thorough enough as a dictionary. Once the various tools on the machine have been negotiated, children should be quite happy to explore alone (though the games are also enjoyable when played with friends).

Educational features

Help
[✓] The help option is more than a simple guide around the Word Machine; basic, though valuable lessons on the structure of English grammar and the function of dictionaries are provided.

Word Wheel
[✓] This option is activated if a word is selected which belongs to a group containing related words. The Word Wheel icon lights up when the user chooses a word which relates to it. For example, if the word 'acorn' is chosen, a red square will flip out from the Word Wheel. Clicking on the square reveals that 'acorn' belongs to the nut group; a list of other nuts is also provided, enabling further exploration. The Word Wheel develops an understanding of linguistic systems as it contextualizes different words and clarifies the relationships between words.
[x] An index of available word groups would be useful; this could help with school projects or homework.

Word Detective
[✓] This operates in the same way as the Word Wheel, but is activated where the dictionary contains any significant facts about the selected word. The Word Detective has the following menu options: Alternative, Word History, Homophone, Homograph, Synonym, Language Note, Word Builder and Idiom. The option(s) which apply to the chosen word will be highlighted so that the user knows where to click for more information. The Word Detective encourages interest in linguistic structures and etymology.
[x] More words could be included in this section as it is the most original/interesting aspect of the dictionary. Also, it would be useful if the words included were indexed in some way; there is no way of knowing which words will activate the Word History option, for example.

Games
[✓] The three games, Hangman, Charades and Spelling, all increase vocabulary and develop the ability to spell correctly; the fact that they are all addictively playable increases their impact.
[x] The educational potential of these games would be improved if they were 'hyperlinked' to the main dictionary. It is highly likely that children will not recognize all of the words involved, but finding a definition requires quitting the games section. This is a slow process and tries the patience of the most determined of players!

Alternative children's dictionaries

Macmillan Dictionary for Children	£24.99
Develops the basics of literacy in a purportedly stimulating multimedia environment. For children aged 6–12	
My First Incredible Amazing Dictionary Dorling Kindersley	£29.00
This is the precursor to the DK *Children's Dictionary*. It is for children aged 4–7, introducing them to 1 000 words through an energetic combination of animation, spoken word, pictures and sound effects. DK's distinctive bright, white and clear interface is utilized to optimum effect, drawing children in to an engaging world of words.	

Atlases

The Atlas could be described as an informatory picture book: a text in which pictures and words carry equal significance. Maps are, of course, very specialized pictures, but they might explain the lack of discrimination between child and adult electronic atlases. Children's electronic reference usually has a strong visual component; a component common to all atlases, regardless of readership. Dorling Kindersley, generally recognized as a publisher of children's reference, have produced a family atlas, while Mindscape's *World Atlas & Almanac*, ostensibly for adults, bears the logo 'Kids to Adults' and suggests an age range of 6 plus. While it is true that many electronic encyclopedias also appeal to a 'family' audience, there are actually encyclopedias with a limited age range designed specifically for children. The only children's products which might be described as atlases are *Where in the World is Carmen Sandiego?* (Broderbund) and *My First Amazing World Explorer* (DK). Certainly they borrow from the basic concept and structure of the atlas; however, they are both based around exploratory adventures which are better described as entertaining geography lessons; for this reason these titles are discussed in the 'Geography' section of this chapter. Like dictionaries, atlases are available in various formats aside from the stand-alone product. Most encyclopedias include maps and geographical information; *Discovery Tree* and *Encarta 96* both include a number of basic maps, though detail is minimal compared to comprehensive atlases. Reference Libraries also usually include atlases; *Microsoft Bookshelf 95* contains *The Hammond Atlas of the World*, as does *Infopedia UK 96*.

Featured product

Title: *Dorling Kindersley World Reference Atlas*
Publisher: Dorling Kindersley

RRP: £39.99

Age Range: ~8+

Reputation

High standards are expected of DK, and their *World Reference Atlas* has not disappointed the critics. DK seem to have bridged the child and adult markets successfully here, for, as *PC Guide* observes:

> Dorling Kindersley ventures further into the adult realm with this disc than perhaps with any other (except for its sex guide). But while the potted histories of countries around the world are written in suitably grown-up wordage, and the array of statistical information is truly enormous, the same clean and clear publishing format that makes DK's kiddier discs so approachable is very much in evidence.[26]

The reputation of *World Reference Atlas* is second only to Microsoft's *Encarta World Atlas*, though this comparison is not usually made with children in mind; DK's atlas must be the favourite if the atlas is to be purchased for young children.

Profile

Once again DK provide no user's guide, but the disc does have an excellent help system which clarifies each possible route. The *World Reference Atlas* is based around 193 country articles. The opening screen offers five avenues of exploration, each represented by a different graphic, all ultimately leading to these articles; these are the Political World, the Physical World, the World in View, the A–Z of Countries and the Index. The most child-friendly option is probably the A–Z, which provides an illustrated catalogue of countries in alphabetical sequence. The more conventional index provides various filters which allow searches focusing on people, physical features or places. The three alternative options allow exploration via maps of variant detail; the World in View gives access to photographs and video clips, which in turn lead to any of the country articles, while the Political and Physical Worlds provide self-explanatory routes to accessing country articles. Each country article contains photographs or video clips, maps, text and up to 50 pop-up windows accessible from the 'navigation panel'. The navigation panel enables movement around the atlas, also giving access to printing, copying and help options. It also contains an extended section of icons representing different aspects of the country; these are politics, aid, tourism, chronology, communications, media, economics, health, world ranking, wealth, people, climate, environment, world affairs, resources, education, defence and crime. The maps provide three different zoom options, where the maximum detail is approximately 100 miles to the inch. All maps are linked to a scrolling system which simulates the effect of a rolling globe; keys and scale bars are also provided for every map. The navigation panel also provides an easy path back to previous screens. Given the clarity and variety of presentation, DK have really succeeded in providing a product for children and adults. It is in this area that they really challenge Microsoft; DK understand the children's market and this shows in the intrinsic design of their product, which gives children gradual access to more complex textual entries. Eight-year-olds will require help negotiating the atlas to begin with, though once the navigation panel has been explained they will enjoy making their own way around the world whether visually or otherwise.

Educational features

Comparable information

[✓] The most valuable aspect of this disc is its ability to compare information on different countries. Clicking on various icons on the navigation panel provides up-to-date (to 1995) statistics on subjects such as weather patterns or consumer goods ownership. Many of these statistical panels have a 'compare' option which brings up the country index; for example, Brazil's health spending can be compared to the United Kingdom's. The potential for classwork, group projects and homework is enormous and, once again, the multimedia format develops cross-referencing skills.
[x] Information is provided on a national scale; in many cases statistical information on key towns and cities would be valuable.

Visual contextualization

[✓] Geographical context is constantly maintained, regardless of zoom intensity. Location is maintained during zoom-ins through a larger-scale country icon which responds to any movements made. Basic geographical-location lessons are thus constantly being taught.

Search routes

[✓] The various indexes allow children to grow with this atlas; more complex searches can be tried as the child develops.
[x] The centre of every search, the country article, is biased towards human geography. The Physical World screen leads to the same country information as the Political World screen, which makes for a rather one-sided perspective.

Video clips

[✓] Video clips can be enlarged to full-screen size, providing an attractive filmic quality to the whole production. These clips are likely to entice the most reluctant learner and can be used alone as a method of searching the globe.
[x] There are only a limited number of video clips and photographs, which partially explains Microsoft's success in the popularity stakes; the *World Reference Atlas* has 250 compared with the 3 000 in *Encarta's World Atlas*.

Alternative atlases

3D Atlas: (Electronic Arts) £65.00

Designed in the guise of a documentary, full of video-clips and animations; its maps are not very detailed.

Encarta 96 World Atlas: (Microsoft) £49.99

This is the market leader, a position earned through the depth and variety of information it offers. It is awarded 'Best Buy' by *What PC?*, who say of it: 'Statistics in over 450 categories are available ... and there's an ingenious way of viewing them too: just choose the statistic you want and as you move the cursor over each country the appropriate figure appears...'[27] *Encarta* is also the winning atlas for *PC Guide*, who describe it as a 'tour de force'.[28] (*Encarta 97* is now available at the same price.)

164 A Guide to Children's Reference Books

Global Explorer: (Logix) £106.93

Most detailed map on the market, providing street names in large towns and cities.

ITN European Video Atlas: (Attica) £29.99

Introduced by Trevor McDonald, it includes 'video profiles of over 30 countries created by the ITN newsroom'.[29]

Times World Map & Database: (HarperCollins) £45.00

Emphasis is on statistics providing detailed information on physical and human geography; a huge amount of information takes up four discs.

World Atlas & Almanac: (Mindscape) £59.99

This claims an age range of 6+ (unrealistic); children will be alienated by an unfriendly interface and options which are difficult to manoeuvre.

Virtual classrooms: single-subject encyclopedias, museums and infotainment

While general encyclopedias are able to cover an enormous breadth of information, the depth in which they are able to discuss individual subjects is necessarily limited. This imbalance is remedied by the plethora of reference titles devoted to in-depth treatment of single subjects; topics run from gardening to Einstein, reflecting both the pursuit of leisure and academic interests. Aside from the advantage of increased depth, the design of these products often suits the subject, making for a more visually stimulating experience. As noted in Dorling Kindersley's book on multimedia:

> The way a title presents information, its 'look and feel,' is known as its interface. General encyclopedias include so many different types of information that they have to use all-purpose interfaces, which are often fairly bland. One-subject titles, however, can build information into a graphical world specially created to entice the user into it.[30]

In many cases this is true, and user enticement has obvious advantages in the classroom. However, Dorling Kindersley have a 'vested interest' in championing the 'one-subject encyclopedia'; it is a format central to their current list of titles. Their *Eyewitness* encyclopedias are beautifully designed, engaging and deeply informative, though, of course, the disadvantage of their approach is its cost; a complete DK encyclopedic library (including *The Ultimate Human Body*, *Eyewitness History of the World*, *World Reference Atlas* and the *Encyclopedias of Science, Nature, Space & the Universe*) costs approximately £240.00 as opposed to £49.99 for *Encarta 96*. Nevertheless, while aesthetic appeal is not enough to win their place in school or home libraries, these CD-ROMs do have another significant benefit. The single-subject CD-ROM is perhaps easier to manage for the cognitively-developing child, since there is a more obvious coherence to its structure. This structural coherence lends the reader/user a greater sense of control over their learning experience. Margaret Meek points out that:

> Most children discover the power of language long before they go to school. As it becomes part of their serious play they find that they can use words to control other people. . . . As they play on the boundaries of sense and nonsense they know that, to a significant extent, they are in charge.[31]

Power acquisition is, then, a central part of the learning process; if children do not feel linguistically empowered by a conversation or text they are likely to reject it. If a CD-ROM refuses user control, if its breadth is disorientating, then the child is likely to lose patience with it very quickly. While both general and one-subject encyclopedias can be poorly structured, and therefore disorientating, the general encyclopedia is more likely to be daunting to children finding their way in the world, because its boundaries are necessarily less clearly defined. Alternatively, a CD-ROM entitled, for example, *Endangered Wildlife* (GSP) sets certain parameters through its title alone, a certainty which is empowering to the user. Computer literacy involves the negotiation of a specialized language system which, if it is clearly signposted, children will adapt to with relative ease.

Naturally, not all single-subject CD-ROMs present themselves as encyclopedias; Flagtower's innovative titles are delivered in the form of documentaries, *Great Artists* (Attica & Marshall Cavendish) is a virtual museum, while *Where in the World is Carmen Sandiego?* is a geography lesson in the guise of a 'whodunit'. Notably ambitious is Dorling Kindersley's *Virtual Reality* series; each edition contributes another level to this virtual museum. Recently *V.R. Bird* (£29.99) and *V.R. Cat* (£29.99) have been joined by a dinosaur wing in the shape of the much celebrated *Dinosaur Hunter* (£29.99). However, the rapidity of technological advances has disadvantaged DK in this case; *Dinosaur Hunter* dates its older companion titles, thus diminishing their combined effect as a complete museum. A representative of DK describes *Dinosaur Hunter* as more 'gamey' than the other 'virtual' titles, reflecting the increasing tendency, in all areas of multimedia, to combine information with entertainment.

Evidently, multimedia allows lessons to be presented in increasingly ingenious ways, many of which will now be explored. The diversity of single-subject titles means that it is impossible to locate definitive 'market leaders' in line with general reference products. Consequently, several titles will be briefly discussed within each subject category, reflecting the varying approaches of different software publishers. Since the focus of this chapter is educational, in this section I have restricted coverage to subjects relevant to the classroom, though schoolchildren are just as likely to be interested (if not more so) in such titles as *Cinemania 97* (Microsoft: £49.99) or the *Ultimate Encyclopedia of Soccer* (Pearson New Media: £29.99). I have decided to concentrate on four core subjects, because it is impossible to cover all available topics; they are Geography, History, Science and the Arts.

Geography

The *Encarta 96 World Atlas* or DK's *World Reference Atlas* should both provide excellent introductions to any geography lesson. Geography, however, contains the two separate disciplines of human and physical geography; distinctions which these general titles do not always recognize. Human geography in particular benefits from multimedia hyperlinks in such encyclopedias, which allow speedy comparison of various world statistics. Physical geography, however, is less well served by atlases and, also, it has always been relatively difficult to represent in a teaching environment; a mountain cannot be contained in a classroom – or can it? Thanks to the virtual environments of multimedia, students can potentially move around physical landforms without leaving their seats. Field trips are not always possible, and though many children have been lucky enough to visit coastlines or hillsides, how many can say they have peered into the eye of a volcano? This is just the type of experience made possible by virtual environments. *Geodome Landforms* (featured below) requires development, but indicates that such experiences will soon be part of school experience. YITM also have an impressive list of extremely promising titles; *The Physical World* (£79.99) is an award-winning title for 11–16 year olds, including full teacher support material, while *Exploring Maps* (£59.99) encourages mapping skills in Key Stage 2 pupils.

While the above titles are primarily aimed at teachers and students in secondary education, there is also a range of geographical edutainment available for youngsters. For instance, Random House includes geography as one of the subjects introduced in its 'Jump Ahead' series; *Discovery Tree* (4–8 yrs) and their *Year 2* CD-ROM (6–7 yrs: £29.99) both introduce basic geographical concepts required by the National Curriculum. Alternatively, ABLAC's geographical adventure *Nigel's World* (6–12 yrs: £34.00) develops reading skills as children learn to recognize continents, countries, cultures and customs from over 40 maps and 90 colour photographs.

Featured Products

Title: *Where in the World is Carmen Sandiego?* and *Carmen Sandiego: Junior Detective Edition*

Publisher: Broderbund

RRP: £29.99 each

Age Range: 9+ and 5–9

Broderbund claim that they defined the term edutainment with the production of this title ten years ago. Its success is perhaps marked by the arrival of a cartoon (shown on Channel 4) inspired by the CD-ROM; it has also sold over 4 million copies worldwide. *Where in the World is Carmen Sandiego?* is a detective adventure based around the concept of an atlas; this edition also includes the printed reference atlas, *Hutchinson's*

Guide to the World. Carmen Sandiego heads an international crime ring (V.I.L.E.) which steals such world treasures as Mount Everest's South Face! The aim is to track down the villains, learning about various geographical locations en route. There are 60 countries to visit, and skills taught include world geography, world cultures, familiarity with maps and deductive reasoning. *Carmen Sandiego: Junior Detective Edition* is also available for younger children, teaching memory and matching skills, familiarity with maps and symbols, and regional and world geography. Both of these products have been localized for the UK.

Title: *My First Amazing World Explorer*

Publisher: Dorling Kindersley

RRP: £29.99

Age Range: ~5–8

Described as a 'CD-ROM Activity Pack', this title includes a poster, picture postcards, stickers, books and a jigsaw puzzle. Once all this has been digested, the CD-ROM itself contains plenty of screens to entertain and inform. The home screen is actually a beautifully illustrated child's bedroom, full of hot spots, which provides access to a world of animated adventure. The most powerful part of the bedroom is 'My Map of the World' which, once personal details have been entered on the on-screen passport, leads to more detailed maps of various places and snippets of basic information. However, the most engaging aspect of this product is its interactive playfulness; postcards can be sent back to the bedroom, stickers can be collected while travelling and the mug-shot chosen for the passport miraculously appears in a picture-frame on the bedroom wall. Once again, this DK product has received extensive critical commendation.

Title: *Exploring Earth Science*

Publisher: Attica Cybernetics

RRP: £99.99

Age Range: ~11+

The advertisements for *Exploring Earth Science* declare that it 'provides support material for the three main subject areas of Geology, Satellites and Space Science within the National Curriculum'.[32] It is then, rather disconcerting to read in the user manual that it, 'is a Multimedia CD-ROM designed to support the teaching of Earth Science in US Secondary schools'.[33] This leads me to question the *extent* to which it supports the UK curriculum, if indeed it is not specifically designed to meet the needs of British students. The CD-ROM itself resembles a poorly-designed encyclopedia, making no use of the visual possibilities described by Dorling Kindersley above (see p.164); the interface is unattractive and often difficult to move around. It is divided into the three main subject areas of Earth, Space and Satellite, which are rather clumsily linked. The text which accompanies the numerous photographs and animations is particularly deficient; it generally lacks substance, is poorly presented and is often grammatically unsound. For example, the text accompanying a picture of mud on a beach (uninspiring in itself) reads as follows: 'mud forms mudstone.' This is hardly a stimulating or informative commentary. The Star Atlas, an interesting feature of this product, 'enables a study of the sky with simulated views from anywhere on Earth at any time over the last two or three thousand years'.[34] However, its presentation is dated and frenetic, making the identification of specific stars difficult. A 'school' version of this product is also available, including project folders for classwork.

Title: *Geodome Landforms*

Publisher: Attica Cybernetics and BBC Education

RRP: £39.99

Age Range: ~11+

The package contains both a clear user guide and an extremely helpful booklet of teacher's notes; its list of CD-ROM contents is particularly useful for class preparation. This is an exquisitely-presented product, covering four subjects: rivers, earthquakes, coasts and volcanoes. These are housed separately in one of the four 'domes' of the title; these futuristic virtual rooms do provide a stimulating environment for learning, but they are really no more than an excuse for the impressive title of this package. Each room contains a Gallery Guide, 3–D Model, Hazard Zone, Slide Projector, Video Screen and Quiz. The Gallery Guide contains a database on the relevant subject and is presented in the style of an electronic encyclopedia. Some articles have further information in the form of photographs, animations, issues (documentary-style reports from the BBC archives) and newsflashes (newsclips from BBC archives). An effective teaching tool is the 'Drag and Drop' screens which are linked to some photographs; the object is to locate specific geographical features using labels at the bottom of the screen. However, while all of these visual teaching aids are excellent, there are too few of them. The quiz section of each dome is another excellent feature of this product; beneficially, its difficulty levels and time limits are variable, allowing for student progression. Unfortunately, while the 3D-Model looks very impressive it actually contains very little information and can only be moved in two directions. Similarly, the Hazard Zone looks promising, and indeed is an excellent idea, but it is little more than a gimmick; pupils must analyse various risk factors in a hazardous situation and predict outcomes, which is fine until it becomes clear that there is only one situation per subject. *Geodome Landforms* has great potential, it is just a pity that it lacks the depth to match its polished surface.

Title: *The Times Perspectives: Planet Earth*

Publisher: News Multimedia

RRP: £39.99

Age Range: ~11+

This package is a delight to use from installation onwards; automatic installation makes this process as simple as switching on a light. The CD-ROM is also sleekly packaged in

Information playgrounds   169

a wallet-style holder which incorporates an excellent user guide. *Planet Earth* presents the evolving story of environmental awareness as reported by *The Times* newspaper. It is an archive of articles on a common theme, supported by photographs and illustrations which provide a consistently engaging backdrop to the text. The highlight of this package, however, is in the simplicity of its design. The material is all presented on a Contents Grid which is divided into eight rows (one for each subject: air, land, water, animals, people, energy, responses and the future) and seven columns (one for each time period: 1831–1971, 1972–75, 1976–79, 1980–83, 1984–87, 1988–91, 1992–95). The distribution of articles and photographs according to subject and year is represented by yellow and red dots strewn over the grid. Movement around the grid is simple; once a subject/period has been chosen, articles can be selected through scrolling list windows which drop onto the various subject screens and are filled with photographs and stimulating headlines. There are several useful aspects for the avid researcher: specific searches can be carried out via the keywords index, a notepad is provided for personal comments, and a backtracking system shows headlines of articles read and a scrapbook of the pictures viewed. A newspaper archive could easily be dull and unattractive; however, if anything will encourage the use of newspapers as a learning/teaching resource it is *Planet Earth*; this is multimedia at its most sophisticated.

History

Historical CD-ROMs bear witness to some of the most significant innovations extant in multimedia. The majority of available CD-ROMs detail modern history, which is perhaps a result of multimedia's effective use of the various forms of communication developed this century; many utilize film, video or newspaper archives and digitized sound. Flagtower have successfully pioneered the documentary-style CD-ROM, integrating encyclopedic information with the moving image; their interactive documentaries include *World War I* (£29.99), *World War II* (£29.99), *Great Generals* (£29.99), *The Space Race* (£29.99) and *A History of Medicine* (£39.99). Newspapers are perhaps the most precise chroniclers of our times (if not the most impartial), which means that *The Times Perspectives* series serves this area particularly well; current titles include *Women's Rights*, *World War I* and *World War II* (of course, *Planet Earth* could also be regarded as a historical title), and forthcoming are: *The Cold War* and *The Industrial Revolution* (all titles currently cost £39.99). News Multimedia state that:

> Each of the first four titles which have been designed for home reference, secondary schools and further education offer new insights into their subjects through the use of original newspaper articles, features, letters, leading articles, augmented by photographs and illustrations.[35]

War is perhaps the most common of all the historical subjects represented on CD-ROM, World War II being the most ubiquitous of human dramas depicted by multimedia. This conceivably reflects the interests of older generations worldwide, whose lives have been personally touched by this war; though, of course, the popularity of this subject could also be attributed to its centrality in the

National Curriculum. Although a large proportion of this market is directed at secondary schools or older enthusiasts, there are several titles suitable for younger children. Dorling Kindersley's *Eyewitness History of the World* is a highly respected and attractive chronicle of history for children and adults alike, while *How Would You Survive?* (Grolier Kids) and *Stowaway* (Dorling Kindersley) are specifically child-centred; the latter provides a unique insight into the workings of an eighteenth-century warship through the magnificent cross-sections illustrated by Stephen Biesty.

Featured products

Title: *How Would You Survive?*

Publisher: Grolier Interactive

RRP: £40.00

Age Range: ~5–11

This is a highly individual multimedia adventure which enters the worlds of the Ancient Egyptians, Vikings and Aztecs. This package encourages children to take an empathetic view of history as they explore the various civilizations through 140 movies, multimedia maps, sound effects and animations. Each world has its own tour guide, a child who provides help whenever it is required. Hand-drawn, scrolling panoramas are lavishly illustrated and packed with hot spots which lead to articles and animations on various subjects, ranging from birth to death. There are also useful hyperlinks between the three lands, allowing the comparison of living conditions or burial practices; for example, Egyptian mummification can be compared with Viking long-boat burials, though be prepared for some ghoulish sound-effects here! Ultimately, there is a game entitled 'Have you Survived?', in which the player can become a pharaoh, king or chief when enough knowledge has been accumulated. A must for all young explorers of the past; though teachers and parents will thoroughly enjoy it too.

Title: *The Journey of Thomas Blue Eagle*

Publisher: YITM

RRP: £29.99

Age Range: ~8+

This has won several awards, including the 1995 EMMA for best visuals; indeed its packaging is sleek and the CD-ROM is atmospherically illustrated. The atmosphere captured is that of a Lakota teepee which provides the setting for a semi-fictional history of this buffalo-hunting tribe. Thomas Blue Eagle is a Lakota boy whose story is told through five different features: the Ledgerbook (a pictorial history of the tribe), the Hide Painter (an interactive painting tool), the Picto Writer (a creative writing/drawing tool), the Winter Count (Chief Iron Arm's chronicle of tribal history from 1865–1880, juxtaposed with US newspapers for each year) and photographs and commentary from the

Carlisle School (a US government school attended by Blue Eagle.) YITM state that this disc was: 'inspired by the ledger drawings of Nineteenth Century Plains Indians and developed with the help of the Lakota';[36] this suggests a certain degree of historical accuracy. The helpful (printed) user guide explains the potential use in schools for this disc; possible curriculum applications range across the disciplines of history, art and design and creative writing. Whatever the application though, *The Journey of Thomas Blue Eagle* is a delight to use and is sure to inspire teachers, parents and children alike.

Title: *The Times Perspectives: Women's Rights*

Publisher: News Multimedia

RRP: £39.99

Age Range: ~11+

The overall feel of this title is similar to *Planet Earth*; multimedia is used to provide a seamless journey through history. However, News Multimedia are not short of creative imagination, for *Women's Rights* has a fresh layout and is every bit as innovative as its stable-mate. *Women's Rights* is divided into three primary compartments (Overview, Issues and Timeline), which are accessed through the Options screen. 'Overview' provides a detailed introduction to various aspects of the fight for women's rights. An audio-visual presentation opens this section which itself is divided into three parts, each presented in a unique manner. 'Women's rights and human rights' is a short essay; 'Equality' is a series of pictures linked to spoken quotations, voicing the opinions of women worldwide as their experiences are compared; 'Turning the Tide' is an interactive model, using dress codes to reflect the changes experienced by women in each decade of this century. 'Issues' contains the main body of articles on this disc; issues are listed in bold type on a home screen and are accessed by a simple click of the mouse; they cover the workplace, women's lib, motherhood, war and peace, family, the vote, image, the law, power, education and the body. Each issue is represented by a series of topics, depicted through articles and photographs which can be placed in the on-screen scrapbook. 'Timeline' has screens holding key headlines, photographs and articles for each decade since 1850; from 1990 each year has its own screen. All three sections can be accessed via the tools window in the bottom-right corner of the screen, as can options such as quit and print. *Women's Rights* maintains user-interest through its imaginative presentation of articles, which portray an often moving chronicle of women's on-going struggle to make a place for themselves in the modern world.

Title: *World War II*

Publisher: Flagtower

RRP: £49.99

Age Range: ~11+

World War II is one in the series of remarkable interactive documentaries from Flagtower. The program is made up of various dramatic narratives using sound, pictures, video, music and animation; many of the film sequences constitute rare footage from this period. There is also a selection of 'text and graphic supplementary screens', providing information in the following areas: air, land, sea, art and propaganda, broadcast, eyewitness, medical, profile, units, technology, tactics and strategy and the home front. The story of World War II can be watched in all of the disc's six hour glory, or gradually through six shorter commentaries labelled 'Theatres of War', which are: Western Europe, The Pacific, The Mediterranean, Eastern Europe, The Atlantic and Asia. There is also a section entitled 'Themes', a selection of extracts from an interview with Norman Stone, Professor of Modern History at Oxford University. It is remarkably easy to move around the various documentaries; each narrative can be paused and previous screens can be accessed by clicking on the appropriate icon. The index provides five different ways of searching for information, through Key Events, People, A–Z, Weapons & Equipment and Contents, which makes this a flexible and effective research tool as well as an entertaining, informative and occasionally harrowing journey through World War II.

Title: *Images of War*

Publisher: Marshall Cavendish

RRP: £39.99

Age Range: ~11+

The title of this CD-ROM is misleading as it actually only deals with World War II; its subheading 'the real story of World War II' should be given more prominence. Nevertheless, this is an excellent title, produced in conjunction with the Imperial War Museum. It contains 35 battle documentaries, 30 minutes of video, over 1 000 pictures, 100 eyewitness accounts, map sequences of battles, a Dossiers section for the collection of project material (this has obviously been designed for schoolchildren and, as such, is suitably user-friendly) and a Compare and Contrast section for military hardware and key people (this section is also impressive, though perhaps has not been used to its full potential; it would be useful if all entries could be compared in this way, rather than the few pre-selected items). However, this is compensated for to some extent by the timelines around which most of the information is stored; the student is given a clear picture of consecutive campaigns being fought on each continent. Though perhaps not as sleek as Flagtower's production, *Images of War* is a worthy competitor, especially notable for its recognition of the schoolchild's needs.

Title: *Makers of the Twentieth Century*

Publisher: News Multimedia

RRP: £44.99

Age Range: 10+

One of the most original pieces of software available and probably the most exciting of the extant introductions to history. *Makers of the Twentieth Century* is based on a series in the *Sunday Times Magazine* which profiled 1 000 key personalities of modern times, although the selection has been narrowed down to 200 for the CD, allowing for an increase in depth. Each profile contains introductory biographies, articles from various papers (from *The Sun* to *The Times*), pictures, sound recordings, interesting facts (actually 'flying facts' which whiz across the screen waiting to be caught) and sometimes film clips. However, the most exciting aspects of this CD-ROM are the six worlds in which the profiles are housed (mind, power, body, senses, discovery and design); each has its own unique design and is fronted by an interactive home screen (though home screen is hardly an adequate description for the three-dimensional space of the Mind World, where the great thinkers and writers of our time lurk in a purple panorama). Probably the most fun is the Design World, where animations of various inventions (with clues to the inventors behind them) spring from the walls in the fashion of a surreal daydream. The biographies can also be accessed through more conventional indexes; in fact there are seven search methods in all, including a timeline and A–Z. Moving from screen to screen is rather slow, though the producers have compensated by flashing quotes and facts onto the screen while the CD reaches for its data. *Makers of the Twentieth Century* does not claim to be a comprehensive view of modern times; as its editors observe, this would be an impossible aim, for 'No single work could say everything there is to say about the life of the century.'[37] Its rich and diverse atmosphere, however, goes a long way in reflecting the multifarious changes witnessed and caused by the people of this century. The ingenuity of design and its inherent playfulness will attract a young audience; although it is relatively advanced linguistically, the adventurous audio-visual component potentially opens up this title to children slightly younger than the suggested ten years.

Science

Some of the most ambitious experiments in multimedia are taking place in the scientific field; its simulated environments are able to reproduce complex processes which would take years to observe in the natural world, or might even be invisible to the naked eye. Furthermore, complicated scientific theories have recently become more accessible to the layperson due to the publication of numerous 'popular science' titles. Indeed, such is their popularity that such books as Gleick's *Chaos* have become best sellers. The fractals it made famous adorn album covers and the bedroom walls of teenagers; they are no longer relegated to geometry textbooks. More significantly, though, there are numerous sophisticated programs which render these stunning geometric patterns with apparent simplicity; a five-year-old could produce a fractal if gently steered in the right direction. An exciting project, due for release in December 1996, combines the talents of Notting Hill (software designers) and Richard Dawkins, author of such successful titles as *The Selfish Gene* and *The Blind Watchmaker*. This CD, *The Evolution of Life* (£39.95), is based on the latter book and deals with Dawkins' theories concerning natural selection, creating various 'semi-virtual', interactive environments. Most exciting however, is the inclusion of Notting Hill's 'evolution' program, *Cybertation*, which actually selects and breeds 3-D-rendered creatures on the screen; the move has been made from Artificial Intelligence to Artificial Life. Less sophisticated examples of Artificial Life can be found in the increasingly popular *Catz* (Mindscape: £14.99) and *Dogz* (Mindscape: £14.00) titles, currently topping the CD-ROM charts; this software allows a virtual pet to live and grow on the hard disc and screen of a PC. 'Cute-factor' aside, however, the educational potential of these programs is vast; for example, children will be able to see Darwin's theory of evolution at work, literally bringing *The Origin of the Species* to life.

While the potential for future scientific exploration is obviously great, existing titles also offer children varied and stimulating avenues into the scientific world. Of course, 'science' denotes a massive subject area and includes several diverse disciplines. Dorling Kindersley's *Eyewitness Encyclopedia of Science* 2.0 (£39.99) involves the four main areas, splitting coverage between physics, chemistry, maths and life sciences. The new edition contains 100 extra articles, the Who's Who section introduces 150 new scientists, and there are several new interactive features and adjustable 3-D models. The *Hutchinson Science Library* (Helicon: £39.99) offers a visually less impressive alternative to GCSE students.

Of course, titles which cover this much ground lack depth by comparison with the scientific software concentrating on specific areas. Biology, or life science, is particularly well presented through the numerous successful discs detailing the human body. One of the most popular (and most terrifying if, like me, you have a phobia of the heart-beat which introduces it) is DK's *The Ultimate Human Body* 2.0 (£39.99), though *A.D.A.M, The Inside Story* (Random House: £29.99) and *BodyWorks 5.0* (Softkey: £46.95) are also highly praised. Perhaps the plethora of nature titles is an attempt to win girls over to the idea of using electronic reference; publishers certainly have more hope of succeeding here than with the multimedia dollies mentioned earlier. In the Roehampton Survey, statistics revealed that girls were less likely than boys to use CD-ROMs, while nominating animals/nature as favourite subject matter (boys tended towards more technical subjects).[38] Of course, this market trend also reflects an escalating concern for the environment; contemporary children are particularly sensitive to problems that, unfortunately, they have inherited from careless parents/ancestors. It is in this area that DK can perhaps claim a victory over Microsoft; their *Eyewitness Encyclopedia of Nature* (£39.99) is a more graceful treatment of natural history than the *Exploropedia World of Nature* (£29.99) and generally rates more highly with critics. *Exploropedia*, however, is more child-centred, and its froggy guide might hold more appeal for the young nature lover. News Multimedia's *Planet Earth* would also sit comfortably in this category; its section on animals provides a stimulating though disturbing account of man's relationship with the animal kingdom. Other highly-praised reference titles involving natural or environmental issues are *Devil's Canyon* (News Multimedia: £29.95), *Wide World of Animals* (Electronic Arts: £39.99) and *Animal Safari* (Marshall Cavendish: £29.99). Alternatively, *Terratopia* (Funsoft: £29.99) is an interactive adventure for 8–12-year-olds, structured around environmental issues.

Physics is presented in a fun way for children in HarperCollins' *The Cartoon Guide to Physics* (£39.99), though its frenetic pace and irritating on-screen guide, Lucy, let it down to some extent. There are also numerous products on the subject of space, astronomy and the planets, aimed at both adult enthusiasts and schoolchildren; again, DK have produced one of the leading titles in *Eyewitness Encyclopedia of Space & The Universe* (£39.99). Science and maths are also core subjects of the edutainment market, featuring prominently in the *Funschool 6* series recently released by Europress (£29.99 each). Children from 4 through to 11 are served by this beautifully animated series, which is produced in conjunction with educational consultants to satisfy elements of the National Curriculum (though I should point out that my computer crashed out of these programs several times and that the lack of a visible 'quit' icon left me with no escape from one of the *Fairyland* games). Europress also produce a *Genius Range* which, though cheap at £9.99 per disc, are unimaginative, dull and repetitive. *Peter Rabbit's Number Garden* (Mindscape: £29.99) provides a creative slant to the field of mathematics, as children are rewarded for numeric dexterity with 'a field of their own' in which to plant selected vegetation. Though such discs are not reference titles, even of the *Discovery Tree's* innovative kind, they 'pave the way' for the reference products intended mostly for slightly older audiences. For this reason, *Maths Workshop* and *Essential Science* merit mention among the featured products below.

Featured products

Title: *Essential Science*

Publisher: Ten out of Ten Educational Systems

RRP: £14.99

Age Range: 5–12

The publishers of *Essential Science* claim to produce award-winning software; this sounds impressive until it becomes apparent that this award was bestowed in 1994, for software produced in 1993. A sticker on the box also claims that the title is linked to the National Curriculum, though there is no suggestion that schools, teaching authorities or exam boards have been consulted in its production. *Essential Science* is comprised of six games which are supposed to provide scientific lessons on: heat and light; solids, liquids and gases; classification; magnetism and electricity; plants and animals; material changes; forces; measuring instruments; the environment and the weather. This is an impressive list, implying that this product provides astounding value for money and that it is perhaps a reference text in disguise; an implication which has no foundation in reality. The games make use of outdated graphics and, more significantly, are really no more than uninspired matching games; they are neither fun nor stimulating. For example, the 'Electromagnet' does not expound upon magnetism; instead, a magnet is the backdrop for a multiple-choice question and answer game. The closest *Essential Science* comes to being scientific is with the questions asked on some of the higher levels; for example: 'Which of the following can be separated by filtration?', where options given are, 'coffee & water', 'sand & water', 'milk & water' and 'sugar & water'. Of course, no explanation is provided as to *why* the answer is 'sand & water'; the child needs recourse to a *proper* science lesson for such explanations, rendering this product entirely ineffectual.

Title: *Maths Workshop*

Publisher: Broderbund

RRP: £30.00

Age Range: 6–10

This compulsive title falls firmly into the realm of edutainment; children are taught mathematical skills while playing really humorous, colourful and amusing games. This package contains an excellent user's guide, equipping parents with a detailed breakdown of which skills are being developed. Poly Gonzales, the daughter of a rocket scientist and a calculus professor, guides children through the six games, supplying help whenever it is required; these games include Bowling for Numbers (a personal favourite, featuring Gus the bowling gorilla), Hidden Picture Puzzles and Rhythm Shop. These games each have a unique design and develop such skills as whole number operations, estimation, spatial sense and logical reasoning. Even the most reluctant mathematicians will be fascinated by *Maths Workshop*.

Title: *David Bellamy's Endangered Wildlife*

Publisher: GSP

RRP: £19.95

Age Range: 8+

David Bellamy fans beware! The hirsute botanist does no more than give his name to the title (and his face to the box). This is not the most polished of products, a lack of sophistication which might discourage older audiences, though it does succeed in its refreshingly cheerful presentation of bestial facts. This program is divided into two sections: the Discovery Tour and the Discovery Game. The Discovery Tour travels the world's continents in pursuit of endangered species. Once an animal has been selected, information is provided on habitat, food, lifestyle and threats; most entries are also accompanied by sounds, photographs and video clips. This section is full of facts, but is dull in comparison to the Discovery Game, which is really central to the success of this title. The object of this game is to save endangered species from extinction by solving a series of puzzles; they include crosswords, word-searches, matching games and more. Each time a game is successfully completed children are rewarded with a piece of information about the animal; this is a fun method of teaching a serious message – it will keep children occupied for hours. However, the ultimate praise for this product comes from eight-year-old Katie Macpherson, who sent the following review to *The Weekend Times*:

> My favourite part is the crossword. If you get it right a picture appears underneath.... Some of the video clips are so good that you would think there was a real animal in front of you. You don't need to be a genius to play this game, and even the adults will want to play – but only let them once you've gone to bed.... This game is excellent for anyone, like me, who is mad on animals.[39]

Title: *The New Encyclopedia of the Living World*

Publisher: Funsoft & Z Multi Media

RRP: £12.99

Age Range: ~8+

The packaging declares that this title is part of 'The Complete Multi Media Collection', though detailed examination reveals that it does nothing to deserve its multimedia tag; the interface and articles are lifeless, which is rather ironic considering its title. The encyclopedia is divided into five sections: *Living World* (a spoken introduction accompanied by photographs of unidentified creatures); *Taxonomy* (another verbal lesson, accompanied by a few photographs and Latinate tables, this time on the classification of plants and animals); *Encyclopedia* (a scant amount of text is accompanied by the occasional photo, video clip or soundtrack); *Biologists* (a series of short biographical texts without pictures); *Origin of the Species* (reams of poorly-presented text and, again, not illustrated). None of these sections is linked to the rest; there are no hyperlinks or hot spots/words and the scope for interaction is non-existent. The verbal commentaries, while informative, cannot be paused or controlled in any manner, which makes them virtually useless as a teaching aid. Even at £12.99 this product is expensive – do not waste your money on it.

Title: *Interactive Periodic Table*

Publisher: Attica Cybernetics

RRP: £24.99

Age Range: ~13+

I must confess to a certain bias towards this title, for the periodic table has always held a mysterious fascination for me, and Attica's interactive version is packed full of periodic delights. A clear and concise user guide is provided, which is necessary for some of the more complex options on this disc. The on-screen 'Tutorial' provides an historical overview of the periodic table and is divided into the following sections: Introduction (an audio-visual presentation); The Elements (Boyle's Dozen, The First Thirty and The New Elements); and The Periodic Table (Mendeleyev's Ideas, Periods & Groups and Periodic Trends), which includes an entertaining rendition of Tom Lehrer's song 'The Elements'. Central to the program is the Periodic Table Screen, providing access to information on each element and a series of research options. Element Information Screens provide the following data for every element: Historical background, Physical, Atomic and Chemical properties and Resources; this information is accompanied by photographs, tables and mobile 3-D models. The Periodic Table itself can be used to display properties according to requirement, while the chosen properties of individual elements, groups and periods can be selected for comparison on a range of graphs; this is the most practical aspect of the disc, providing a flexible approach to the comparative investigation of elements. Potentially, this is an excellent teaching aid, though there are a few problems: it is perhaps a little dry in its presentation of facts, the labelling on graphs is sometimes unclear, and there is a bug in the provision of the element's 'year of discovery' (1987 appears as

1,987.00). Nevertheless, the *Interactive Periodic Table* is an enjoyable package for those with a penchant for chemical investigations.

The Arts

The arts and computer technology do not complement each other in such obvious ways as science and multimedia, but the possibilities are equally exciting. Literature, music and art are all represented through multimedia in different ways, particularly exploiting the audio-visual aspects of this electronic environment. The majesty of Shakespearean drama is never fully conveyed through textual examination; theatrical performance is the optimum medium for this, though live productions are not always available as a text is being studied. Video/film screenings can be a solution, but there is now another answer; *Romeo and Juliet* (HarperCollins & BBC: £40.00) offers an entire audio-recording of the play, detailed background notes and nine BBC video-clips. Alternatively, *Karaoke Macbeth* (Beaufort Publications: £50.00) satisfies thespian yearnings, inviting users to act out their favourite *Macbeth* characters. Predominantly reference-based titles are also available: *The Jack Kerouac Romnibus* (Beaufort Publications: £49.99) includes archival photographs and text in addition to the complete text of *The Dharma Bums*, while a powerful search function makes *William Shakespeare* (Andromeda Interactive: £35.00), containing his complete works, a useful source for research. The possibilities for encyclopedic works are clear, but although Microsoft include *The Bloomsbury Treasury of Quotations* in their newly localized *Bookshelf* (£49.99), as yet there is a lack of such comprehensive literary guides as *The Cambridge Guide to English Literature*. Classical music is increasingly well served by the hardware accompanying computers; highly-developed sound cards and speakers enhance most multimedia experiences, though they have particular advantages in relation to musically-oriented discs. Attica's *Orchestra* (£39.99) takes a symphonic journey through Simon Rattle's world via a series of interviews, animations, musical themes and an audio-visual performance of Britten's *The Young Person's Guide to the Orchestra*. A more practical and comprehensive, albeit less inspiring, title is also produced by Attica in the form of *The Attica Guide to Classical Music* (£24.99); it contains 62 biographies of composers, descriptions of 200 pieces of audio-accompanied music, and a timeline dating back to 1659. For younger enthusiasts, *Beethoven Lives Upstairs* (BMG: £29.99) makes an animated inspection of Beethoven's living quarters, providing games, video clips and an art gallery on the way round. A growing number of art galleries are also appearing on CD-ROM, a recent addition to which is Macmillan's *The Mystery of Magritte* (£39.99) which *CD-ROM Today* describes as 'visually breathtaking'.[40] This might well appeal to parents and children who have enjoyed Anthony Browne's picture books; much of his work is inspired by Magritte, in particular *Through the Magic Mirror* (1976). Multimedia has long been used by London's National Gallery; its Micro Gallery allows visitors to pinpoint pictures, listen to individual analyses and take one of four guided tours. Two discs are also produced in conjunction with the National Gallery: Microsoft's *Art Gallery* (£39.99) and Attica's *Great Artists* (designed for educational purposes in schools: £39.99). Attica have also produced a title in conjunction with the Tate Gallery, called *Investigating Twentieth Century Art* (£116.32), which includes teacher's notes. An intriguing twist in the tail of this marriage between art and technology is that technology is becoming recognised as an art-form in itself, as witnessed by Jan Howells:

> Technology has spawned a new school of artists. William Latham, for example, went from fine art to an IBM independent research fellowship and is now renowned for his Organic Art CD-Rom.... Latham's desire to mate computers with art was simple. 'Modern art just wasn't going anywhere – it was covering the same old ground and had got itself in a rut,' he says.... Dr Rachel Armstrong, producer for OCC multimedia, has worked with a number of artists merging their skills with technology.... 'Technology empowers,' she says. 'It does not replace the artist; it attaches different techniques and enhances what they do.'[41]

Featured products

Title: *Great Artists*

Publisher: Attica Cybernetics & Marshal Cavendish

RRP: £19.99

Age Range: ~8+

Great Artists scrutinizes 40 celebrated paintings from the National Gallery, such as Botticelli's *Venus and Mars* and Van Gogh's *Sunflowers*, making them particularly accessible to a young audience. The disc is structured around these paintings, allowing in-depth study of the canvas, while supplementary information on the artists and their social and historical contexts is also provided. Although, there are only 40 primary paintings (allowing detailed examination) there are an additional 1 960 paintings illustrating the various textual commentaries. The interface is elegantly rendered, harmonizing with its subject matter, and each section is clearly introduced and labelled, while hyperlinks facilitate mobility around the disc. The home screen depicts an artist's studio, which provides entry to each of the available options. 'Artists' leads to a scrolling series of 40 artist portraits (or silhouettes where no portrait is available). Once an artist has been selected, details of life history, key paintings, studio practices, fellow artists and social background are provided through textual, pictorial and sometimes spoken commentary. 'Paintings' leads to a scrolling tableau of 40 paintings which can be selected for further information and examination. 'Topics' is divided into three sections (Themes, Materials and Methods), providing a basic art-history lesson on such topics as the symbolic relevance of death, the use of perspective and the importance of the artist's chosen media. The art atlas contains ten historical maps of Europe (dating from 1250–1910), detailing places of artistic significance during ten different time periods; commentaries are supplied for each area of importance. The timeline divides the history of art into ten periods, supplying information on technology, music, famous people, literature, world events, artists, paintings and fashion. Finally, the workshop allows the disfiguring of each masterpiece; it enables the user to crop, deface or discolour paintings at will (the purpose of these options is not always clear – perhaps we are intended to purge ourselves of the vandal within). This disc has a depth far beyond the canvas of its 40 chosen paintings, making up for necessary absences; a must for art-lovers everywhere.

Title: *The Magical Music Box: Swan Lake*

Publisher: Marshall Cavendish

RRP: £29.99

Age Range: ~6+

The Magical Music Box comes complete with a descant recorder which, parents will be delighted to hear, can actually be used in 'the rehearsal studio'. This CD is made up of three virtual environments: the theatre, the composer's room and the rehearsal room, of which the latter is the most exciting. The theatre houses an animated version of *Swan Lake* (reminiscent of the animated Shakespeare television series) which can be watched either Act by Act or in its entirety. I must confess to disappointment here; I had expected a ballet performance (perhaps shown through video clips) since, after all, *Swan Lake* is a ballet, but the emphasis of this disc is on music rather than dance. However, this gripe is forgotten on entrance to the vibrant virtual environment of the rehearsal studio, where students are introduced to various instruments and styles of music (a glossary of musical terms is also provided to help decipher textual commentaries). More ingeniously, however, it provides an interactive fingering chart for recorder students and teaches them to play along to an extract from *Swan Lake* – piano accompaniment is even provided. Finally, the composer's room provides historical information on the composer and his work which, while interesting, lacks the depth necessary to involve older children for long. Information is also provided on three other composers, Bizet, Rimsky-Korsakov and Grieg, though no explanation is given for their inclusion over the exclusion of others. This is a highly enjoyable title and, even though it is a little inadequate in places, I did not want to leave *The Magical Music Box* once I had entered.

Which, where and how?: A basic guide to purchasing CD-ROMs

Since the multimedia market advances with such rapidity, frequently-updated specialist journals are probably the best indicators of market trends; they provide professional and mostly objective information on what is available and how different products compare. Alternative sources of help are also available to parents and teachers, and some of them are outlined below. However, the final decision as to which products to buy must ultimately rest with the individual; a decision which need not be stress-laden or overly bank-breaking, if certain ground rules are followed. Consideration of the following points should result in a fairly painless purchasing process:

- **Specification:** Ensure that the product you have bought is of the correct

specification for your system; boxes are usually labelled with minimum requirements.
- **Price watch:** Always shop around for the product you've decided on; the RRP only serves as a pointer as to what you should be paying.
- **Mail-Order:** Mail-Order should certainly be considered, as mail-order companies usually offer extremely competitive prices and frequently charge less than high-street shops; listings can be found in most PC or software magazines. It's worth checking all listings each time you make a purchase, as the same company may be cheap in one area and expensive in another.

Selected Mail-Order Companies

CD Concepts	0181 993 7117
CD-Direct	0800 317 864
CD-ROM Systems	0171 352 2127
Gameplay	0113 234 0444
Heaven Software	0143 816411
Microworld	01425 610699
Multimax	01652 651651
Ridgeway	01844 342411
Simply Sales	0181 498 2100
Software First	01268 531222
Software Warehouse	01675 466467
Watford Electronics	01582 745555

- **Retail:** Many people still favour the high street as the product is immediately accessible. The problem is that limited shelf-space means that you may not be able to find the title you want; again, shop around and watch out for special offers. CD-ROMs are widely available now in book stores, record shops, electrical retailers and more; my recommended software retailer is Electronics Boutique, since they have an excellent range of stock and a ten-day returns policy.
- **Returns:** It is extremely rare to find shops with 'customer-friendly' returns policies; most will only accept faulty software, with no provision for unsuitable or disliked goods. However, Waterstones and HMV will exchange a credit note for unwanted goods, while Electronics Boutique will give a refund provided the product is returned within ten days.
- **VAT:** Ensure that quoted prices are inclusive of VAT; many companies craftily exclude this from their price lists, giving a false impression to the consumer.

182   A Guide to Children's Reference Books

- **Freebies:** Buying PCs or subscribing to magazines and clubs often involves a selection of free software. For example *CD-ROM Today* is currently offering one of the following titles to all subscribers: *Flight Unlimited* (Virgin), *Monty Python & the Quest for the Holy Grail* (7th Level), *Eyewitness Encyclopedia of Space & the Universe* and *My Very First Incredible Amazing World Explorer* (Dorling Kindersley). It is also worth considering that PCs are often sold with 'bundles' of free software.
- **Magazines:** An invaluable indication of all that is good and bad in the world of multimedia can be found in specialist journals; it pays to research titles prior to buying them. There are many PC/software magazines on the market, all of which review software as it is released. However, some perform this service better than others; some are extremely technical, while others are games-oriented. The following titles are recommended because they offer lucid, informed advice and frequently discuss children's titles and educational issues.

Recommended journals

CD-ROM Today
The best multimedia magazine on the market; it is visually inviting with clearly-written, enlightening articles and reviews on reference, information, education, and games. It contains an excellent buyer's guide and a comparative disc directory. Its cover disc generally has excellent demos of selected new releases.
Monthly
☎ For subscriptions phone: 01225 822511
Price: £4.99

Parents & Computers
A relatively new title which provides 'a guide to education for 3–11 year olds'. This is packed with excellent articles on family, school and educational matters. It also reviews numerous child-centred titles. It does not have a cover disc, but this is reflected in its low price.
Tri-Monthly
☎ For subscriptions phone: 0151 3571275
Price: £2.25

- **PIN:** The Parents Information Network offers advice to parents who want to introduce children to the world of multimedia. PIN costs £20.00 to join and can be contacted for further information on: 0181 248 4666. They also publish the following titles: *Computers in the Home: What Parents Want* and *Parent's Guide to Computers Supporting Homework*.
- **RomRats:** The RomRats Club is an interactive guide to software, intended for children aged 3–12. The £19.95 membership buys three CDs a year and monthly newsletters. (Phone: 0990 143053)
- *Kid's Kit*: This is a multimedia starter kit for children, produced by Sierra

Edutainment (01734 303322), and costs £45.00. There are two kits available: the blue kit is for 4–7-year-olds and includes *Alphabet Blocks*, *Uncle Archibald* and *Mother Goose*; the red kit is for 8–12-year-olds and includes *ADI*, *Incredible Toons* and *Woodruff*.

- **Libraries:** The Ramesis project has initiated a lending scheme in selected libraries, allowing users to borrow from their range of CD-ROMs. (Phone: 01274 737376)
- **Books:** Usborne publish a series called 'Computer Guides', designed to introduce children to the world of computer technology. Also, Dorling Kindersley have produced an excellent illustrated guide to multimedia called *Multimedia: The Complete Guide* (£19.99).
- **Internet:** Information can be downloaded from an almost infinite number of sources; a selection of useful addresses follows:

Dinosaurs	http://www.dinosauria.com
Dorling Kindersley	http://www.dk.com
Dr Seuss	http://www.seussville.com
Electronic Telegraph	http://www.telegraph.co.uk
Europress	http://www.europress.co.uk
Flagtower	http://www.flagtower.com
Guardian Newspaper	http://www.guardian.co.uk
Kids Only	http://www.access.victoria.bc.ca/kidsonly.html
Microsoft	http://www.microsoft.com
Natural History Museum	http://www.nhm.ac.uk
News Multimedia	http://www.newsmultimedia.co.uk
Oxford University Press	http://www.oup.co.uk
Parents Place	http://www.parentsplace.com
Times Newspaper	http://www.the-times.co.uk
Yahooligans: Web Site for Kids	http://www.yahooligans.com

Glossary of technical jargon

Bundle: This is a collective term for different software titles sold together; it can refer either to separate titles included with a hardware purchase, or to various titles grouped together on one CD-ROM.

CD-ROM: An acronym for Compact Disc Read-Only Memory: a data storage medium capable of holding vast amounts of information (approximately 600 Megabytes of data).

Database: A collection of related pieces of data stored in a logical structure; its design enables data to be written to it or read from it rapidly.

Edutainment: Education and entertainment combined on a multimedia CD-ROM.

Hardware: The physical components of a computer such as the monitor, printer or modem; the 'grey boxes' that sit on your desk.

Home Page: The initial page for locations on the Internet is known as the site's home page.

Home Screen: The main menu or contents page of a multimedia application.

Hot Spot: An on-screen graphic which, on selection, conveys the user to a different part of the program.

Hot Word: An on-screen word which, on selection, conveys the user to a different part of the program.

Hyperlink: Synonymous with hot spot or hot word; an on-screen button which, on selection, conveys the user to a different part of the text.

Hypermedia: The collective term used to encompass all hyperlinks in documents or multimedia applications, including hypertext, hot spots and hot words.

Hypertext: The term used to describe a document or page within a multimedia application that contains hot spots and hot word links.

Icon: A pictorial symbol denoting a common function or command within an application.

Information Superhighway: The global communications network, destined to provide high-speed access to information through a fibre-optic data medium.

Infotainment: Information and entertainment combined on a multimedia CD-ROM

Interactive: A title is described as interactive if the user is able to control any element of its on-screen displays.

Interface: The medium through which information is made accessible to the user; otherwise known as the human-computer interface.

Internet: A global network of computer networks owned by organizations, educational institutions and the general public.

MAC: An abbreviation for Apple Macintosh computers. (MACs are distinct from PCs, which have a different hardware architecture, requiring alternative software.)

Megabyte: A unit used to describe the amount of information available on a computer, hard disc, floppy disc or CD-ROM. One megabyte is equivalent to over one million individual characters.

Menu: A list of commands available in an application that are typically grouped around a logical set of operations; analogous to the contents page of a book.

Mouse: A 'touch-sensitive' hardware device, used to convey input from the user to the computer.

Network: The connection of two or more computers and/or other computer hardware, such as printers, through physical cabling or telecommunication links.

PC: An acronym for Personal Computer; this refers to an IBM compatible computer. (PCs are distinct from Apple Macintosh computers, which have a different hardware architecture, requiring alternative software.)

Program: A list of commands developed in a computer language that when compiled will perform an operation or function. Computer games, multimedia applications and word-processing packages are all forms of computer program.

Software: A term used to describe all forms of computer program.

Sound Card: A hardware device that enables computers to generate and reproduce music or sounds from commands issued through the software.

Toolbar: An interactive, on-screen device (often situated at the top of the screen) which allows the user to carry out such various functions as printing or moving text.

Virtual Reality: A computer-generated simulation of reality, providing the illusion of a real situation using three-dimensional modelling.

Window: An on-screen frame containing information; its size can be altered both horizontally and vertically to suit the requirements of the user.

World Wide Web: A graphical interface used to access the Internet, based upon a hypertext system for searching, accessing and finding information.

Notes

1. Since CD-ROM is the most common medium for multimedia, it is the medium which sets the standard for this chapter. However, it should be noted that some titles are also available on floppy disk (e.g. many of ABLAC's titles are produced both on 3.5" disk and CD-ROM).
2. From *The American Heritage Dictionary of the English Language* on *Microsoft Office Professional Version 7.0/Bookshelf* 1995 edition. (N.B. – A localized version of *Bookshelf* is due for release as this goes to press: the *British Reference Collection* will cost £49.99.)
3. Montaigne, M. *Essays*, bk1, ch. 22, 'Of Custom' (1580, tr. by John Florio). Taken from: *The Columbia Dictionary of Quotations* (1993) on *Microsoft Office Professional Version 7.0/Bookshelf* 1995 edition.
4. Slogan taken from the back sleeve of the CD-ROM: *Fun School 6 – Fairyland* (Europress 1996).
5. Turnbull, P. (1996) 'We Don't Need A New Computer' in *Parents & Computers*, Autumn, p.33.

6. Bruner, J. (1986) *Actual Minds, Possible Worlds*. Cambridge, Mass: Harvard University Press, p.11
7. Sainsbury, L. 'Looking to the future: Alternative Forms of Children's Books' in Reynolds, K. et al., *Young People's Reading at the End of the Century*. Survey report from the National Centre for Research in Children's Literature at the Roehampton Institute (awaiting publication). Further information from Dr Kimberley Reynolds, Director NCRCL, Roehampton Institute London, Downshire House, Roehampton Lane, London SW15 4HT
8. Norris, T. (1995) 'New Children's Discs' in *CD-ROM Today*, September, Issue 17, p.35.
9. Dickens, C. (1985) *Hard Times*. Harmondsworth: Penguin (first published in 1854), p.47.
10. Meek, M. (1991) *On Being Literate*. London: Bodley Head (first published in 1971) p.222.
11. Richards, M. (1996) 'Editor's Corner' in *CD-ROM Today*, January, Issue 21, p.16.
12. Taken from a press release for Funsoft's Barbie™ series. Contact: Funsoft (UK) Ltd, 77 Fulham Palace Road, London SW6 8JA.
13. Reynolds, K. et al., *Young People's Reading at the End of the Century*. Survey report from the National Centre for Research in Children's Literature at the Roehampton Institute (awaiting publication). Further information from Dr Kimberley Reynolds, Director NCRCL, Roehampton Institute London, Downshire House, Roehampton Lane, London SW15 4HT
14. Geer, S. (1996) 'A Lifeline for CD-ROM' in *The Daily Telegraph: Connected* (supplement), Tuesday September 17, p.12.
15. Montaigne, M. (1965) *Montaigne's Essays: Vol.1*, tr. J. Florio, London: J.M. Dent & Son (first published in 1908), p.107
16. Geer, S. (1996) 'A Lifeline for CD-ROM' in *The Daily Telegraph: Connected* (supplement), Tuesday September 17, p.12.
17. Since the PC is the most common platform for multimedia software, it is the platform which sets the standard for this chapter. However, it should be noted that most titles are also available for use on the MAC.
18. Sainsbury, L. 'Looking to the Future: Alternative Forms of Children's Books' in Reynolds, Kimberley et al., *Young People's Reading at the End of the Century*. Survey report from the National Centre for Research in Children's Literature at the Roehampton Institute (awaiting publication). Further information from Dr Kimberley Reynolds, Director NCRCL, Roehampton Institute London, Downshire House, Roehampton Lane, London SW15 4HT
19. Richards, M. (1996) 'Six of the Best' in *CD-ROM Today* July, Issue 27, p.84.
20. Taken from a press release for 'The Jump Ahead Series'. Contact: Random House UK New Media, 20 Vauxhall Bridge Road. London SW1V 2SA.
21. PIN (1996), *Parent's Guide: Jump Ahead Discovery Tree*. London: Random House, p.8.
22. 'Children Literature' Microsoft[R] Encarta[R] 96 Encyclopedia[C] 1993–1995 Microsoft Corporation [C] Funk & Wagnalls Corporation.
23. Turnbull, P. (1996) 'We Don't Need A New Computer' in *Parents & Computers*, Autumn, p.33.
24. McNicholas, C. (1996) 'Do your Homework' in *CD-ROM Magazine*, June vol. 2, no. 9, p.27.

25. Harrison, R. & Richards, M. (1996) 'Top Kids' Discs' in *CD-ROM Today*, September, Issue 29, pp. 34–47.
26. Editorial panel (1996) 'All-Time Top 50 Multimedia CD-ROMs' in *PC Guide*, October, Issue 4, vol. 4, p.86.
27. Editorial Panel (1996) 'Fact Finders' in *What PC and Software?*, October, vol. 15 Issue 10, p.73.
28. Editorial panel (1996) 'All-Time Top 50 Multimedia CD-ROMs' in *PC Guide*, October, Issue 4, vol. 4, p.86.
29. Taken from a press release for the *ITN European Video Atlas*. Contact: Attica, Media House, Presley Way, Crownhill, Milton Keynes MK8 0ES
30. Elliot, J. & Worsley, T. eds (1996) *Multimedia: The Complete Guide*. London: Dorling Kindersley, p.22.
31. Meek, M. (1991) *On Being Literate*. London: Bodley Head (first published in 1971) p.55.
32. Taken from a press release for *Exploring Earth Science* published by Attica Cybernetics. Contact: Attica, Media House, Presley Way, Crownhill, Milton Keynes MK8 0ES.
33. Clarke, E. et al. (1993) *Exploring Earth Science: Users Guide*. Oxford: Attica Cybernetics.
34. Taken from packaging of the CD-ROM *Exploring Earth Science* published by Attica Cybernetics.
35. Taken from a press release for 'The Times Perspectives series'. Contact: News Multimedia Ltd, PO Box 495, Virginia Street London E1 9XY.
36. Taken from a press release for *The Journey of Thomas Blue Eagle*. Contact: YITM Ltd, Television Centre, Kirkstall Road, Leeds LS3 1JS.
37. Bastable, J & Charlton, H. eds(1996) 'The Making of Makers,' in printed introduction to **Makers of the Twentieth Century**, Leighton Buzzard: News Multimedia, p.3.
38. Pinsent, P. 'Information Books' in Reynolds, K. et al., *Young People's Reading at the End of the Century*. Survey report from the National Centre for Research in Children's Literature at the Roehampton Institute (awaiting publication). Further information from Dr Kimberley Reynolds, Director NCRCL, Roehampton Institute London, Downshire House, Roehampton Lane, London SW15 4HT
39. Quoted by: Wapshott, T. (1996) 'Computer Games and Pastimes' in *The Weekend Times*, 22 June.
40. Tipp, G. (1996) 'The Mystery of Magritte' in *CD-ROM Today*, November, Issue 31, p.47.
41. Howells, J. (1996) 'Cyber Art goes Mainstream' in *The Daily Telegraph: Connected* (supplement), Tuesday 10 September, p.6.

Bibliography

Historical Survey

Avery, G. & Briggs, J. (1989) (eds) *Children and Their Books*. Oxford: Clarendon Press

Avery, G. (1995) 'The Beginnings of Children's Reading to c.1700' in Hunt, P. (ed.) (1995) *Children's Literature: An Illustrated History*. Oxford: University Press

Brooks, R.G. & Pugh, A.K. (eds) (1984) *Studies in the History of Reading*. Reading: Centre for the Teaching of Reading with the United Kingdom Reading Association

Brown, A. et al. (1971/2) *Chambers' Young Set Dictionaries*. London

Carpenter, H. & Prichard, M. (1984) *The Oxford Companion to Children's Literature*. Oxford: University Press

The Children's Picture Dictionary (1951). London: Collins

Coleman, J. (1981) *English Literature in History: 1350–1400*. London: Hutchinson

Comenius, J. (1659) *Orbis Sensualium Pictus* facsimile (1968). London: Oxford University Press

Courtney, J.L. & Speck, G.E. (1970) *Encyclopedia for Boys and Girls*. London: Ward Lock

Duffy, E. (1992) *The Stripping of the Altars: Traditional Religion in England 1400–1580*. New Haven & London: Yale University Press

Fenning, D. (4th edn, 1779) *A New and Easy Guide to the Use of the Globes*. London: S. Crowder

Guillot, R. (1956) (trans. Michael, M., 1958) *The New Encyclopedia for the Younger Generation*. London: Spring Books

Harvey Darton, F.N. (1982) *Children's Books in England*. (3rd edition, revised by Brian Alderson). Cambridge: University Press

Krapp, P. (1964) 'Encyclopedia', in Halsey, L. et al., *Collier's Encyclopedia* vol.9. USA: Crowell-Collier

Manchester, E.A. (n.d., c.1942) *Collins Clear School Atlas*. London: Collins

Mee, A. (n.d., c.1925) (ed.) *The Children's Encyclopedia* (10 volumes). London: Educational Book Company

My First Atlas (n.d., c.1952). Edinburgh: W. & A. Johnston

My Picture Dictionary: A Picture with Every Word. London: Publicity Products (n.d.)

O'Donnell, M. et al. (1956) *Words I Like to Read and Write*. Edinburgh: James Nisbet

Ogan, E. (n.d., c.1933) (ed.) *The Wonderland of Knowledge* (12 volumes). London: Odhams

Philip, G. (n.d., c.1910?) *Philips' Elementary Atlas of Comparative Geography*. London: Philips

Roxburgh, J.F. (n.d., c.1935) *General Knowledge Illustrated*. London: Associated Newspapers

Umphelby, F. ('A Lady', with additions by Bartlett, B.) (1858, 28th Edn) *The Child's Guide to Knowledge*. London

Waddington, M. (1952) *Cassell's Picture Dictionary*. London: Cassell

Walker's Universal Atlases for the Use of Schools (1811;1828). London: W.Wilson

General

Bruner, J. (1986) *Actual Minds, Possible Worlds*. Cambridge, Mass.: Harvard University Press

Clarke, E. et al. (1993) *Exploring Earth Science: Users Guide*. Oxford: Attica Cybernetics.

Department for Education (1995) *The National Curriculum: England*. London: HMSO

Dickens, C. (1985) *Hard Times*. Harmondsworth: Penguin (first published in 1854)

Editorial panel (1996) 'All-Time Top 50 Multimedia CD-ROMs' in *PC Guide* 4 (4), October

Editorial Panel (1996) 'Fact Finders' in *What PC and Software?*, 15 (10), October

Elliot, J. & Worsley, T. (eds) (1996) *Multimedia: The Complete Guide*. London: Dorling Kindersley

Geer, S. (1996) 'A Lifeline for CD-ROM' in *The Daily Telegraph: Connected* (supplement) Tuesday 17 September

Harrison, R. & Richards, M. (1996) 'Top Kids' Discs' in *CD-ROM Today* (29), September

Howells, J. (1996) 'Cyber Art goes Mainstream' in *The Daily Telegraph: Connected* (supplement), Tuesday 10 September

McNicholas, C. (1996) 'Do your Homework' in *CD-ROM Magazine*, 2 (9), June

Meek, M. (1991) *On Being Literate*. London: Bodley Head (first published in 1971)

Meek, M. et al. (1977) *The Cool Web: The Pattern of Children's Reading.* London: The Bodley Head
Montaigne, M. (1580) 'Of Custom' in *Essays*, bk.1, (tr. by Cotton, C.)
Moss, E. (1977) 'The "Peppermint" lesson' in Meek, M., et al. *The Cool Web: The Pattern of Children's Reading.* London: The Bodley Head
Norris, T. (1995) 'New Children's Discs' in *CD-ROM Today*, (17), September
Pinsent, P. (awaiting publication) 'Information Books' in Reynolds, K. et al., *Young People's Reading at the End of the Century*
Reynolds, K. et al. (awaiting publication) *Young People's Reading at the End of the Century.* Survey report from the National Centre for Research in Children's Literature at the Roehampton Institute. Further information from Dr Kimberley Reynolds, Director NCRCL, Roehampton Institute London, Downshire House, Roehampton Lane, London SW15 4HT
Richards, M. (1996) 'Editor's Corner' in *CD-ROM Today*, (21), January
Richards, M. (1996) 'Six of the Best' in *CD-ROM Today*, (27), July
Sainsbury, L. (awaiting publication) 'Looking to the future: Alternative Forms of Children's Books' in Reynolds, K. et al., *Young People's Reading at the End of the Century*
Tipp, G. (1996) 'The Mystery of Magritte' in *CD-ROM Today*, (31), November
Tucker, N. (1990) *The Child and the Book: A Psychological and Literary Exploration.* Cambridge & New York: Cambridge University Press (first published in 1981)
Turnbull, P. (1996) 'We Don't Need A New Computer' in *Parents & Computers,* Autumn
Wapshott, T. (1996) 'Computer Games and Pastimes' in *The Weekend Times,* 22 June

Author Index

Adams, Simon 141, 142
Alderton, David 93, 94, 96
Allaby, Michael 65
Allen, Sarah 36
Ardley, Bridget 67
Ardley, Neil 67, 121, 122
Augarde, A.J. (comp.) 60
Ayto, John 117

Bateman, Dick 66
Bingham, Jane 30
Bingham, Jane (ed.) 61
Bond, Shirley 71
Bremner, Tony 84
Bresler, Lynn 83
Briquebec, John 141
Brooks, Felicity 71
Burnie, David 120
Butterworth, John (comp.) 60

Campbell, Fiona 94, 95
Campbell, Tessa 76
Carpenter, Humphrey 67
Champion, Neil 83
Chisholm, Jane 75
Civardi, Anne 84
Claybourne, A. 41
Claybourne, Anna 74, 131
Colvin, Leslie 70
Cook, Janet 71
Couper, Heather 109
Cunningham, Antonia 74
Curtis, Neil 65

Dixon, Dougal 36, 96

Edom, Helen 71
Edwards, Richard 12
Elliott, Jane 82
Evans, Charlotte 92
Evans, Charlotte (ed.) 125

Farndon, John 82, 137
Flood, Mike 129

Ganeri, Anita 20, 50, 83, 108
Gifford, Clive 134
Glover, David 67
Goldsmith, Evelyn 10, 28, 55, 57
Grabham, Sue (ed.) 123
Grant, Neil 110
Gribbin, Mary 38
Grisewood, John (ed.) 54

Harper, Don 95
Hart, M. 72
Hawkins, Joyce M. (comp.) 114
Hawkins, Joyce M. (ed.) 114
Headlam, Catherine (ed.) 127
Henbest, Nigel 92, 109
Hindley, Judy 84
Hope, Colin (comp.) 60
Hopkinson, Christina 132

Jennings, Terry 67
Jones, Louise 91

Kerrod, Robin 67
Khanduri, Kamini 74
Kilpatrick, Cathy 84
King, Colin 82
Kramer, Ann 141, 142

Langley, Andrew 89, 139, 140
Lapage, Ginny 26
Lapage, Ginny (comp.) 56
Lindsay, William 110
Locke, Ann 9

McGough, Roger 11
McNeil, Mary Jean 84
Mason, Antony 19, 50
Mayes, Susan 39, 40, 41
Meredith, Susan 40, 41, 130
Miles, Lisa 69, 111
Millard, Anne 73, 110
Morris, Mike 37
Muirden, James 65
Myring, Lynn 75

Needham, Kate 41

Oakley, Mark 96
Oxlade, Chris 134

Parker, Steve 119
Paton, John (ed.) 137
Pemberton, Sheila (comp.) 11
Philip, Neil (ed.) 121

Ransford, Sandy 36
Rawson, Christopher 84
Reid, Dee (comp.) 29, 58, 59
Reid, Struan 83, 128
Roche, Hannah 14
Ruders, Poul 122

Sansome, Rosemary (comp.) 29, 58, 59
Schofield, Dene 92
Selburg, I. 72
Snowden, Sheila 75

Speare, Emma 70
Spooner, Alan (comp.) 58, 59, 62
Spurgeon, Richard 129
Stephens, M. 72
Stockley, Corinne 134
Stubbs, Dawn 94

Tahta, Sophy 40, 41, 42
Tarsky, S. 72
Taylor, Barbara 110
Taylor, Geraldine 27
Treays, Rebecca et al. 134
Tyler, Jenny 49, 50, 76

Unwin, Mike 41

van Rose, Susanna 110
Vanags, Patricia 73
Varley, Carol 69

Wardley, Rachel 30
Wardley, Rachel (ed.) 62
Watt, Fiona 129
Watts, Lisa 49, 50, 76
Webster, Charlie 37
Wertheim, Jane 134
Weston, John (comp.) 58
Wiegand, Patrick 13, 21
Wiegand, Patrick (ed.) 47, 48, 106
Wilkes, Angela 29
Williams, Brenda 89, 139
Williams, Brian 65
Wilson, Francis 129
Wingate, Philippa 134
Wood, Tim 90, 91
Woodward, Kate 40, 41
Wright, David 50, 104
Wright, Jill 50, 104

Index of Reviewed Titles

Electronic reference material and multimedia are indicated by (rmm) following a page number

ADI 182(rmm)
Alphabet Blocks 182(rmm)
Animal Atlas, The 110
Animal World 86
Animal Safari 174(rmm)
Art Gallery 178(rmm)
[Astronomy] Planets 92
Atlas of Ancient Worlds, The 110
Attica Guide to Classical Music, The 178(rmm)

Barbie Fashion Designer 149(rmm)
Beethoven Lives Upstairs 178(rmm)
[Beginning biology] Food 92
[Beginning biology] Plants 93
[Beginning biology] The Body 93
Big Animals 38
Big Bugs 38
Big Buildings 38
Big Farm Animals 38
Big Machines 38
Big Ocean Creatures 38
'Big . . .' series 37, 43, 44
Big Trucks 38
Big Wonders of the World 38
Biggest, Tallest, Greatest, Bestest! 79
Bird Atlas, The 110
Blind Watchmaker, The 173(rmm)
Bloomsbury Treasury of Quotations, The 178(rmm)
Body Atlas, The 119
Body Facts 87
Body Works 5.0 174(rmm)
Bookshelf 178(rmm)
Brain Blasters 79

Britain 1901–1945 91
British Multimedia Encyclopedia 157(rmm)

Cambridge Guide to English Literature, The 178(rmm)
Carmen Sandiego: Junior Detective Edition 166(rmm), 167(rmm)
Cartoon Guide to Physics, The 174(rmm)
Castles 87
Cats 36
CD-ROM Today 182
Chambers Children's Illustrated Dictionary, The 52, 54, 100
Chambers First Dictionary 23, 25
Children's Britannica 77, 137
Children's Encyclopedia of History, The: Dark Ages to 1914 73
Children's Encyclopedia of History, The: First Civilisations to the Fall of Rome 73
Children's Encyclopedia of Our World, The 50, 76
Cinemania 97 165(rmm)
Cold War, The 169(rmm)
Collins Children's Dictionary 51, 55
Collins COBUILD on CD-ROM 158(rmm)
Collins COBUILD Student's Dictionary 158(rmm)
Collins Concise School Dictionary 113
Collins Electronic Dictionary & Thesaurus 158(rmm)
Collins 'Faxfinder' series 86, 99, 100
Collins First Dictionary 23, 26
Collins First Word Book 10
Collins Illustrated Children's Dictionary 51, 55

Collins Junior Dictionary 52, 56
Collins 'Little Gems' 35, 44
Collins Pocket Primary Dictionary 51, 57
Collins Primary Dictionary 51, 57
Collins School Dictionary 113
Collins Shorter School Dictionary 112, 113
Compton's Interactive Encyclopedia 157(rmm)
Computers 97
Computers in the Home 182(rmm)
Concise Oxford Dictionary 155(rmm), 157(rmm), 158(rmm)
Corel Super Ten Reference Pack 158(rmm)
Countries of the World Facts 83
Cybertation 173(rmm)

David Bellamy's Endangered Wildlife 176(rmm)
[De Agostini] 'My First Weather Books' collection 14, 15
Devil's Canyon 174(rmm)
Dharma Bums, The 178(rmm)
Dictionary of Nature 120, 143, 144
Dictionary of Science 121, 143, 144
Dinosaur Hunter 165(rmm)
Dinosaurs 36
Discovery Tree 152(rmm), 153(rmm), 154(rmm), 161(rmm), 175(rmm)
Dogs 36
Dogz 173(rmm)
Dorling Kindersley Children's Dictionary, The 159(rmm)
Dorling Kindersley Illustrated Factopedia, The 135, 143, 144
Dorling Kindersley World Reference Atlas 161(rmm)
Dreadful Dinosaurs 79

Earth and Space 87
Earth Atlas, The 110
Earth Facts 83
Ecology 129
Encarta '96 Encyclopedia: World English Edition 155(rmm), 157(rmm)
Encarta '96 World Atlas 161(rmm), 163(rmm), 166(rmm)
Endangered Wildlife 165(rmm)
Energy & Power 129
Essential Biology 134
Essential Chemistry 134
Essential Physics 134

Essential Science 133, 143, 144, 175(rmm)
Exploring Earth Science 167(rmm)
Exploropedia World of Nature 174(rmm)
Eyewitness Atlas of the World 103, 169(rmm)
Eyewitness Encyclopedia of Nature 174(rmm)
Eyewitness Encyclopedia of Science 2.0 173(rmm)
Eyewitness Encyclopedia of Space & The Universe 174(rmm), 181(rmm)

Flight Unlimited 181(rmm)
Fly with the Birds: an Oxford Word and Rhyme Book 12, 14, 15
Funschool 6 series 174(rmm)

Genius Range 174(rmm)
Geodome Landforms 166, 168(rmm)
Georgian Britain: 1714 to 1837 89, 140
Georgians, The 91
Global Explorer 164(rmm)
Grassland Wildlife 74
Great Artists 165(rmm), 178(rmm), 179(rmm)
Great Atlas of Discovery, The 110
Great Dinosaur Atlas, The 110
Great Generals 169(rmm)
Great Inventions 87
Grolier Multimedia Encyclopedia 1996 157(rmm)

Hammond Atlas of the World, The 161(rmm)
Historical Atlas. Ancient World: From the Earliest Civilizations to the Roman Empire 30,000BC–AD456 141
Historical Atlas. Exploration & Empire: Empire-builders, European. Expansion & the Development of Science 1450–1760 142
Historical Atlas. Revolution and Technology: Rapid Change and the Growth of the Modern World 1760 – to the Present Day 142
Historical Atlas. Trade and Religion: Barbarian Invasions, Empires around the World & Medieval Europe AD456–1450 141
'History of Britain' series 88, 89, 98, 100, 138
History of Medicine, A 169(rmm)
Horses and Ponies 36
How Animals Live 84
How Birds Live 84
How do Animals Talk? 40, 42, 43

Index of Reviewed Titles   195

How do Bees Make Honey? 41, 43
How Does a Bird Fly? 40, 42, 43
How Machines Work 84
How Things Are Built 71
How Things Are Made 71
How Things Began 84
How Would You Survive? 169(rmm), 170(rmm)
How Your Body Works 84
Hutchinson Encyclopedia 1996 157(rmm)
Hutchinson Science Library 174(rmm)

I can say apple 9
I can say blanket 9
I can say boat 9
I can say teddy 9
Illustrated Book of Myths: Tales & Legends of the World 121, 143
Images of War 172(rmm)
Incredible Toons 182(rmm)
Industrial Revolution, The 169(rmm)
Infopedia UK '96 158(rmm)
Inside Story, The 174(rmm)
Interactive Periodic Table 177(rmm)
Investigating Twentieth Century Art 178(rmm)
ITN European Video Atlas 164(rmm)

Jack Kerouac Romnibus, The 178(rmm)
Journey of Thomas Blue Eagle, The 170(rmm)
Jump Ahead series 166(rmm)

Karaoke Macbeth 177(rmm)
Karl's Kite 14
Kid's Kit 182(rmm)
Kingfisher Beano Book of Amazing Facts, The 78
Kingfisher Beano Book of Britain, The 79
Kingfisher Beano File, The 79
Kingfisher Children's Encyclopedia 79, 137, 154(rmm)
Kingfisher Children's Micropedia '96 154(rmm)
Kingfisher Child's World Encyclopedia 24, 32, 44
Kingfisher Encyclopedia of Lands and Peoples, The 123, 125, 143, 144
Kingfisher First Encyclopedia 24, 33
Kingfisher First Picture Atlas, The 19, 50
Kingfisher 'Historical Atlas' series, The 140

Kingfisher History Encyclopedia, The 125, 127, 143, 144
Kingfisher Illustrated History of the World, The 125
Kingfisher Science Encyclopedia, The 127, 128
Kingfisher Visual Encyclopedia of Science 65, 100
Kings & Queens of England: Part 1 871–1485 91
Kings & Queens of England: Part 2 1485 to The Present Day 91

Ladybird Dictionary with colour illustrations 23, 27
Ladybird 'Discovery' Series 91, 98
Ladybird Picture Atlas 20, 43, 44, 50
Ladybird Picture Dictionary 23, 27
[Lifestyles and Living] Castles 93
[Lifestyles and Living] Clothes and Costume 94
[Lifestyles and Living] Flight 94
Little Horrors 79
Little Ladybird abc, A 9, 14, 15

Macmillan Dictionary for Children 161(rmm)
Magical Music Box, The: Swan Lake 179(rmm)
Major Disasters 87
Makers of the Twentieth Century 172(rmm)
Maths Workshop 175(rmm)
Medieval Britain: 1066 to 1485 89, 139
Microsoft Bookshelf 95 158(rmm)
Microsoft Bookshelf: British Reference Collection 158(rmm)
Middle Ages, The 90
Mini Oxford School Dictionary, The 112, 114, 143, 144
Mini Oxford School Speller, The 63, 99, 100
Mini Oxford School Thesaurus, The 116, 143, 144
Modern Britain 1901 to the 1990s 89, 140
Monty Python & the Quest for the Holy Grail 181(rmm)
Mother Goose 182(rmm)
Mountain Wildlife 74
Multimedia: The Complete Guide 182(rmm)
My First Alphabet Book 10, 14, 15
My First Amazing World Explorer 161(rmm), 167(rmm)
My First Encyclopedia 152(rmm)

196   Index of Reviewed Titles

My First Incredible Amazing Dictionary 161(rmm)
My First Oxford Dictionary 23, 28, 43, 44
My First Oxford Dictionary Activities 43, 44
My Oxford ABC Picture Rhyme Book 11, 14, 15
My Oxford Picture Word Book 11, 14, 15
Mystery of Magritte, The 178(rmm)

[Natural Habitats] Polar Animals 95
[Natural Habitats] Rainforest Animals 94
New Encyclopedia of the Living World, The 176(rmm)
New Oxford School Atlas, The 106, 143, 144
New Oxford School Dictionary, The 114
Nigel's World 166(rmm)

Oceans Atlas, The 108, 143
Orchestra 178(rmm)
Our Earth 75
[Our Earth] Thunder and Lightning 95
[Our Earth] Volcanoes and Earthquakes 95
Oxford Children's A to Z of Geography, The 66
Oxford Children's A to Z of Mathematics, The 67
Oxford Children's A to Z of Music, The 67
Oxford Children's A to Z of Science, The 67
Oxford Children's A to Z of Technology, The 67
Oxford Children's A to Z of the Human Body, The 67
Oxford Children's Dictionary, The 58
Oxford Children's Encyclopedia 77, 80, 99, 137, 152(rmm), 154(rmm)
Oxford Children's Encyclopedia of Science Video. Video 1: Acid to Evolution 81
Oxford Children's Encyclopedia of Science Video. Video 2: Fire to Metals 81
Oxford Children's Encyclopedia of Science Video. Video 3: Nuclear to X-rays 81
Oxford Children's Thesaurus, The 62
Oxford Compendium 158(rmm)
Oxford Dictionary of Quotations & Modern Quotations 158(rmm)
Oxford English Dictionary 158(rmm)
Oxford Illustrated Junior Dictionary, The 24, 29, 51, 58
Oxford Infant Atlas, The 13, 14, 15, 21
Oxford Junior Atlas, The 47
Oxford Junior Dictionary, The 51, 59

Oxford Practical Atlas, The 107
Oxford Primary School Dictionary, The 52, 60, 98, 154(rmm)
Oxford Rainbow Atlas, The 48
Oxford Reference Shelf 158(rmm)
Oxford School A-Z of English, The 117, 143, 144
Oxford School Dictionary, The 112, 114
Oxford Study Dictionary, The 113, 115, 143, 144
Oxford Study Thesaurus, The 117
Oxford Thesaurus 158(rmm)

Parents & Computers 142(rmm), 182
Parent's Guide to Computers Supporting Handbook 182(rmm)
Penguin Hutchinson Reference Library 158(rmm)
Pesky Pirates 79
Peter Rabbit's Number Garden 148(rmm), 174(rmm)
Pete's Puddles 14
Physical World, The 166(rmm)
Planet Earth 129, 169(rmm), 174(rmm)
Pocket Atlas 50, 99, 100, 104
Polar Wildlife 74

Rainforest Wildlife 74
Random House Kid's Encyclopedia 154(rmm)
Religions of the World 97
Revolting Recipes 79
Rhymes and Riddles 79
Rockets and Spaceflight 75
Roman Britain: 55BC to AD406 89, 140
Romans, The 90
Romeo and Juliet 177(rmm)

Sainsbury's Children's Encyclopedia 82, 137
Saxons and the Normans, The 90
Saxons and Vikings, The: 406 to 1066 89, 140
School Rules 79
Scientists and Inventors 97
Sea, The 97
Selfish Gene, The 173(rmm)
Space Atlas, The 109, 143
Space Facts 83
Space Race, The 169(rmm)
Spell it yourself 63
Stuarts, The 91

Stuarts, The: 1603 to 1714 89, 140
Suki's Sun Hat 14
Sun, Moon and Planets 75
Superbikes 37
Supercars 37
Su's Snowgirl 14

Terratopia 174(rmm)
Threatened Planet 97
3D Atlas 163(rmm)
Through the Magic Mirror 178(rmm)
Times Perspectives: Planet Earth, The 168(rmm)
Times Perspectives: Women's Rights 169(rmm), 171(rmm)
Times World Map & Database 164(rmm)
Tudors, The 90
Tudors, The: 1485 to 1603 89, 139

Ultimate Encyclopedia of Soccer 165(rmm)
Ultimate Human Body, The 174(rmm)
Uncle Archibald 182(rmm)
Unsolved Mysteries 87
Usborne Book of Facts and Lists, The: Omnibus Edition 83
Usborne Book of Knowledge, The 84
Usborne Book of the Countryside, The 72, 99, 100
Usborne Book of the Earth, The 76, 129, 143, 144
Usborne Book of the Seas, The 76
Usborne Book of World History, The 73
Usborne Book of World Religions, The 130, 143
Usborne Book of World Wildlife, The 74, 99, 100
Usborne Children's Atlas of the World, The 49
Usborne Children's Encyclopedia, The 82
Usborne Computer Dictionary for Beginners, The 131, 143
Usborne First Dictionary, The 23, 30
Usborne First Guide to the Universe, The 75
Usborne Geography Encyclopedia, The 69, 85, 98
Usborne History of the Twentieth Century, The 132
Usborne Illustrated Atlas of World History, The 111
Usborne Illustrated Dictionary, The 52, 61

Usborne Illustrated Dictionary of Biology, The 135
Usborne Illustrated Dictionary of Chemistry, The 135
Usborne Illustrated Dictionary of Physics, The 135
Usborne Illustrated Dictionary of Science, The 134
Usborne Illustrated Encyclopedia: Science & Technology 67
Usborne Illustrated Encyclopedia: The Natural World 68
Usborne Illustrated Handbook of Invention & Discovery, The 128
Usborne Living World Encyclopedia, The 70, 85
Usborne NatureTrail Book of Birdwatching, The 72
Usborne NatureTrail Book of Trees & Leaves, The 72
Usborne NatureTrail Book of Wild Flowers, The 72
Usborne NatureTrail Omnibus, The 73
Usborne Picture Atlas, The 50, 76
Usborne Picture Dictionary, The 24, 29
Usborne Pocket Dictionary, The 53, 62, 99, 100
Usborne Science Encyclopedia, The 71, 85
Usborne Starting Point Science 38, 97
Usborne Starting Point Science: Earth and Space 43, 44
Usborne Starting Point Science: Life on Earth 43, 44
Usborne Starting Point Science: Volume 1 42
Usborne Starting Point Science: Volume 2 42
Usborne Starting Point Science: Volume 3 42
Usborne Starting Point Science: Volume 4 42
Usborne Starting Point Science: You and Your Body 43, 44
Usborne World of Knowledge Encyclopedia, The 85
Using the Oxford Primary School Dictionary 98
Using the Oxford School Dictionary 115

Victorian Britain: 1837 to 1901 89, 140
Victorians, The 91
Virtual Reality series 165(rmm)
V.R. Bird 165(rmm)
V.R. Cat 165(rmm)

Weather & Climate 129

Weather Facts 83
Webster's World Encyclopedia 157(rmm)
What Makes a Car Go? 42
What Makes a Flower Grow? 39, 42, 43
What Makes it Rain? 39, 42, 43
What Makes you Ill? 41, 42, 43
What Parents Want 182(rmm)
What's Inside You? 40, 42, 43
What's Out in Space? 40, 42, 43
What's the Earth Made of? 41, 43
What's Under the Ground? 39, 42, 43
What's Under the Sea? 41, 43
Where did Dinosaurs Go? 41, 42, 43
Where do Babies Come From? 40, 42, 43
Where does Electricity Come from? 40, 42
Where does Rubbish Go? 40, 42
Where Food Comes From 71
Where in the World is Carmen Sandiego? 161(rmm), 166(rmm), 165(rmm)
Where Things Come From and How Things are Made 71

Why are People Different? 41, 42, 43
Why do People Eat? 41, 42, 43
Why do Tigers have Stripes? 41, 42, 43
Why is Night Dark? 40, 42, 43
Wide World of Animals 174(rmm)
[Wildlife] Birds 95
[Wildlife] Dinosaurs 96
[Wildlife] Quest for New Animals 96
[Wildlife] Sharks 96
[Wildlife] Whales and Dolphins 96
William Shakespeare 178(rmm)
Women's Rights 169(rmm), 171(rmm)
Woodruff 182(rmm)
World Atlas & Almanac 161(rmm), 164(rmm)
World Facts 88
World Reference Atlas 162(rmm), 166(rmm)
World War I 169(rmm)
World War II 169(rmm), 171(rmm)

Young Person's Guide to Music, A 122, 143

Subject Index

Electronic reference material and multimedia are indicated by (rmm) following a page number

Alphabet books xiii–xiv, 8–13
    editor's personal selection 14–15
Animals 38, 40, 41, 42, 43, 84, 86, 94, 95, 96, 110
    see also Cats; Dogs; Farm animals; Horses; Ponies; Reptiles; Tigers
Arts 177–80(rmm)
Astronomy 91, 92
Atlases xv–xvii, 13, 161–4(rmm)
    Key Stage 1 18, 19–22
    Key Stage 2 47–51, 76
    Key Stage 3 102–11

Babies 40, 42, 43
Bees 41, 43
Biology 91, 92, 93, 134, 135
Birds 40, 42, 43, 84, 95, 110
Birdwatching 72
Britain 79, 88, 89, 91, 138, 139
Bugs 38
Building 71
Buildings 38

Cars 37, 42
Castles 87, 93
Cats 36
CD-ROMS
    guide to purchasing 180–2(rmm)
    see also Reference and multimedia
Chemistry 134, 135
Children's assessments
    Key Stage 1 18, 19, 25, 31, 32, 34, 43
    Key Stage 2 46, 47, 53, 64
    Key Stage 3 101–2

Clams 38
Climate 129
Clothes and costume 94
Computers 97, 131
Countries 83
Countryside 72

'Desire to know', Key Stage 1 16–17
Dictionaries xiv–xv, 157–61(rmm)
    Key Stage 1 18, 23–31
    Key Stage 2 51–76
    Key Stage 3 112–18
Dinosaurs 36, 41, 42, 79, 96, 110
Disasters 87
Discovery 110, 128
Disease 41, 42, 43
Dogs 36
Dolphins 96

Earth 41, 43, 75, 76, 83, 87, 91, 95, 110, 129, 168(rmm)
Earth science 167(rmm)
Earthquakes 95
Ecology 129
Education Reform Act 1988 6
Electricity 40, 42
Electronic reference library 151–7(rmm)
    see also Reference and multimedia
Encyclopedias xvii–xxi, 151–7(rmm), 164–80(rmm)
    Key Stage 1 18, 31–4
    Key Stage 2 64–85
    Key Stage 3 118–38
Energy 129

England 91
English 117
Environment 97
Exploration 167(rmm)

Facts 78, 83, 86, 88
Farm animals 38
First words books 8–13
　editor's personal selection 14–15
Flight 94
Flowers 39, 42, 43, 72
Food 41, 42, 43, 71, 92

Geography 19, 66, 69, 85, 166(rmm)
Georgians 89, 91, 140
Grasslands 74

History 73, 88, 89, 90, 111, 125, 127, 132, 138, 139, 140, 141, 142, 169–73(rmm)
　see also Kings and queens; Middle Ages; Museums; Romans; Saxons; Stuarts; Tudors; Victorians; Vikings
Honey 41, 43
Horses 36
Human body 40, 42, 43, 67, 84, 87, 93, 119

Illness 41, 42, 43
Information retrieval skills 16
Infotainment 164–80(rmm)
Insects 38
　see also Bees; Bugs; Spiders
Inventions 87, 97, 128
ISBN 2

Key Stage 1 6, 16–44
　atlases 18, 19–22
　children's assessment 18, 19, 25, 31, 32, 34, 43
　'desire to know' 16–17
　dictionaries 18, 23–31
　editor's personal selection 43–4
　encyclopedias 18, 31–4
　mini-libraries 35–43
　National Curriculum coverage 19, 24–5, 31–2
Key Stage 2 6, 45–100
　atlases 47–51, 76
　children's assessments 46, 47, 53, 64
　dictionaries (and related texts) 51–64

dictionaries (single-subject) 64–76
editor's personal selection 98–100
encyclopedias (general) and books of facts 76–85
encyclopedias (single-subject) 64–76
mini-libraries 85–97
National Curriculum coverage 46, 47, 53, 64, 85–6
Key Stage 3 6, 101–44
　atlases 102–11
　children's assessment 101–2
　dictionaries (and related texts) 112–18
　editor's personal selection 143
　encyclopedias 118–38
　mini-libraries 138–43
　National Curriculum coverage 102, 116, 118, 120
Key Stage 4 6
Kings and Queens 91

Landforms 168(rmm)
Lands 123, 125
Language reference 157–61(rmm)
Legends 121
Life 43, 84
Lifestyles 91
Lightning 95
Lists 83
Living world 70, 85

Machines 38, 84
Making things 71
Mathematics 67, 175(rmm)
Medieval history 89
Middle Ages 90
Mini-libraries
　Key Stage 1 35–43
　Key Stage 2 85–97
　Key Stage 3 138–43
Moon 75
Motorbikes 37
Mountains 74
Multimedia. See Reference and multimedia
Museums 164–80(rmm)
Music 67, 122, 179(rmm)
Mysteries 87
Myths 121

National Curriculum coverage 3, 5–6

Key Stage 1 19, 24–5, 31–2
Key Stage 2 46, 47, 53, 64, 85–6
Key Stage 3 102, 116, 118, 120
Natural world 68
Nature 120
Nature lovers 73
Night 40, 42, 43
Normans 90

Oceans 108

People 41, 42, 43
Peoples 123, 125
Periodic table 177(rmm)
Physics 134, 135
Planets 75, 92
Plants 93
Polar regions 95
Polar wildlife 74
Ponies 36
Power 129
Pre-school children 8–15

Rain 39, 43
Rainforests 74, 94
Reference and multimedia 145–87(rmm)
    advantages 150–1(rmm)
    disadvantages 151(rmm)
Reference books, brief historical survey xii–xiii
Religions 97, 130
Reptiles 96
Retrieval devices 3
Rockets 75
Romans 89, 90
Rubbish 40, 42

Saxons 89, 90
Science 38, 42, 43, 65, 67, 71, 85, 97, 121, 127, 128, 133, 134, 135, 173–7(rmm)
    see also Chemistry; Energy; Physics; Space
Sea 41, 43, 76, 97
Seals 38
Sharks 96
Space 40, 42, 43, 83, 87, 109
Spaceflight 75, 94
Spiders 38
Stuarts 89, 91, 140
Sun 75

Technology 67, 142
Thunder 95
Tigers 41, 43
Trees 72
Trucks 38
Tudors 89, 90, 139
Twentieth century 132, 172(rmm)

Underground 39, 42, 43
Universe 75

Victorians 89, 91
Vikings 89
Virtual classrooms 164–80(rmm)
Volcanoes 95

Weather 14, 39, 43, 83, 129
Whales 38, 96
Wild flowers 72
Wildlife 74, 95, 96, 176(rmm)
Wonders of the world 38
World 76

Index of Illustrators

for reviewed titles

Addarro, Susanna 93

Baker, Julian 38
Barnett, Russell 110
Batchelor, Louise 9
Baxendale, Kathy 58
Berry, Gaynor 27
Biro, Val 11
Boni, S. 94, 95, 96
Bonson, Richard 110
Bull, Peter 38, 60
Burton, Andy 131

Cecchi, Lorenzo 92, 93, 94, 95
Corbella, Luciano 108

Dann, Penny 57
Davies, Robin 91
Dennis, Peter 90, 91, 129, 132
Dillow, John 20, 50, 90, 91
Donnelly, Strawberrie 10

Edwards, Brin 129
Ewan, Caroline 129

Finney, Denise 129
Fleury, Eugene 19, 50
Fornari, Giuliano 110, 119

Galante, L.R. 94, 95, 96
Gliori, Debi 11
Gower, Jeremy 130
Gower, Teri 30

Hart, Celia 58
Hersey, Bob 49, 76
Hewetson, Nicholas 130

Khan, Aziz 129
King, Colin 29, 84
Kitamura, Satoshi 12
Kuo Kang Chen 129

le Fever, Bill 58
Lilly, Kenneth 110

McEwan, Joseph 75, 129
Mistry, Nilesh 121
Morter, Peter 110
Mousdale, Peter 76

Nevett, Louise 75
Newton, Martin 75
Nicholls, Mike 27

Orr, Richard 110

Park, Julie 10, 28
Pieri, Lorenzo 93, 97
Pratt, Pierre 14

Rees, Gary 55
Rowe, Barry 29, 58

Schramm, Philip 75
Scott, Peter David 36
Shields, Chris 129

Smith, Guy 75
Stalio, Ivan 93, 94, 95, 96
Studio Boni/Galante 92, 93, 94, 95, 96, 97

Tansley, Elizabeth 9
Tewson, Andrew 38
Thomas, Paul 58

Thompson, George 84
Trotter, Stuart 30

Walster, Robert 134
Wilkinson, Sean 134
Wood, Judith 27
Woodcock, John 19, 50

For Product Safety Concerns and Information please contact our EU
representative GPSR@taylorandfrancis.com
Taylor & Francis Verlag GmbH, Kaufingerstraße 24, 80331 München, Germany

www.ingramcontent.com/pod-product-compliance
Lightning Source LLC
Chambersburg PA
CBHW052110300426
44116CB00010B/1607